LIFE AND LETTERS OF ROBERT BROWNING

Mrs. Sutherland Orr

Copyright © 2015 by Astounding Stories

No part of this book may be reproduced in any written, electronic, recording, or photocopying without written permission of the publisher or author. The exception would be in the case of brief quotations embodied in the critical articles or reviews and pages where permission is specifically granted by the publisher or author.

Although every precaution has been taken to verify the accuracy of the information contained herein, the publisher assume no responsibility for any errors or omissions. No liability is assumed for damages that may result from the use of information contained within.

For permission requests, write to the publisher, put in subject "Attention: "Permissions Coordinator,' at the address below, or contact us using our web site.

www.Astounding-Stories.com
Admin@ Astounding - Stories.com

Whenever new book is published by Astounding Stories we will send you FREE eBook for your honest review
www.astounding-stories.com/reviews
Join Our Email List NOW and get 5 FREE eBooks

All books in this Million Book Project by Astounding Stories are in Public Domain. They are published first time before 1923, or before 1963 and copyright was not renewed.

Proudly Created in the United States of America

TABLE OF CONTENTS

Preface 5
Chapter 1
    Origin of the Browning Family—Robert Browning's 6
Chapter 2
    Robert Browning's Father—His Position in Life—Comparison 6
Chapter 3
    1812-1826 Birth of Robert Browning—His Childhood 6
Chapter 4
    1826-1833 First Impressions of Keats and Shelley—Prolonged 6
Chapter 5
    1833-1835 'Pauline'—Letters to Mr. Fox—Publication of the 6
Chapter 6
    1835-1838 Removal to Hatcham; some Particulars—Renewed 7
Chapter 7
    1838-1841 First Italian Journey—Letters to Miss Haworth—Mr. 7
Chapter 8
    1841-1844 'A Blot in the 'Scutcheon'—Letters to Mr. 7
Chapter 9
    1844-1849 Introduction to Miss Barrett—Engagement—Motives 7
Chapter 10
    1849-1852 Death of Mr. Browning's Mother—Birth of his 7
Chapter 11
    1852-1855 M. Joseph Milsand—His close Friendship with 8
Chapter 12
    1855-1858 'Men and Women'—'Karshook'—'Two in the 8
Chapter 13
    1858-1861 Mrs. Browning's Illness—Siena—Letter from Mr. 8
Chapter 14
    1861-1863 Miss Blagden—Letters from Mr. Browning to 8
Chapter 15
    1863-1869 Pornic—'James Lee's Wife'—Meeting at Mr. F. 8
Chapter 16
    1869-1873 Lord Dufferin; Helen's Tower—Scotland; Visit to 9
Chapter 17
    1873-1878 London Life—Love of Music—Miss 9
Chapter 18
    1878-1884 He revisits Italy; Asolo; Letters to Mrs. 9
Chapter 19
    1881-1887 The Browning Society; Mr. Furnivall; Miss E. 9
Chapter 20
    Constancy to Habit—Optimism—Belief in Providence—Political 9
Chapter 21
    1887-1889 Marriage of Mr. Barrett Browning—Removal to De 10
Chapter 22
    1889 Proposed Purchase of Land at Asolo—Venice—Letter 10
    LIFE AND LETTERS OF ROBERT BROWNING 11
Chapter 1 11
Chapter 2 13
Chapter 3
    1812-1826 16

Chapter 4
   1826-1833 20
Chapter 5
   1833-1835 23
Chapter 6
   1835-1838 29
Chapter 7
   1838-1841 34
Chapter 8
   1841-1844 39
Chapter 9
   1844-1849 44
Chapter 10
   1849-1852 50
Chapter 11
   1852-1855 54
Chapter 12
   1855-1858 60
Chapter 13
   1858-1861 65
Chapter 14
   1861-1863 70
Chapter 15
   1863-1869 75
Chapter 16
   1869-1873 80
Chapter 17
   1873-1878 84
Chapter 18
   1878-1884 89
Chapter 19
   1881-1887 94
Chapter 20 .... *100*
Chapter 21
   1887-1889 107
Chapter 22
   1889 112
   Conclusion 115

Preface

Such letters of Mr. Browning's as appear, whole or in part, in the present volume have been in most cases given to me by the persons to whom they were addressed, or copied by Miss Browning from the originals under her care; but I owe to the daughter of the Rev. W. J. Fox—Mrs. Bridell Fox—those written to her father and to Miss Flower; the two interesting extracts from her father's correspondence with herself and Mr. Browning's note to Mr. Robertson.

For my general material I have been largely indebted to Miss Browning. Her memory was the only existing record of her brother's boyhood and youth. It has been to me an unfailing as well as always accessible authority for that subsequent period of his life which I could only know in disconnected facts or his own fragmentary reminiscences. It is less true, indeed, to say that she has greatly helped me in writing this short biography than that without her help it could never have been undertaken.

I thank my friends Mrs. R. Courtenay Bell and Miss Hickey for their invaluable assistance in preparing the book for, and carrying it through the press; and I acknowledge with real gratitude the advantages derived by it from Mr. Dykes Campbell's large literary experience in his very careful final revision of the proofs.

A. Orr. April 22, 1891.

CONTENTS LIFE AND LETTERS OF ROBERT BROWNING Chapter 1 Chapter 2 Chapter 3 Chapter 4 Chapter 5 Chapter 6 Chapter 7 Chapter 8 Chapter 9 Chapter 10 Chapter 11 Chapter 12 Chapter 13 Chapter 14 Chapter 15 Chapter 16 Chapter 17 Chapter 18 Chapter 19 Chapter 20 Chapter 21 Chapter 22 Conclusion Index

Chapter 1

Origin of the Browning Family—Robert Browning's

Grandfather—His position and Character—His first and second Marriage—Unkindness towards his eldest Son, Robert Browning's Father—Alleged Infusion of West Indian Blood through Robert Browning's Grandmother—Existing Evidence against it—The Grandmother's Portrait.

Chapter 2

Robert Browning's Father—His Position in Life—Comparison

between him and his Son—Tenderness towards his Son—Outline of his Habits and Character—His Death—Significant Newspaper Paragraph—Letter of Mr. Locker—Lampson—Robert Browning's Mother—Her Character and Antecedents—Their Influence upon her Son—Nervous Delicacy imparted to both her Children—Its special Evidences in her Son.

Chapter 3

1812-1826 Birth of Robert Browning—His Childhood

and Schooldays—Restless Temperament—Brilliant Mental Endowments—Incidental Peculiarities—Strong Religious Feeling—Passionate Attachment to his Mother; Grief at first Separation—Fondness for Animals—Experiences of School Life—Extensive Reading—Early Attempts in Verse—Letter from his Father concerning them—Spurious Poems in Circulation—'Incondita'—Mr. Fox—Miss Flower.

Chapter 4

1826-1833 First Impressions of Keats and Shelley—Prolonged

Influence of Shelley—Details of Home Education—Its Effects—Youthful Restlessness—Counteracting Love of Home—Early Friendships: Alfred Domett, Joseph Arnould, the Silverthornes—Choice of Poetry as a Profession—Alternative Suggestions; mistaken Rumours concerning them—Interest in Art—Love of good Theatrical Performances—Talent for Acting—Final Preparation for Literary Life.

Chapter 5

1833-1835 'Pauline'—Letters to Mr. Fox—Publication of the

Poem; chief Biographical and Literary Characteristics—Mr. Fox's Review in the 'Monthly Repository'; other Notices—Russian Journey—Desired diplomatic Appointment—Minor Poems; first Sonnet; their Mode of Appearance—'The Trifler'—M. de Ripert-Monclar—'Paracelsus'—Letters to Mr. Fox concerning it; its Publication—Incidental Origin of

'Paracelsus'; its inspiring Motive; its Relation to 'Pauline'—Mr. Fox's Review of it in the 'Monthly Repository'—Article in the 'Examiner' by John Forster.

Chapter 6

1835-1838 Removal to Hatcham; some Particulars—Renewed

Intercourse with the second Family of Robert Browning's Grandfather—Reuben Browning—William Shergold Browning—Visitors at Hatcham—Thomas Carlyle—Social Life—New Friends and Acquaintance—Introduction to Macready—New Year's Eve at Elm Place—Introduction to John Forster—Miss Fanny Haworth—Miss Martineau—Serjeant Talfourd—The 'Ion' Supper—'Strafford'—Relations with Macready—Performance of 'Strafford'—Letters concerning it from Mr. Browning and Miss Flower—Personal Glimpses of Robert Browning—Rival Forms of Dramatic Inspiration—Relation of 'Strafford' to 'Sordello'—Mr. Robertson and the 'Westminster Review'.

Chapter 7

1838-1841 First Italian Journey—Letters to Miss Haworth—Mr.

John Kenyon—'Sordello'—Letter to Miss Flower—'Pippa Passes'—'Bells and Pomegranates'.

Chapter 8

1841-1844 'A Blot in the 'Scutcheon'—Letters to Mr.

Frank Hill; Lady Martin—Charles Dickens—Other Dramas and Minor Poems—Letters to Miss Lee; Miss Haworth; Miss Flower—Second Italian Journey; Naples—E. J. Trelawney—Stendhal.

Chapter 9

1844-1849 Introduction to Miss Barrett—Engagement—Motives

for Secrecy—Marriage—Journey to Italy—Extract of Letter from Mr. Fox—Mrs. Browning's Letters to Miss Mitford—Life at Pisa—Vallombrosa—Florence; Mr. Powers; Miss Boyle—Proposed British Mission to the Vatican—Father Prout—Palazzo Guidi—Fano; Ancona—'A Blot in the 'Scutcheon' at Sadler's Wells.

Chapter 10

1849-1852 Death of Mr. Browning's Mother—Birth of his

Son—Mrs. Browning's Letters continued—Baths of Lucca—Florence again—Venice—Margaret Fuller Ossoli—Visit to England—Winter in Paris—Carlyle—George Sand—Alfred de Musset.

Chapter 11

1852-1855 M. Joseph Milsand—His close Friendship with

Mr. Browning; Mrs. Browning's Impression of him—New Edition of Mr. Browning's Poems—'Christmas Eve and Easter Day'—'Essay' on Shelley—Summer in London—Dante Gabriel Rossetti—Florence; secluded Life—Letters from Mr. and Mrs. Browning—'Colombe's Birthday'—Baths of Lucca—Mrs. Browning's Letters—Winter in Rome—Mr. and Mrs. Story—Mrs. Sartoris—Mrs. Fanny Kemble—Summer in London—Tennyson—Ruskin.

Chapter 12

1855-1858 'Men and Women'—'Karshook'—'Two in the

Campagna'—Winter in Paris; Lady Elgin—'Aurora Leigh'—Death of Mr. Kenyon and Mr. Barrett—Penini—Mrs. Browning's Letters to Miss Browning—The Florentine Carnival—Baths of Lucca—Spiritualism—Mr. Kirkup; Count Ginnasi—Letter from Mr. Browning to Mr. Fox—Havre.

Chapter 13

1858-1861 Mrs. Browning's Illness—Siena—Letter from Mr.

Browning to Mr. Leighton—Mrs. Browning's Letters continued—Walter Savage Landor—Winter in Rome—Mr. Val Prinsep—Friends in Rome: Mr. and Mrs. Cartwright—Multiplying Social Relations—Massimo d'Azeglio—Siena again—Illness and Death of Mrs. Browning's Sister—Mr. Browning's Occupations—Madame du Quaire—Mrs. Browning's last Illness and Death.

Chapter 14

1861-1863 Miss Blagden—Letters from Mr. Browning to

Miss Haworth and Mr. Leighton—His Feeling in regard to Funeral Ceremonies—Establishment in London—Plan of Life—Letter to Madame du Quaire—Miss Arabel Barrett—Biarritz—Letters to Miss Blagden—Conception of 'The Ring and the Book'—Biographical Indiscretion—New Edition of his Works—Mr. and Mrs. Procter.

Chapter 15

1863-1869 Pornic—'James Lee's Wife'—Meeting at Mr. F.

Palgrave's—Letters to Miss Blagden—His own Estimate of his Work—His Father's Illness and Death; Miss Browning—Le Croisic—Academic Honours; Letter to the Master of Balliol—Death of Miss Barrett—Audierne—Uniform Edition of his Works—His rising Fame—'Dramatis Personae'—'The Ring and the Book'; Character of Pompilia.

Chapter 16

1869-1873 Lord Dufferin; Helen's Tower—Scotland; Visit to

Lady Ashburton—Letters to Miss Blagden—St.-Aubin; The Franco-Prussian War—'Herve Riel'—Letter to Mr. G. M. Smith—'Balaustion's Adventure'; 'Prince Hohenstiel—Schwangau'—'Fifine at the Fair'—Mistaken Theories of Mr. Browning's Work—St.-Aubin; 'Red Cotton Nightcap Country'.

Chapter 17

1873-1878 London Life—Love of Music—Miss

Egerton-Smith—Periodical Nervous Exhaustion—Mers; 'Aristophanes' Apology'—'Agamemnon'—'The Inn Album'—'Pacchiarotto and other Poems'—Visits to Oxford and Cambridge—Letters to Mrs. Fitz-Gerald—St. Andrews; Letter from Professor Knight—In the Savoyard Mountains—Death of Miss Egerton-Smith—'La Saisiaz'; 'The Two Poets of Croisic'—Selections from his Works.

Chapter 18

1878-1884 He revisits Italy; Asolo; Letters to Mrs.

Fitz-Gerald—Venice—Favourite Alpine Retreats—Mrs. Arthur Bronson—Life in Venice—A Tragedy at Saint-Pierre—Mr. Cholmondeley—Mr. Browning's Patriotic Feeling; Extract from Letter to Mrs. Charles Skirrow—'Dramatic Idyls'—'Jocoseria'—'Ferishtah's Fancies'.

Chapter 19

1881-1887 The Browning Society; Mr. Furnivall; Miss E.

H. Hickey—His Attitude towards the Society; Letter to Mrs. Fitz-Gerald—Mr. Thaxter, Mrs. Celia Thaxter—Letter to Miss Hickey; 'Strafford'—Shakspere and Wordsworth Societies—Letters to Professor Knight—Appreciation in Italy; Professor Nencioni—The Goldoni Sonnet—Mr. Barrett Browning; Palazzo Manzoni—Letters to Mrs. Charles Skirrow—Mrs. Bloomfield Moore—Llangollen; Sir Theodore and Lady Martin—Loss of old Friends—Foreign Correspondent of the Royal Academy—'Parleyings with certain People of Importance in their Day'.

Chapter 20

Constancy to Habit—Optimism—Belief in Providence—Political

Opinions—His Friendships—Reverence for Genius—Attitude towards his Public—Attitude towards his Work—Habits of Work—His Reading—Conversational Powers—Impulsiveness and Reserve—Nervous Peculiarities—His Benevolence—His Attitude towards Women.

Chapter 21

1887-1889 Marriage of Mr. Barrett Browning—Removal to De

Vere Gardens—Symptoms of failing Strength—New Poems; New Edition of his Works—Letters to Mr. George Bainton, Mr. Smith, and Lady Martin—Primiero and Venice—Letters to Miss Keep—The last Year in London—Asolo—Letters to Mrs. Fitz-Gerald, Mrs. Skirrow, and Mr. G. M. Smith.

Chapter 22

1889 Proposed Purchase of Land at Asolo—Venice—Letter

to Mr. G. Moulton-Barrett—Lines in the 'Athenaeum'—Letter to Miss Keep—Illness—Death—Funeral Ceremonial at Venice—Publication of 'Asolando'—Interment in Poets' Corner.

LIFE AND LETTERS OF ROBERT BROWNING

Chapter 1

Origin of the Browning Family—Robert Browning's Grandfather—His position and Character—His first and second Marriage—Unkindness towards his eldest Son, Robert Browning's Father—Alleged Infusion of West Indian Blood through Robert Browning's Grandmother—Existing Evidence against it—The Grandmother's Portrait.

A belief was current in Mr. Browning's lifetime that he had Jewish blood in his veins. It received outward support from certain accidents of his life, from his known interest in the Hebrew language and literature, from his friendship for various members of the Jewish community in London. It might well have yielded to the fact of his never claiming the kinship, which could not have existed without his knowledge, and which, if he had known it, he would, by reason of these very sympathies, have been the last person to disavow. The results of more recent and more systematic inquiry have shown the belief to be unfounded.

Our poet sprang, on the father's side, from an obscure or, as family tradition asserts, a decayed branch, of an Anglo-Saxon stock settled, at an early period of our history, in the south, and probably also south-west, of England. A line of Brownings owned the manors of Melbury-Sampford and Melbury-Osmond, in north-west Dorsetshire; their last representative disappeared—or was believed to do so—in the time of Henry VII., their manors passing into the hands of the Earls of Ilchester, who still hold them.* The name occurs after 1542 in different parts of the country: in two cases with the affix of 'esquire', in two also, though not in both coincidently, within twenty miles of Pentridge, where the first distinct traces of the poet's family appear. Its cradle, as he called it, was Woodyates, in the parish of Pentridge, on the Wiltshire confines of Dorsetshire; and there his ancestors, of the third and fourth generations, held, as we understand, a modest but independent social position.

* I am indebted for these facts, as well as for some others referring to, or supplied by, Mr. Browning's uncles, to some notes made for the Browning Society by Dr. Furnivall.

This fragment of history, if we may so call it, accords better with our impression of Mr. Browning's genius than could any pedigree which more palpably connected him with the 'knightly' and 'squirely' families whose name he bore. It supplies the strong roots of English national life to which we instinctively refer it. Both the vivid originality of that genius and its healthy assimilative power stamp it as, in some sense, the product of virgin soil; and although the varied elements which entered into its growth were racial as well as cultural, and inherited as well as absorbed, the evidence of its strong natural or physical basis remains undisturbed.

Mr. Browning, for his own part, maintained a neutral attitude in the matter. He neither claimed nor disclaimed the more remote genealogical past which had presented itself as a certainty to some older members of his family. He preserved the old framed coat-of-arms handed down to him from his grandfather; and used, without misgiving as to his right to do so, a signet-ring engraved from it, the gift of a favourite uncle, in years gone by. But, so long as he was young, he had no reason to think about his ancestors; and, when he was old, he had no reason to care about them; he knew himself to be, in every possible case, the most important fact in his family history.

Roi ne suis, ni Prince aussi, Suis le seigneur de Conti,

he wrote, a few years back, to a friend who had incidentally questioned him about it.

Our immediate knowledge of the family begins with Mr. Browning's grandfather, also a Robert Browning, who obtained through Lord Shaftesbury's influence a clerkship in the Bank of England, and entered on it when barely twenty, in 1769. He served fifty years, and rose to the position of Principal of the Bank Stock Office, then an important one, and which brought him into contact with the leading financiers of the day. He became also a lieutenant in the Honourable Artillery Company, and took part in the defence of the Bank in the Gordon Riots of 1789. He was an able, energetic, and worldly man: an Englishman, very much of the provincial type; his literary tastes being limited to the Bible and 'Tom Jones', both of which he is said to have read through once a year. He possessed a handsome person and, probably, a vigorous constitution, since he lived to the age of eighty-four, though frequently tormented by gout; a circumstance which may help to account for his not having seen much of his grandchildren, the poet and his sister; we are indeed told that he particularly dreaded the lively boy's vicinity to his afflicted foot. He married, in 1778, Margaret, daughter of a Mr. Tittle by his marriage with Miss Seymour; and who was born in the West Indies and had inherited property there. They had three children: Robert, the poet's father; a daughter, who lived an uneventful life and plays no part in the family history; and another son who died an infant. The Creole mother died also when her eldest boy was only seven years old, and passed out of his memory in all but an indistinct impression of having seen her lying in her coffin. Five years later the widower married a Miss Smith, who gave him a large family.

This second marriage of Mr. Browning's was a critical event in the life of his eldest son; it gave him, to all appearance, two step-parents instead of one. There could have been little sympathy between his father and himself, for no two persons were ever more unlike, but there was yet another cause for the systematic unkindness under which the lad grew up. Mr. Browning fell, as a hard man easily does, greatly under the influence of his second wife, and this influence was made by her to subserve the interests of a more than natural jealousy of her predecessor. An early instance of this was her banishing the dead lady's portrait to a garret, on the plea that her husband did not need two wives. The son could be no burden upon her because he had a little income, derived from his mother's brother; but this, probably, only heightened her ill-will towards him. When he was old enough to go to a University, and very desirous of going—when, moreover, he offered to do so at his own cost—she induced his father to forbid it, because, she urged, they could not afford to send their other sons to college. An earlier ambition of his had been to become an artist; but when he showed his first completed picture to his father, the latter turned away and refused to look at it. He gave himself the finishing stroke in the parental eyes, by throwing up a lucrative employment which he had held for a short time on his mother's West Indian property, in disgust at the system of slave labour which was still in force there; and he paid for this unpractical conduct as soon as he was of age, by the compulsory reimbursement of all the expenses which his father, up to that date, had incurred for him; and by the loss of his mother's fortune, which, at the time of her marriage, had not been settled upon her. It was probably in despair of doing anything better, that, soon after this, in his twenty-second year, he also became a clerk in the Bank of England. He married and settled in Camberwell, in 1811; his son and daughter were born, respectively, in 1812 and 1814. He became a widower in 1849; and when, four years later, he had completed his term of service at the Bank, he went with his daughter to Paris, where they resided until his death in 1866.

Dr. Furnivall has originated a theory, and maintains it as a conviction, that Mr. Browning's grandmother was more than a Creole in the strict sense of the term, that of a person born of white parents in the West Indies, and that an unmistakable dash of dark blood passed from her to her son and grandson. Such an occurrence was, on the face of it, not impossible, and would be absolutely unimportant to my mind, and, I think I may add, to that of Mr. Browning's sister and son. The poet and his father were what we know them, and if negro blood had any part in their composition, it was no worse for them, and so much the better for the negro. But many persons among us are very averse to the idea of such a cross; I believe its assertion, in the present case, to be entirely mistaken; I prefer, therefore, touching on the facts alleged in favour of it, to passing them over in a silence which might be taken to mean indifference, but might also be interpreted into assent.

We are told that Mr. Browning was so dark in early life, that a nephew who saw him in Paris, in 1837, mistook him for an Italian. He neither had nor could have had a nephew; and he was not out of England at the time specified. It is said that when Mr. Browning senior was residing on his mother's sugar plantation at St. Kitt's, his appearance was held to justify his being placed in church among the coloured members of the congregation. We are assured in the strongest terms that the story has no foundation, and this by a gentleman whose authority in all matters concerning the Browning family Dr. Furnivall has otherwise accepted as conclusive. If the anecdote were true it would be a singular circumstance that Mr. Browning senior was always fond of drawing negro heads, and thus obviously disclaimed any unpleasant association with them.

I do not know the exact physical indications by which a dark strain is perceived; but if they are to be sought in the colouring of eyes, hair, and skin, they have been conspicuously absent in the two persons who in the present case are supposed to have borne them. The poet's father had light blue eyes and, I am assured by those who knew him best, a clear, ruddy complexion. His appearance induced strangers passing him in the Paris streets to remark, 'C'est un Anglais!' The absolute whiteness of Miss Browning's skin was modified in her brother by a sallow tinge sufficiently explained by frequent disturbance of the liver; but it never affected the clearness of his large blue-grey eyes; and his hair, which grew dark as he approached manhood, though it never became black, is spoken of, by everyone who remembers him in childhood and youth, as golden. It is no less worthy of note that the daughter of his early friend Mr. Fox, who grew up in the little social circle to which he belonged, never even heard of the dark cross now imputed to him; and a lady who made his acquaintance during his twenty-fourth year, wrote a sonnet upon him, beginning with these words:

Thy brow is calm, young Poet—pale and clear As a moonlighted statue.

The suggestion of Italian characteristics in the Poet's face may serve, however, to introduce a curious fact, which can have no bearing on the main lines of his descent, but holds collateral possibilities concerning it. His mother's name Wiedemann or Wiedeman appears in a merely contracted form as that of one of the oldest families naturalized in Venice. It became united by marriage with the Rezzonico; and, by a strange coincidence, the last of these who occupied the palace now owned by Mr. Barrett Browning was a Widman-Rezzonico. The present Contessa Widman has lately restored her own palace, which was falling into ruin.

That portrait of the first Mrs. Browning, which gave so much umbrage to her husband's second wife, has hung for many years in her grandson's dining-room, and is well known to all his friends. It represents a stately woman with an unmistakably fair skin; and if the face or hair betrays any indication of possible dark blood, it is imperceptible to the general observer, and must be of too slight and fugitive a nature to enter into the discussion. A long curl touches one shoulder. One hand rests upon a copy of Thomson's 'Seasons', which was held to be the proper study and recreation of cultivated women in those days. The picture was painted by Wright of Derby.

A brother of this lady was an adventurous traveller, and was said to have penetrated farther into the interior of Africa than any other European of his time. His violent death will be found recorded in a singular experience of the poet's middle life.

Chapter 2

Robert Browning's Father—His Position in Life—Comparison between him and his Son—Tenderness towards his Son—Outline of his Habits and Character—His Death—Significant Newspaper Paragraph—Letter of Mr. Locker-Lampson—Robert Browning's Mother—Her Character and Antecedents—Their Influence upon her Son—Nervous Delicacy imparted to both her Children—Its special Evidences in her Son.

It was almost a matter of course that Robert Browning's father should be disinclined for bank work. We are told, and can easily imagine, that he was not so good an official as the grandfather; we know that he did not rise so high, nor draw so large a salary. But he made the best of his position for his family's sake, and it was at that time both more important and more lucrative than such appointments have since become. Its emoluments could be increased by many honourable means not covered by the regular salary. The working-day was short, and every additional hour's service well paid. To be enrolled on the night-watch was also very remunerative; there were enormous perquisites in pens, paper, and sealing-wax.* Mr. Browning availed himself of these opportunities of adding to his income, and was thus enabled, with the help of his private means, to gratify his scholarly and artistic tastes, and give his children the benefit of a very liberal education—the one distinct ideal of success in life which such a nature as his could form. Constituted as he was, he probably suffered very little through the paternal unkindness which had forced him into an uncongenial career. Its only palpable result was to make him a more anxiously indulgent parent when his own time came.

* I have been told that, far from becoming careless in the use of these things from his practically unbounded command of them, he developed for them an almost superstitious reverence. He could never endure to see a scrap of writing-paper wasted.

Many circumstances conspired to secure to the coming poet a happier childhood and youth than his father had had. His path was to be smoothed not only by natural affection and conscientious care, but by literary and artistic sympathy. The second Mr. Browning differed, in certain respects, as much from the third as from the first. There were, nevertheless, strong points in which, if he did not resemble, he at least distinctly foreshadowed him; and the genius of the one would lack some possible explanation if we did not recognize in great measure its organized material in the other. Much, indeed, that was genius in the son existed as talent in the father. The moral nature of the younger man diverged from that of the older, though retaining strong points of similarity; but the mental equipments of the two differed far less in themselves than in the different uses to which temperament and circumstances trained them.

The most salient intellectual characteristic of Mr. Browning senior was his passion for reading. In his daughter's words, 'he read in season, and out of season;' and he not only read, but remembered. As a schoolboy, he knew by heart the first book of the 'Iliad', and all the odes of Horace; and it shows how deeply the classical part of his training must have entered into him, that he was wont, in later life, to soothe his little boy to sleep by humming to him an ode of Anacreon. It was one of his amusements at school to organize Homeric combats among the boys, in which the fighting was carried on in the manner of the Greeks and Trojans, and he and his friend Kenyon would arm themselves with swords and shields, and hack at each other lustily, exciting themselves to battle by insulting speeches derived from the Homeric text.*

* This anecdote is partly quoted from Mrs. Andrew Crosse, who has introduced it into her article 'John Kenyon and his Friends', 'Temple Bar', April 1890. She herself received it from Mr. Dykes Campbell.

Mr. Browning had also an extraordinary power of versifying, and taught his son from babyhood the words he wished him to remember, by joining them to a grotesque rhyme; the child learned all his Latin declensions in this way. His love of art had been proved by his desire to adopt it as a profession; his talent for it was evidenced by the life and power of the sketches, often caricatures, which fell from his pen or pencil as easily as written words. Mr. Barrett Browning remembers gaining a very early elementary knowledge of anatomy from comic illustrated rhymes now in the possession of their old friend, Mrs. Fraser Corkran through which his grandfather impressed upon him the names and position of the principal bones of the human body.

Even more remarkable than his delight in reading was the manner in which Mr. Browning read. He carried into it all the preciseness of the scholar. It was his habit when he bought a book—which was generally an old one allowing of this addition—to have some pages of blank paper bound into it. These he filled with notes, chronological tables, or such other supplementary matter as would enhance the interest, or assist the mastering, of its contents; all written in a clear and firm though by no means formal handwriting. More than one book thus treated by him has passed through my hands, leaving in me, it need hardly be said, a stronger impression of the owner's intellectual quality than the acquisition by him of the finest library could have conveyed. One of the experiences which disgusted him with St. Kitt's was the frustration by its authorities of an attempt he was making to teach a negro boy to read, and the understanding that all such educative action was prohibited.

In his faculties and attainments, as in his pleasures and appreciations, he showed the simplicity and genuineness of a child. He was not only ready to amuse, he could always identify himself with children, his love for whom never failed him in even his latest years. His more than childlike indifference to pecuniary advantages had been shown in early life. He gave another proof of it after his wife's death, when he declined a proposal, made to him by the Bank of England, to assist in founding one of its branch establishments in Liverpool. He never indeed, personally, cared for money, except as a means of acquiring old, i.e. rare books, for which he had, as an acquaintance declared, the scent of a hound and the snap of a bulldog. His eagerness to possess such treasures was only matched by the generosity with which he parted with them; and his daughter well remembers the feeling of angry suspicion with which she and her brother noted the periodical arrival of a certain visitor who would be closeted with their father for hours, and steal away before the supper time, when the family would meet, with some precious parcel of books or prints under his arm.

It is almost superfluous to say that he was indifferent to creature comforts. Miss Browning was convinced that, if on any occasion she had said to him, 'There will be no dinner to-day,' he would only have looked up from his book to reply, 'All right, my dear, it is of no consequence.' In his bank-clerk days, when he sometimes dined in Town, he left one restaurant with which he was not otherwise dissatisfied, because the waiter always gave him the trouble of specifying what he would have to eat. A hundred times that trouble would not have deterred him from a kindly act. Of his goodness of heart, indeed, many distinct instances might be given; but even this scanty outline of his life has rendered them superfluous.

Mr. Browning enjoyed splendid physical health. His early love of reading had not precluded a wholesome enjoyment of athletic sports; and he was, as a boy, the fastest runner and best base-ball player in his school. He died, like his father, at eighty-four or rather, within a few days of eighty-five, but, unlike him, he had never been ill; a French friend exclaimed when all was over, 'Il n'a jamais ete vieux.' His faculties were so unclouded up to the last moment that he could watch himself dying, and speculate on the nature of the change which was befalling him. 'What do you think death is, Robert?' he said to his son; 'is it a fainting, or is it a pang?' A notice of his decease appeared in an American newspaper. It was written by an unknown hand, and bears a stamp of genuineness which renders the greater part of it worth quoting.

'He was not only a ruddy, active man, with fine hair, that retained its strength and brownness to the last, but he had a courageous spirit and a remarkably intelligent mind. He was a man of the finest culture, and was often, and never vainly, consulted by his son Robert concerning the more recondite facts relating to the old characters, whose bones that poet liked so well to disturb. His knowledge of old French, Spanish, and Italian literature was wonderful. The old man went smiling and peaceful to his long rest, preserving his faculties to the last, insomuch that the physician, astonished at his continued calmness and good humour, turned to his daughter, and said in a low voice, "Does this gentleman know that he is dying?" The daughter said in a voice which the father could hear, "He knows it;" and the old man said with a quiet smile, "Death is no enemy in my eyes." His last words were spoken to his son Robert, who was fanning him, "I fear I am wearying you, dear."'

Four years later one of his English acquaintances in Paris, Mr. Frederick Locker, now Mr. Locker-Lampson, wrote to Robert Browning as follows:

Dec. 26, 1870.

My dear Browning,—I have always thought that you or Miss Browning, or some other capable person, should draw up a sketch of your excellent father so that, hereafter, it might be known what an interesting man he was.

I used often to meet you in Paris, at Lady Elgin's. She had a genuine taste for poetry, and she liked being read to, and I remember you gave her a copy of Keats' poems, and you used often to read his poetry to her. Lady Elgin died in 1860, and I think it was in that year that Lady Charlotte and I saw the most of Mr. Browning.* He was then quite an elderly man, if years could make him so, but he had so much vivacity of manner, and such simplicity and freshness of mind, that it was difficult to think him old.

* Mr. Locker was then married to Lady Charlotte Bruce, Lady Elgin's daughter.

I remember, he and your sister lived in an apartment in the Rue de Grenelle, St. Germain, in quite a simple fashion, much in the way that most people live in Paris, and in the way that all sensible people would wish to live all over the world.

Your father and I had at least one taste and affection in common. He liked hunting the old bookstalls on the 'quais', and he had a great love and admiration for Hogarth; and he possessed several of Hogarth's engravings, some in rare and early states of the plate; and he would relate with glee the circumstances under which he had picked them up, and at so small a price too! However, he had none of the 'petit-maitre' weakness of the ordinary collector, which is so common, and which I own to!—such as an infatuation for tall copies, and wide margins.

I remember your father was fond of drawing in a rough and ready fashion; he had plenty of talent, I should think not very great cultivation; but quite enough to serve his purpose, and to amuse his friends. He had a thoroughly lively and *healthy* interest in your poetry, and he showed me some of your boyish attempts at versification.

Taking your dear father altogether, I quite believe him to have been one of those men—interesting men—whom the world never hears of. Perhaps he was shy—at any rate he was much less known than he ought to have been; and now, perhaps, he only remains in the recollection of his family, and of one or two superior people like myself! who were capable of appreciating him. My dear Browning, I really hope you will draw up a slight sketch of your father before it is too late. Yours, Frederick Locker.

The judgments thus expressed twenty years ago are cordially re-stated in the letter in which Mr. Locker-Lampson authorizes me to publish them. The desired memoir was never written; but the few details which I have given of the older Mr. Browning's life and character may perhaps stand for it.

With regard to the 'strict dissent' with which her parents have been taxed, Miss Browning writes to me: 'My father was born and educated in the Church of England, and, for many years before his death, lived in her communion. He became a Dissenter in middle life, and my mother, born and brought up in the Kirk of Scotland, became one also; but they could not be called bigoted, since we always in the evening attended the preaching of the Rev. Henry Melvill* afterwards Canon of St. Paul's, whose sermons Robert much admired.'**

* At Camden Chapel, Camberwell. ** Mr. Browning was much interested, in later years, in hearing Canon, perhaps then already Archdeacon, Farrar extol his eloquence and ask whether he had known him. Mr. Ruskin also spoke of him with admiration.

Little need be said about the poet's mother. She was spoken of by Carlyle as 'the true type of a Scottish gentlewoman.' Mr. Kenyon declared that such as she had no need to go to heaven, because they made it wherever they were. But her character was all resumed in her son's words, spoken with the tremulous emotion which so often accompanied his allusion to those he had loved and lost: 'She was a divine woman.' She was Scotch on the maternal side, and her kindly, gentle, but distinctly evangelical Christianity must have been derived from that source. Her father, William Wiedemann, a ship-owner, was a Hamburg German settled in Dundee, and has been described by Mr. Browning as an accomplished draughtsman and musician. She herself had nothing of the artist about her, though we hear of her sometimes playing the piano; in all her goodness and sweetness she seems to have been somewhat matter-of-fact. But there is abundant indirect evidence of Mr. Browning's love of music having come to him through her, and we are certainly justified in holding the Scottish-German descent as accountable, in great measure at least, for the metaphysical quality so early apparent in the poet's mind, and of which we find no evidence in that of his father. His strong religious instincts must have been derived from both parents, though most anxiously fostered by his mother.

There is yet another point on which Mrs. Browning must have influenced the life and destinies of her son, that of physical health, or, at least, nervous constitution. She was a delicate woman, very anaemic during her later years, and a martyr to neuralgia, which was perhaps a symptom of this condition. The acute ailment reproduced itself in her daughter in spite of an otherwise vigorous constitution. With the brother, the inheritance of suffering was not less surely present, if more difficult to trace. We have been accustomed to speaking of him as a brilliantly healthy man; he was healthy, even strong, in many essential respects. Until past the age of seventy he could take long walks without fatigue, and endure an amount of social and general physical strain which would have tried many younger men. He carried on until the last a large, if not always serious, correspondence, and only within the latest months, perhaps weeks of his life, did his letters even suggest that physical brain-power was failing him. He had, within the limits which his death has assigned to it, a considerable recuperative power. His consciousness of health was vivid, so long as he was well; and it was only towards the end that the faith in his probable length of days occasionally deserted him. But he died of no acute disease, more than seven years younger than his father, having long carried with him external marks of age from which his father remained exempt. Till towards the age of forty he suffered from attacks of sore-throat, not frequent, but of an angry kind. He was constantly troubled by imperfect action of the liver, though no doctor pronounced the evil serious. I have spoken of this in reference to his complexion. During the last twenty years, if not for longer, he rarely spent a winter without a suffocating cold and cough; within the last five, asthmatic symptoms established themselves; and when he sank under what was perhaps his first real attack of bronchitis it was not because the attack was very severe, but because the heart was exhausted. The circumstances of his death recalled that of his mother; and we might carry the sad analogy still farther in his increasing pallor, and the slow and not strong pulse which always characterized him. This would perhaps be a mistake. It is difficult to reconcile any idea of bloodlessness with the bounding vitality of his younger body and mind. Any symptom of organic disease could scarcely, in his case, have been overlooked. But so much is certain: he was conscious of what he called a nervousness of nature which neither father nor grandfather could have bequeathed to him. He imputed to this, or, in other words, to an undue physical sensitiveness to mental causes of irritation, his proneness to deranged liver, and the asthmatic conditions which he believed, rightly or wrongly, to be produced by it. He was perhaps mistaken in some of his inferences, but he was not mistaken in the fact. He had the pleasures as well as the pains of this nervous temperament; its quick response to every congenial stimulus of physical atmosphere, and human contact. It heightened the enjoyment, perhaps exaggerated the consciousness of his physical powers. It also certainly in his later years led him to overdraw them. Many persons have believed that he could not live without society; a prolonged seclusion from it would, for obvious reasons, have been unsuited to him. But the excited gaiety which to the last he carried into every social gathering was often primarily the result of a moral and physical effort which his temperament prompted, but his strength could not always justify. Nature avenged herself in recurrent periods of exhaustion, long before the closing stage had set in.

I shall subsequently have occasion to trace this nervous impressibility through various aspects and relations of his life; all I now seek to show is that this healthiest of poets and most real of men was not compounded of elements of pure health, and perhaps never could have been so. It might sound grotesque to say that only a delicate woman could have been the mother of Robert Browning. The fact remains that of such a one, and no other, he was born; and we may imagine, without being fanciful, that his father's placid intellectual powers required for their transmutation into poetic genius just this infusion of a vital element not only charged with other racial and individual qualities, but physically and morally more nearly allied to pain. Perhaps, even for his happiness as a man, we could not have wished it otherwise.

Chapter 3

1812-1826

Birth of Robert Browning—His Childhood and Schooldays—Restless Temperament—Brilliant Mental Endowments—Incidental Peculiarities—Strong Religious Feeling—Passionate Attachment to his Mother; Grief at first Separation—Fondness for Animals—Experiences of School Life—Extensive Reading—Early Attempts in Verse—Letter from his Father concerning them—Spurious Poems in Circulation—'Incondita'—Mr. Fox—Miss Flower.

Robert Browning was born, as has been often repeated, at Camberwell, on May 7, 1812, soon after a great comet had disappeared from the sky. He was a handsome, vigorous, fearless child, and soon developed an unresting activity and a fiery temper. He clamoured for occupation from the moment he could speak. His mother could only keep him quiet when once he had emerged from infancy by telling him stories—doubtless Bible stories—while holding him on her knee. His energies were of course destructive till they had found their proper outlet; but we do not hear of his ever having destroyed anything for the mere sake of doing so. His first recorded piece of mischief was putting a handsome Brussels lace veil of his mother's into the fire; but the motive, which he was just old enough to lisp out, was also his excuse: 'A pitty baze [pretty blaze], mamma.' Imagination soon came to his rescue. It has often been told how he extemporized verse aloud while walking round and round the dining-room table supporting himself by his hands, when he was still so small that his head was scarcely above it. He remembered having entertained his mother in the very first walk he was considered old enough to take with her, by a fantastic account of his possessions in houses, &c., of which the topographical details elicited from her the remark, 'Why, sir, you are quite a geographer.' And though this kind of romancing is common enough among intelligent children, it distinguishes itself in this case by the strong impression which the incident had left on his own mind. It seems to have been a first real flight of dramatic fancy, confusing his identity for the time being.

The power of inventing did not, however, interfere with his readiness to learn, and the facility with which he acquired whatever knowledge came in his way had, on one occasion, inconvenient results. A lady of reduced fortunes kept a small elementary school for boys, a stone's-throw from his home; and he was sent to it as a day boarder at so tender an age that his parents, it is supposed, had no object in view but to get rid of his turbulent activity for an hour or two every morning and afternoon. Nevertheless, his proficiency in reading and spelling was soon so much ahead of that of the biggest boy, that complaints broke out among the mammas, who were sure there was not fair play. Mrs.——was neglecting her other pupils for the sake of 'bringing on Master Browning;' and the poor lady found it necessary to discourage Master Browning's attendance lest she should lose the remainder of her flock. This, at least, was the story as he himself remembered it. According to Miss Browning his instructress did not yield without a parting shot. She retorted on the discontented parents that, if she could give their children 'Master Browning's intellect', she would have no difficulty in satisfying them. After this came the interlude of home-teaching, in which all his elementary knowledge must have been gained. As an older child he was placed with two Misses Ready, who prepared boys for entering their brother's the Rev. Thomas Ready's school; and in due time he passed into the latter, where he remained up to the age of fourteen.

He seems in those early days to have had few playmates beyond his sister, two years younger than himself, and whom his irrepressible spirit must sometimes have frightened or repelled. Nor do we hear anything of childish loves; and though an entry appeared in his diary one Sunday in about the seventh or eighth year of his age, 'married two wives this morning,' it only referred to a vague imaginary appropriation of two girls whom he had just seen in church, and whose charm probably lay in their being much bigger than he. He was, however, capable of a self-conscious shyness in the presence of even a little girl; and his sense of certain proprieties was extraordinarily keen. He told a friend that on one occasion, when the merest child, he had edged his way by the wall from one point of his bedroom to another, because he was not fully clothed, and his reflection in the glass could otherwise have been seen through the partly open door.*

* Another anecdote, of a very different kind, belongs to an earlier period, and to that category of pure naughtiness which could not fail to be sometimes represented in the conduct of so gifted a child. An old lady who visited his mother, and was characterized in the family as 'Aunt Betsy', had irritated him by pronouncing the word 'lovers' with the contemptuous jerk which the typical old maid is sometimes apt to impart to it, when once the question had arisen why a certain 'Lovers' Walk' was so called. He was too nearly a baby to imagine what a 'lover' was; he supposed the name denoted a trade or occupation. But his human sympathy resented Aunt Betsy's manner as an affront; and he determined, after probably repeated provocation, to show her something worse than a 'lover', whatever this might be. So one night he slipped out of bed, exchanged his nightgown for what he considered the appropriate undress of a devil, completed this by a paper tail, and the ugliest face he could make, and rushed into the drawing-room, where the old lady and his mother were drinking tea. He was snatched up and carried away before he had had time to judge the effect of his apparition; but he did not think, looking back upon the circumstances in later life, that Aunt Betsy had deserved quite so ill of her fellow-creatures as he then believed.

His imaginative emotions were largely absorbed by religion. The early Biblical training had had its effect, and he was, to use his own words, 'passionately religious' in those nursery years; but during them and many succeeding ones, his mother filled his heart. He loved her so much, he has been heard to say, that even as a grown man he could not sit by her otherwise than with an arm round her waist. It is difficult to measure the influence which this feeling may have exercised on his later life; it led, even now, to a strange and touching little incident which had in it the incipient poet no less than the loving child. His attendance at Miss Ready's school only kept him from home from Monday till Saturday of every week; but when called upon to confront his first five days of banishment he felt sure that he would not survive them. A leaden cistern belonging to the school had in, or outside it, the raised image of a face. He chose the cistern for his place of burial, and converted the face into his epitaph by passing his hand over and over it to a continuous chant of: 'In memory of unhappy Browning'—the ceremony being renewed in his spare moments, till the acute stage of the feeling had passed away.

The fondness for animals for which through life he was noted, was conspicuous in his very earliest days. His urgent demand for 'something to do' would constantly include 'something to be caught' for him: 'they were to catch him an eft;' 'they were to catch him a frog.' He would refuse to take his medicine unless bribed by the gift of a speckled frog from among the strawberries; and the maternal parasol, hovering above the strawberry bed during the search for this object of his desires, remained a standing picture in his remembrance. But the love of the uncommon was already asserting itself; and one of his very juvenile projects was a collection of rare creatures, the first contribution to which was a couple of ladybirds, picked up one winter's day on a wall and immediately consigned to a box lined with cotton-wool, and labelled, 'Animals found surviving in the depths of a severe winter.' Nor did curiosity in this case weaken the power of sympathy. His passion for birds and beasts was the counterpart of his father's love of children, only displaying itself before the age at which child-love naturally appears. His mother used to read Croxall's Fables to his little sister and him. The story contained in them of a lion who was kicked to death by an ass affected him so painfully that he could no longer endure the sight of the book; and as he dared not destroy it, he buried it between the stuffing and the woodwork of an old dining-room chair, where it stood for lost, at all events for the time being. When first he heard the adventures of the parrot who insisted on leaving his cage, and who enjoyed himself for a little while and then died of hunger and cold, he—and his sister with him—cried so bitterly that it was found necessary to invent a different ending, according to which the parrot was rescued just in time and brought back to his cage to live peacefully in it ever after.

As a boy, he kept owls and monkeys, magpies and hedgehogs, an eagle, and even a couple of large snakes, constantly bringing home the more portable creatures in his pockets, and transferring them to his mother for immediate care. I have heard him speak admiringly of the skilful tenderness with which she took into her lap a lacerated cat, washed and sewed up its ghastly wound, and nursed it back to health. The great intimacy with the life and habits of animals which reveals itself in his works is readily explained by these facts.

Mr. Ready's establishment was chosen for him as the best in the neighbourhood; and both there and under the preparatory training of that gentleman's sisters, the young Robert was well and kindly cared for. The Misses Ready especially concerned themselves with the spiritual welfare of their pupils. The periodical hair-brushings were accompanied by the singing, and fell naturally into the measure, of Watts's hymns; and Mr. Browning has given his friends some very hearty laughs by illustrating with voice and gesture the ferocious emphasis with which the brush would swoop down in the accentuated syllables of the following lines:

Lord, 'tis a pleasant thing to stand In gardens planted by Thy hand. . . . . . Fools never raise their thoughts so high, Like 'brutes' they live, like brutes they die.

He even compelled his mother to laugh at it, though it was sorely against her nature to lend herself to any burlesquing of piously intended things.* He had become a bigger boy since the episode of the cistern, and had probably in some degree outgrown the intense piety of his earlier childhood. This little incident seems to prove it. On the whole, however, his religious instincts did not need strengthening, though his sense of humour might get the better of them for a moment; and of secular instruction he seems to have received as little from the one set of teachers as from the other. I do not suppose that the mental training at Mr. Ready's was more shallow or more mechanical than that of most other schools of his own or, indeed, of a much later period; but the brilliant abilities of Robert Browning inspired him with a certain contempt for it, as also for the average schoolboy intelligence to which it was apparently adapted. It must be for this reason that, as he himself declared, he never gained a prize, although these rewards were showered in such profusion that the only difficulty was to avoid them; and if he did not make friends at school for this also has been somewhere observed,** it can only be explained in the same way. He was at an intolerant age, and if his schoolfellows struck him as more backward or more stupid than they need be, he is not likely to have taken pains to conceal the impression. It is difficult, at all events, to think of him as unsociable, and his talents certainly had their amusing side. Miss Browning tells me that he made his schoolfellows act plays, some of which he had written for them; and he delighted his friends, not long ago, by mimicking his own solemn appearance on some breaking-up or commemorative day, when, according to programme, 'Master Browning' ascended a platform in the presence of assembled parents and friends, and, in best jacket, white gloves, and carefully curled hair, with a circular bow to the company and the then prescribed waving of alternate arms, delivered a high-flown rhymed address of his own composition.

* In spite of this ludicrous association Mr. Browning always recognized great merit in Watts's hymns, and still more in Dr. Watts himself, who had devoted to this comparatively humble work intellectual powers competent to far higher things. ** It was in no case literally true. William, afterwards Sir William, Channel was leaving Mr. Ready when Browning went to him; but a friendly acquaintance began, and was afterwards continued, between the two boys; and a closer friendship, formed with a younger brother Frank, was only interrupted by his death. Another school friend or acquaintance recalled himself as such to the poet's memory some ten or twelve years ago. A man who has reached the age at which his boyhood becomes of interest to the world may even have survived many such relations.

And during the busy idleness of his schooldays, or, at all events, in the holidays in which he rested from it, he was learning, as perhaps only those do learn whose real education is derived from home. His father's house was, Miss Browning tells me, literally crammed with books; and, she adds, 'it was in this way that Robert became very early familiar with subjects generally unknown to boys.' He read omnivorously, though certainly not without guidance. One of the books he best and earliest loved was 'Quarles' Emblemes', which his father possessed in a seventeenth century edition, and which contains one or two very tentative specimens of his early handwriting. Its quaint, powerful lines and still quainter illustrations combined the marvellous with what he believed to be true; and he seemed specially identified with its world of religious fancies by the fact that the soul in it was always depicted as a child. On its more general grounds his reading was at once largely literary and very historical; and it was in this direction that the paternal influence was most strongly revealed. 'Quarles' Emblemes' was only one of the large collection of old books which Mr. Browning possessed; and the young Robert learnt to know each favourite author in the dress as well as the language which carried with it the life of his period. The first edition of 'Robinson Crusoe'; the first edition of Milton's works, bought for him by his father; a treatise on astrology published twenty years after the introduction of printing; the original pamphlet 'Killing no Murder' 1559, which Carlyle borrowed for his 'Life of Cromwell'; an equally early copy of Bernard Mandeville's 'Bees'; very ancient Bibles—are some of the instances which occur to me. Among more modern publications, 'Walpole's Letters' were familiar to him in boyhood, as well as the 'Letters of Junius' and all the works of Voltaire.

Ancient poets and poetry also played their necessary part in the mental culture superintended by Robert Browning's father: we can indeed imagine no case in which they would not have found their way into the boy's life. Latin poets and Greek dramatists came to him in their due time, though his special delight in the Greek language only developed itself later. But his loving, lifelong familiarity with the Elizabethan school, and indeed with the whole range of English poetry, seems to point to a more constant study of our national literature. Byron was his chief master in those early poetic days. He never ceased to honour him as the one poet who combined a constructive imagination with the more technical qualities of his art; and the result of this period of aesthetic training was a volume of short poems produced, we are told, when he was only twelve, in which the Byronic influence was predominant.

The young author gave his work the title of 'Incondita', which conveyed a certain idea of deprecation. He was, nevertheless, very anxious to see it in print; and his father and mother, poetry-lovers of the old school, also found in it sufficient merit to justify its publication. No publisher, however, could be found; and we can easily believe that he soon afterwards destroyed the little manuscript, in some mingled reaction of disappointment and disgust. But his mother, meanwhile, had shown it to an acquaintance of hers, Miss Flower, who herself admired its contents so much as to make a copy of them for the inspection of her friend, the well-known Unitarian minister, Mr. W. J. Fox. The copy was transmitted to Mr. Browning after Mr. Fox's death by his daughter, Mrs. Bridell-Fox; and this, if no other, was in existence in 1871, when, at his urgent request, that lady also returned to him a fragment of verse contained in a letter from Miss Sarah Flower. Nor was it till much later that a friend, who had earnestly begged for a sight of it, definitely heard of its destruction. The fragment, which doubtless shared the same fate, was, I am told, a direct imitation of Coleridge's 'Fire, Famine, and Slaughter'.

These poems were not Mr. Browning's first. It would be impossible to believe them such when we remember that he composed verses long before he could write; and a curious proof of the opposite fact has recently appeared. Two letters of the elder Mr. Browning have found their way into the market, and have been bought respectively by Mr. Dykes Campbell and Sir F. Leighton. I give the more important of them. It was addressed to Mr. Thomas Powell:

Dear Sir,—I hope the enclosed may be acceptable as curiosities. They were written by Robert when quite a child. I once had nearly a hundred of them. But he has destroyed all that ever came in his way, having a great aversion to the practice of many biographers in recording every trifling incident that falls in their way. He has not the slightest suspicion that any of his very juvenile performances are in existence. I have several of the originals by me. They are all extemporaneous productions, nor has any one a single alteration. There was one amongst them 'On Bonaparte'—remarkably beautiful—and had I not seen it in his own handwriting I never would have believed it to have been the production of a child. It is destroyed. Pardon my troubling you with these specimens, and requesting you never to mention it, as Robert would be very much hurt. I remain, dear sir, Your obedient servant, R. Browning. Bank: March 11, 1843.

The letter was accompanied by a sheet of verses which have been sold and resold, doubtless in perfect good faith, as being those to which the writer alludes. But Miss Browning has recognized them as her father's own impromptu epigrams, well remembered in the family, together with the occasion on which they were written. The substitution may, from the first, have been accidental.

We cannot think of all these vanished first-fruits of Mr. Browning's genius without a sense of loss, all the greater perhaps that there can have been little in them to prefigure its later forms. Their faults seem to have lain in the direction of too great splendour of language and too little wealth of thought; and Mr. Fox, who had read 'Incondita' and been struck by its promise, confessed afterwards to Mr. Browning that he had feared these tendencies as his future snare. But the imitative first note of a young poet's voice may hold a rapture of inspiration which his most original later utterances will never convey. It is the child Sordello, singing against the lark.

Not even the poet's sister ever saw 'Incondita'. It was the only one of his finished productions which Miss Browning did not read, or even help him to write out. She was then too young to be taken into his confidence. Its writing, however, had one important result. It procured for the boy-poet a preliminary introduction to the valuable literary patron and friend Mr. Fox was subsequently to be. It also supplies the first substantial record of an acquaintance which made a considerable impression on his personal life.

The Miss Flower, of whom mention has been made, was one of two sisters, both sufficiently noted for their artistic gifts to have found a place in the new Dictionary of National Biography. The elder, Eliza or Lizzie, was a musical composer; the younger, best known as Sarah Flower Adams, a writer of sacred verse. Her songs and hymns, including the well-known 'Nearer, my God, to Thee', were often set to music by her sister.* They sang, I am told, delightfully together, and often without accompaniment, their voices perfectly harmonizing with each other. Both were, in their different ways, very attractive; both interesting, not only from their talents, but from their attachment to each other, and the delicacy which shortened their lives. They died of consumption, the elder in 1846, at the age of forty-three; the younger a year later. They became acquainted with Mrs. Browning through a common friend, Miss Sturtevant; and the young Robert conceived a warm admiration for Miss Flower's talents, and a boyish love for herself. She was nine years his senior; her own affections became probably engaged, and, as time advanced, his feeling seems to have subsided into one of warm and very loyal friendship. We hear, indeed, of his falling in love, as he was emerging from his teens, with a handsome girl who was on a visit at his father's house. But the fancy died out 'for want of root.' The admiration, even tenderness, for Miss Flower had so deep a 'root' that he never in latest life mentioned her name with indifference. In a letter to Mr. Dykes Campbell, in 1881, he spoke of her as 'a very remarkable person.' If, in spite of his denials, any woman inspired 'Pauline', it can have been no other than she. He began writing to her at twelve or thirteen, probably on the occasion of her expressed sympathy with his first distinct effort at authorship; and what he afterwards called 'the few utterly insignificant scraps of letters and verse' which formed his part of the correspondence were preserved by her as long as she lived. But he recovered and destroyed them after his return to England, with all the other reminiscences of those early years. Some notes, however, are extant, dated respectively, 1841, 1842, and 1845, and will be given in their due place.

* She also wrote a dramatic poem in five acts, entitled 'Vivia Perpetua', referred to by Mrs. Jameson in her 'Sacred and Legendary Art', and by Leigh Hunt, when he spoke of her in 'Blue-Stocking Revels', as 'Mrs. Adams, rare mistress of thought and of tears.'

Mr. Fox was a friend of Miss Flower's father Benjamin Flower, known as editor of the 'Cambridge Intelligencer', and, at his death, in 1829, became co-executor to his will, and a kind of guardian to his daughters, then both unmarried, and motherless from their infancy. Eliza's principal work was a collection of hymns and anthems, originally composed for

Mr. Fox's chapel, where she had assumed the entire management of the choral part of the service. Her abilities were not confined to music; she possessed, I am told, an instinctive taste and judgment in literary matters which caused her opinion to be much valued by literary men. But Mr. Browning's genuine appreciation of her musical genius was probably the strongest permanent bond between them. We shall hear of this in his own words.

Chapter 4

1826-1833

First Impressions of Keats and Shelley—Prolonged Influence of Shelley—Details of Home Education—Its Effects—Youthful Restlessness—Counteracting Love of Home—Early Friendships: Alfred Domett, Joseph Arnould, the Silverthornes—Choice of Poetry as a Profession—Alternative Suggestions; mistaken Rumours concerning them—Interest in Art—Love of good Theatrical Performances—Talent for Acting—Final Preparation for Literary Life.

At the period at which we have arrived, which is that of his leaving school and completing his fourteenth year, another and a significant influence was dawning on Robert Browning's life—the influence of the poet Shelley. Mr. Sharp writes,* and I could only state the facts in similar words, 'Passing a bookstall one day, he saw, in a box of second-hand volumes, a little book advertised as "Mr. Shelley's Atheistical Poem: very scarce."' . . . 'From vague remarks in reply to his inquiries, and from one or two casual allusions, he learned that there really was a poet called Shelley; that he had written several volumes; that he was dead.' . . . 'He begged his mother to procure him Shelley's works, a request not easily complied with, for the excellent reason that not one of the local booksellers had even heard of the poet's name. Ultimately, however, Mrs. Browning learned that what she sought was procurable at the Olliers', in Vere Street, London.'

* 'Life of Browning', pp. 30, 31.

Mrs. Browning went to Messrs. Ollier, and brought back 'most of Shelley's writings, all in their first edition, with the exception of "The Cenci".' She brought also three volumes of the still less known John Keats, on being assured that one who liked Shelley's works would like these also.

Keats and Shelley must always remain connected in this epoch of Mr. Browning's poetic growth. They indeed came to him as the two nightingales which, he told some friends, sang together in the May-night which closed this eventful day: one in the laburnum in his father's garden, the other in a copper beech which stood on adjoining ground—with the difference indeed, that he must often have listened to the feathered singers before, while the two new human voices sounded from what were to him, as to so many later hearers, unknown heights and depths of the imaginative world. Their utterance was, to such a spirit as his, the last, as in a certain sense the first, word of what poetry can say; and no one who has ever heard him read the 'Ode to a Nightingale', and repeat in the same subdued tones, as if continuing his own thoughts, some line from 'Epipsychidion', can doubt that they retained a lasting and almost equal place in his poet's heart. But the two cannot be regarded as equals in their relation to his life, and it would be a great mistake to impute to either any important influence upon his genius. We may catch some fleeting echoes of Keats's melody in 'Pippa Passes'; it is almost a commonplace that some measure of Shelleyan fancy is recognizable in 'Pauline'. But the poetic individuality of Robert Browning was stronger than any circumstance through which it could be fed. It would have found nourishment in desert air. With his first accepted work he threw off what was foreign to his poetic nature, to be thenceforward his own never-to-be-subdued and never-to-be-mistaken self. If Shelley became, and long remained for him, the greatest poet of his age—of almost any age—it was not because he held him greatest in the poetic art, but because in his case, beyond all others, he believed its exercise to have been prompted by the truest spiritual inspiration.

It is difficult to trace the process by which this conviction formed itself in the boy's mind; still more to account for the strong personal tenderness which accompanied it. The facts can have been scarcely known which were to present Shelley to his imagination as a maligned and persecuted man. It is hard to judge how far such human qualities as we now read into his work, could be apparent to one who only approached him through it. But the extra-human note in Shelley's genius irresistibly suggested to the Browning of fourteen, as it still did to the Browning of forty, the presence of a lofty spirit, one dwelling in the communion of higher things. There was often a deep sadness in his utterance; the consecration of an early death was upon him. And so the worship rooted itself and grew. It was to find its lyrical expression in 'Pauline'; its rational and, from the writer's point of view, philosophic justification in the prose essay on Shelley, published eighteen years afterwards.

It may appear inconsistent with the nature of this influence that it began by appealing to him in a subversive form. The Shelley whom Browning first loved was the Shelley of 'Queen Mab', the Shelley who would have remodelled the whole system of religious belief, as of human duty and rights; and the earliest result of the new development was that he became a professing atheist, and, for two years, a practising vegetarian. He returned to his natural diet when he found his eyesight becoming weak. The atheism cured itself; we do not exactly know when or how. What we do know is, that it was with him a passing state of moral or imaginative rebellion, and not one of rational doubt. His mind was not so constituted that such doubt could fasten itself upon it; nor did he ever in after-life speak of this period of negation except as an access of boyish folly, with which his maturer self could have no concern. The return to religious belief did not shake his faith in his new prophet. It only made him willing to admit that he had misread him.

This Shelley period of Robert Browning's life—that which intervened between 'Incondita' and 'Pauline'—remained, nevertheless, one of rebellion and unrest, to which many circumstances may have contributed besides the influence of the one mind. It had been decided that he was to complete, or at all events continue, his education at home; and, knowing the elder Mr. Browning as we do, we cannot doubt that the best reasons, of kindness or expediency, led to his so deciding. It was none the less, probably, a mistake, for the time being. The conditions of home life were the more favourable for the young poet's imaginative growth; but there can rarely have been a boy whose moral and mental health had more to gain by the combined discipline and freedom of a public school. His home training was made to include everything which in those days went to the production of an accomplished gentleman, and a great deal therefore that was physically good. He learned music, singing, dancing, riding, boxing, and fencing, and excelled in the more active of these pursuits. The study of music was also serious, and carried on under two masters. Mr. John Relfe, author of a valuable work on counterpoint, was his instructor in thorough-bass; Mr. Abel, a pupil of Moscheles, in execution. He wrote music for songs which he himself sang; among them Donne's 'Go and catch a falling star'; Hood's 'I will not have the mad Clytie'; Peacock's 'The mountain sheep are sweeter'; and his settings, all of which he subsequently destroyed, were, I am told, very spirited. His education seems otherwise to have been purely literary. For two years, from the age of fourteen to that of sixteen, he studied with a French tutor, who, whether this was intended or not, imparted to him very little but a good knowledge of the French language and literature. In his eighteenth year he attended, for a term or two, a Greek class at the London University. His classical and other reading was probably continued. But we hear nothing in the programme of mathematics, or logic—of any, in short, of those subjects which train, even coerce, the thinking powers, and which were doubly requisite for a nature in which the creative imagination was predominant over all the other mental faculties, great as these other faculties were. And, even as poet, he suffered from this omission: since the involutions and overlappings of thought and phrase, which occur in his earlier and again in his latest works, must have been partly due to his never learning to follow the processes of more normally constituted minds. It would be a great error to suppose that they ever arose from the absence of a meaning clearly felt, if not always clearly thought out, by himself. He was storing his memory and enriching his mind; but precisely in so doing he was nourishing the consciousness of a very vivid and urgent personality; and, under the restrictions inseparable from the life of a home-bred youth, it was becoming a burden to him. What outlet he found in verse we do not know, because nothing survives of what he may then have written. It is possible that the fate of his early poems, and, still more, the change of ideals, retarded the definite impulse towards poetic production. It would be a relief to him to sketch out and elaborate the plan of his future work—his great mental portrait gallery of typical men and women; and he was doing so during at least the later years which preceded the birth of 'Pauline'. But even this must have been the result of some protracted travail with himself; because it was only the inward sense of very varied possibilities of existence which could have impelled him towards this kind of creation. No character he ever produced was merely a figment of the brain.

It was natural, therefore, that during this time of growth he should have been, not only more restless, but less amiable than at any other. The always impatient temper assumed a quality of aggressiveness. He behaved as a youth will who knows himself to be clever, and believes that he is not appreciated, because the crude or paradoxical forms which his cleverness assumes do not recommend it to his elders' minds. He set the judgments of those about him at defiance, and gratuitously proclaimed himself everything that he was, and some things that he was not. All this subdued itself as time advanced, and the coming man in him could throw off the wayward child. It was all so natural that it might well be forgotten. But it distressed his mother, the one being in the world whom he entirely loved; and deserves remembering in the tender sorrow with which he himself remembered it. He was always ready to say that he had been worth little in his young days; indeed, his self-depreciation covered the greater part of his life. This was, perhaps, one reason of the difficulty of inducing him to dwell upon his past. 'I am better now,' he has said more than once, when its reminiscences have been invoked.

One tender little bond maintained itself between his mother and himself so long as he lived under the paternal roof; it was his rule never to go to bed without giving her a good-night kiss. If he was out so late that he had to admit himself with a latch-key, he nevertheless went to her in her room. Nor did he submit to this as a necessary restraint; for, except on the occasions of his going abroad, it is scarcely on record that he ever willingly spent a night away from home. It may not stand for much, or it may stand to the credit of his restlessness, that, when he had been placed with some gentleman in Gower Street, for the convenience of attending the University lectures, or for the sake of preparing for them, he broke through the arrangement at the end of a week; but even an agreeable visit had no power to detain him beyond a few days.

This home-loving quality was in curious contrast to the natural bohemianism of youthful genius, and the inclination to wildness which asserted itself in his boyish days. It became the more striking as he entered upon the age at which no reasonable amount of freedom can have been denied to him. Something, perhaps, must be allowed for the pecuniary dependence which forbade his forming any expensive habits of amusement; but he also claims the credit of having been unable to accept any low-life pleasures in place of them. I do not know how the idea can have arisen that he willingly sought his experience in the society of 'gipsies and tramps'. I remember nothing in his works which even suggests such association; and it is certain that a few hours spent at a fair would at all times have exhausted his capability of enduring it. In the most audacious imaginings of his later life, in the most undisciplined acts of his early youth, were always present curious delicacies and reserves. There was always latent in him the real goodness of heart which would not allow him to trifle consciously with other lives. Work must also have been his safeguard when the habit of it had been acquired, and when imagination, once his master, had learned to serve him.

One tangible cause of his youthful restlessness has been implied in the foregoing remarks, but deserves stating in his sister's words: 'The fact was, poor boy, he had outgrown his social surroundings. They were absolutely good, but they were narrow; it could not be otherwise; he chafed under them.' He was not, however, quite without congenial society even before the turning-point in his outward existence which was reached in the publication of 'Pauline'; and one long friendly acquaintance, together with one lasting friendship, had their roots in these early Camberwell days. The families of Joseph Arnould and Alfred Domett both lived at Camberwell. These two young men were bred to the legal profession, and the former, afterwards Sir Joseph Arnould, became a judge in Bombay. But the father of Alfred Domett had been one of Nelson's captains, and the roving sailor spirit was apparent in his son; for he had scarcely been called to the Bar when he started for New Zealand on the instance of a cousin who had preceded him, but who was drowned in the course of a day's surveying before he could arrive. He became a member of the New Zealand Parliament, and ultimately, for a short time, of its Cabinet; only returning to England after an absence of thirty years. This Mr. Domett seems to have been a very modest man, besides a devoted friend of Robert Browning's, and on occasion a warm defender of his works. When he read the apostrophe to 'Alfred, dear friend,' in the 'Guardian Angel', he had reached the last line before it occurred to him that the person invoked could be he. I do not think that this poem, and that directly addressed to him under the pseudonym of 'Waring', were the only ones inspired by the affectionate remembrance which he had left in their author's mind.

Among his boy companions were also the three Silverthornes, his neighbours at Camberwell, and cousins on the maternal side. They appear to have been wild youths, and had certainly no part in his intellectual or literary life; but the group is interesting to his biographer. The three brothers were all gifted musicians; having also, probably, received this endowment from their mother's father. Mr. Browning conceived a great affection for the eldest, and on the whole most talented of the cousins; and when he had died—young, as they all did—he wrote 'May and Death' in remembrance of him. The name of 'Charles' stands there for the old, familiar 'Jim', so often uttered by him in half-pitying, and all-affectionate allusion, in his later years. Mrs. Silverthorne was the aunt who paid for the printing of 'Pauline'.

It was at about the time of his short attendance at University College that the choice of poetry as his future profession was formally made. It was a foregone conclusion in the young Robert's mind; and little less in that of his father, who took too sympathetic an interest in his son's life not to have seen in what direction his desires were tending. He must, it is true, at some time or other, have played with the thought of becoming an artist; but the thought can never have represented a wish. If he had entertained such a one, it would have met not only with no opposition on his father's part, but with a very ready assent, nor does the question ever seem to have been seriously mooted in the family councils. It would be strange, perhaps, if it had. Mr. Browning became very early familiar with the names of the great painters, and also learned something about their work; for the Dulwich Gallery was within a pleasant walk of his home, and his father constantly took him there. He retained through life a deep interest in art and artists, and became a very familiar figure in one or two London studios. Some drawings made by him from the nude, in Italy, and for which he had prepared himself by assiduous copying of casts and study of human anatomy, had, I believe, great merit. But painting was one of the subjects in which he never received instruction, though he modelled, under the direction of his friend Mr. Story; and a letter of his own will presently show that, in his youth at least, he never credited himself with exceptional artistic power. That he might have become an artist, and perhaps a great one, is difficult to doubt, in the face of his brilliant general ability and special gifts. The power to do a thing is, however, distinct from the impulse to do it, and proved so in the present case.

More importance may be given to an idea of his father's that he should qualify himself for the Bar. It would naturally coincide with the widening of the social horizon which his University College classes supplied; it was possibly suggested by the fact that the closest friends he had already made, and others whom he was perhaps now making, were barristers. But this also remained an idea. He might have been placed in the Bank of England, where the virtual offer of an appointment had been made to him through his father; but the elder Browning spontaneously rejected this, as unworthy of his son's powers. He had never, he said, liked bank work himself, and could not, therefore, impose it on him.

We have still to notice another, and a more mistaken view of the possibilities of Mr. Browning's life. It has been recently stated, doubtless on the authority of some words of his own, that the Church was a profession to which he once felt himself drawn. But an admission of this kind could only refer to that period of his childhood when natural impulse, combined with his mother's teaching and guidance, frequently caused his fancy and his feelings to assume a religious form.

From the time when he was a free agent he ceased to be even a regular churchgoer, though religion became more, rather than less, an integral part of his inner life; and his alleged fondness for a variety of preachers meant really that he only listened to those who, from personal association or conspicuous merit, were interesting to him. I have mentioned Canon Melvill as one of these; the Rev. Thomas Jones was, as will be seen, another. In Venice he constantly, with his sister, joined the congregation of an Italian minister of the little Vaudois church there.*

* Mr. Browning's memory recalled a first and last effort at preaching, inspired by one of his very earliest visits to a place of worship. He extemporized a surplice or gown, climbed into an arm-chair by way of pulpit, and held forth so vehemently that his scarcely more than baby sister was frightened and began to cry; whereupon he turned to an imaginary presence, and said, with all the sternness which the occasion required, 'Pew-opener, remove that child.'

It would be far less surprising if we were told, on sufficient authority, that he had been disturbed by hankerings for the stage. He was a passionate admirer of good acting, and would walk from London to Richmond and back again to see Edmund Kean when he was performing there. We know how Macready impressed him, though the finer genius of Kean became very apparent to his retrospective judgment of the two; and it was impossible to see or hear him, as even an old man, in some momentary personation of one of Shakespeare's characters, above all of Richard III., and not feel that a great actor had been lost in him.

So few professions were thought open to gentlemen in Robert Browning's eighteenth year, that his father's acquiescence in that which he had chosen might seem a matter scarcely less of necessity than of kindness. But we must seek the kindness not only in this first, almost inevitable, assent to his son's becoming a writer, but in the subsequent unfailing readiness to support him in his literary career. 'Paracelsus', 'Sordello', and the whole of 'Bells and Pomegranates' were published at his father's expense, and, incredible as it appears, brought no return to him. This was vividly present to Mr. Browning's mind in what Mrs. Kemble so justly defines as those 'remembering days' which are the natural prelude to the forgetting ones. He declared, in the course of these, to a friend, that for it alone he owed more to his father than to anyone else in the world. Words to this effect, spoken in conversation with his sister, have since, as it was right they should, found their way into print. The more justly will the world interpret any incidental admission he may ever have made, of intellectual disagreement between that father and himself.

When the die was cast, and young Browning was definitely to adopt literature as his profession, he qualified himself for it by reading and digesting the whole of Johnson's Dictionary. We cannot be surprised to hear this of one who displayed so great a mastery of words, and so deep a knowledge of the capacities of the English language.

Chapter 5

1833-1835

'Pauline'—Letters to Mr. Fox—Publication of the Poem; chief Biographical and Literary Characteristics—Mr. Fox's Review in the 'Monthly Repository'; other Notices—Russian Journey—Desired diplomatic Appointment—Minor Poems; first Sonnet; their Mode of Appearance—'The Trifler'—M. de Ripert-Monclar—'Paracelsus'—Letters to Mr. Fox concerning it; its Publication—Incidental Origin of 'Paracelsus'; its inspiring Motive; its Relation to 'Pauline'—Mr. Fox's Review of it in the 'Monthly Repository'—Article in the 'Examiner' by John Forster.

Before Mr. Browning had half completed his twenty-first year he had written 'Pauline, a Fragment of a Confession'. His sister was in the secret, but this time his parents were not. This is why his aunt, hearing that 'Robert' had 'written a poem,' volunteered the sum requisite for its publication. Even this first instalment of success did not inspire much hope in the family mind, and Miss Browning made pencil copies of her favourite passages for the event, which seemed only too possible, of her never seeing the whole poem again. It was, however, accepted by Saunders and Otley, and appeared anonymously in 1833. Meanwhile the young author had bethought himself of his early sympathizer, Mr. Fox, and he wrote to him as follows the letter is undated:

Dear Sir,—Perhaps by the aid of the subjoined initials and a little reflection, you may recollect an oddish sort of boy, who had the honour of being introduced to you at Hackney some years back—at that time a sayer of verse and a doer of it, and whose doings you had a little previously commended after a fashion—whether in earnest or not God knows: that individual it is who takes the liberty of addressing one whose slight commendation then, was more thought of than all the gun drum and trumpet of praise would be now, and to submit to you a free and easy sort of thing which he wrote some months ago 'on one leg' and which comes out this week—having either heard or dreamed that you contribute to the 'Westminster'.

Should it be found too insignificant for cutting up, I shall no less remain, Dear sir, Your most obedient servant, R. B.

I have forgotten the main thing—which is to beg you not to spoil a loophole I have kept for backing out of the thing if necessary, 'sympathy of dear friends,' &c. &c., none of whom know anything about it.

Monday Morning; Rev.—Fox.

The answer was clearly encouraging, and Mr. Browning wrote again:

Dear Sir,—In consequence of your kind permission I send, or will send, a dozen copies of 'Pauline' and to mitigate the infliction Shelley's Poem—on account of what you mentioned this morning. It will perhaps be as well that you let me know their safe arrival by a line to R. B. junior, Hanover Cottage, Southampton Street, Camberwell. You must not think me too encroaching, if I make the getting back 'Rosalind and Helen' an excuse for calling on you some evening—the said 'R. and H.' has, I observe, been well thumbed and sedulously marked by an acquaintance of mine, but I have not time to rub out his labour of love. I am, dear sir, Yours very really, R. Browning. Camberwell: 2 o'clock.

At the left-hand corner of the first page of this note is written: 'The parcel—a "Pauline" parcel—is come. I send one as a witness.'

On the inner page is written:

'Impromptu on hearing a sermon by the Rev. T. R.—pronounced "heavy"—

'A *heavy* sermon!—sure the error's great, For not a word Tom uttered *had its weight*.'

A third letter, also undated, but post-marked March 29, 1833, refers probably to the promise or announcement of a favourable notice. A fourth conveys Mr. Browning's thanks for the notice itself:

My dear Sir,—I have just received your letter, which I am desirous of acknowledging before any further mark of your kindness reaches me;—I can only offer you my simple thanks—but they are of the sort that one can give only once or twice in a life: all things considered, I think you are almost repaid, if you imagine what I must feel—and it will have been worth while to have made a fool of myself, only to have obtained a 'case' which leaves my fine fellow Mandeville at a dead lock.

As for the book—I hope ere long to better it, and to deserve your goodness.

In the meantime I shall not forget the extent to which I am, dear sir, Your most obliged and obedient servant R. B. S. & O.'s, Conduit St., Thursday m-g.

I must intrude on your attention, my dear sir, once more than I had intended—but a notice like the one I have read will have its effect at all hazards.

I can only say that I am very proud to feel as grateful as I do, and not altogether hopeless of justifying, by effort at least, your most generous 'coming forward'. Hazlitt wrote his essays, as he somewhere tells us, mainly to send them to some one in the country who had 'always prophesied he would be something'!—I shall never write a line without thinking of the source of my first praise, be assured. I am, dear sir, Yours most truly and obliged, Robert Browning. March 31, 1833.

Mr. Fox was then editor of a periodical called the 'Monthly Repository', which, as his daughter, Mrs. Bridell-Fox, writes in her graceful article on Robert Browning, in the 'Argosy' for February 1890, he was endeavouring to raise from its original denominational character into a first-class literary and political journal. The articles comprised in the volume for 1833 are certainly full of interest and variety, at once more popular and more solid than those prescribed by the present fashion of monthly magazines. He reviewed 'Pauline' favourably in its April number—that is, as soon as it had appeared; and the young poet thus received from him an introduction to what should have been, though it probably was not, a large circle of intelligent readers.

The poem was characterized by its author, five years later, in a fantastic note appended to a copy of it, as 'the only remaining crab of the shapely Tree of Life in my Fool's Paradise.' This name is ill bestowed upon a work which, however wild a fruit of Mr. Browning's genius, contains, in its many lines of exquisite fancy and deep pathos, so much that is rich and sweet. It had also, to discard metaphor, its faults of exaggeration and confusion; and it is of these that Mr. Browning was probably thinking when he wrote his more serious apologetic preface to its reprint in 1868. But these faults were partly due to his conception of the character which he had tried to depict; and partly to the inherent difficulty of depicting one so complex, in a succession of mental and moral states, irrespectively of the conditions of time, place, and circumstance which were involved in them. Only a very powerful imagination could have inspired such an attempt. A still more conspicuous effort of creative genius reveals itself at its close. The moment chosen for the 'Confession' has been that of a supreme moral or physical crisis. The exhaustion attendant on this is directly expressed by the person who makes it, and may also be recognized in the vivid, yet confusing, intensity of the reminiscences of which it consists. But we are left in complete doubt as to whether the crisis is that of approaching death or incipient convalescence, or which character it bears in the sufferer's mind; and the language used in the closing pages is such as to suggest, without the slightest break in poetic continuity, alternately the one conclusion and the other. This was intended by Browning to assist his anonymity; and when the writer in 'Tait's Magazine' spoke of the poem as a piece of pure bewilderment, he expressed the natural judgment of the Philistine, while proving himself such. If the notice by J. S. Mill, which this criticism excluded, was indeed—as Mr. Browning always believed—much more sympathetic, I can only record my astonishment; for there never was a large and cultivated intelligence one can imagine less in harmony than his with the poetic excesses, or even the poetic qualities, of 'Pauline'. But this is a digression.

Mr. Fox, though an accomplished critic, made very light of the artistic blemishes of the work. His admiration for it was as generous as it was genuine; and, having recognized in it the hand of a rising poet, it was more congenial to him to hail that poet's advent than to register his shortcomings.

'The poem,' he says, 'though evidently a hasty and imperfect sketch, has truth and life in it, which gave us the thrill, and laid hold of us with the power, the sensation of which has never yet failed us as a test of genius.'

But it had also, in his mind, a distinguishing characteristic, which raised it above the sphere of merely artistic criticism. The article continues:

'We have never read anything more purely confessional. The whole composition is of the spirit, spiritual. The scenery is in the chambers of thought; the agencies are powers and passions; the events are transitions from one state of spiritual existence to another.'

And we learn from the context that he accepted this confessional and introspective quality as an expression of the highest emotional life—of the essence, therefore, of religion. On this point the sincerest admirers of the poem may find themselves at issue with Mr. Fox. Its sentiment is warmly religious; it is always, in a certain sense, spiritual; but its intellectual activities are exercised on entirely temporal ground, and this fact would generally be admitted as the negation of spirituality in the religious sense of the word. No difference, however, of opinion as to his judgment of 'Pauline' can lessen our appreciation of Mr. Fox's encouraging kindness to its author. No one who loved Mr. Browning in himself, or in his work, can read the last lines of this review without a throb of affectionate gratitude for the sympathy so ungrudgingly, and—as he wrote during his latest years—so opportunely given:

'In recognizing a poet we cannot stand upon trifles nor fret ourselves about such matters [as a few blemishes]. Time enough for that afterwards, when larger works come before us. Archimedes in the bath had many particulars to settle about specific gravities and Hiero's crown, but he first gave a glorious leap and shouted 'Eureka!''

Many persons have discovered Mr. Browning since he has been known to fame. One only discovered him in his obscurity.

Next to that of Mr. Fox stands the name of John Forster among the first spontaneous appreciators of Mr. Browning's genius; and his admiration was, in its own way, the more valuable for the circumstances which precluded in it all possible, even unconscious, bias of personal interest or sympathy. But this belongs to a somewhat later period of our history.

I am dwelling at some length on this first experience of Mr. Browning's literary career, because the confidence which it gave him determined its immediate future, if not its ultimate course—because, also, the poem itself is more important to the understanding of his mind than perhaps any other of his isolated works. It was the earliest of his dramatic creations; it was therefore inevitably the most instinct with himself; and we may regard the 'Confession' as to a great extent his own, without for an instant ignoring the imaginative element which necessarily and certainly entered into it. At one moment, indeed, his utterance is so emphatic that we should feel it to be direct, even if we did not know it to be true. The passage beginning, 'I am made up of an intensest life,' conveys something more than the writer's actual psychological state. The feverish desire of life became gradually modified into a more or less active intellectual and imaginative curiosity; but the sense of an individual, self-centred, and, as it presented itself to him, unconditioned existence, survived all the teachings of experience, and often indeed unconsciously imposed itself upon them.

I have already alluded to that other and more pathetic fragment of distinct autobiography which is to be found in the invocation to the 'Sun-treader'. Mr. Fox, who has quoted great part of it, justly declares that 'the fervency, the remembrance, the half-regret mingling with its exultation, are as true as its leading image is beautiful.' The 'exultation' is in the triumph of Shelley's rising fame; the regret, for the lost privilege of worshipping in solitary tenderness at an obscure shrine. The double mood would have been characteristic of any period of Mr. Browning's life.

The artistic influence of Shelley is also discernible in the natural imagery of the poem, which reflects a fitful and emotional fancy instead of the direct poetic vision of the author's later work.

'Pauline' received another and graceful tribute two months later than the review. In an article of the 'Monthly Repository', and in the course of a description of some luxuriant wood-scenery, the following passage occurs:

'Shelley and Tennyson are the best books for this place. . . . They are natives of this soil; literally so; and if planted would grow as surely as a crowbar in Kentucky sprouts tenpenny nails. 'Probatum est.' Last autumn L——dropped a poem of Shelley's down there in the wood,* amongst the thick, damp, rotting leaves, and this spring some one found a delicate exotic-looking plant, growing wild on the very spot, with 'Pauline' hanging from its slender stalk. Unripe fruit it may be, but of pleasant flavour and promise, and a mellower produce, it may be hoped, will follow.'

* Mr. Browning's copy of 'Rosalind and Helen', which he had lent to Miss Flower, and which she lost in this wood on a picnic. This and a bald though well-meant notice in the 'Athenaeum' exhaust its literary history for this period.* * Not quite, it appears. Since I wrote the above words, Mr. Dykes Campbell has kindly copied for me the following extract from

the 'Literary Gazette' of March 23, 1833: 'Pauline: a Fragment of a Confession', pp. 71. London, 1833. Saunders and Otley. 'Somewhat mystical, somewhat poetical, somewhat sensual, and not a little unintelligible,—this is a dreamy volume, without an object, and unfit for publication.'

The anonymity of the poem was not long preserved; there was no reason why it should be. But 'Pauline' was, from the first, little known or discussed beyond the immediate circle of the poet's friends; and when, twenty years later, Dante Gabriel Rossetti unexpectedly came upon it in the library of the British Museum, he could only surmise that it had been written by the author of 'Paracelsus'.

The only recorded event of the next two years was Mr. Browning's visit to Russia, which took place in the winter of 1833-4. The Russian consul-general, Mr. Benckhausen, had taken a great liking to him, and being sent to St. Petersburg on some special mission, proposed that he should accompany him, nominally in the character of secretary. The letters written to his sister during this, as during every other absence, were full of graphic description, and would have been a mine of interest for the student of his imaginative life. They are, unfortunately, all destroyed, and we have only scattered reminiscences of what they had to tell; but we know how strangely he was impressed by some of the circumstances of the journey: above all, by the endless monotony of snow-covered pine-forest, through which he and his companion rushed for days and nights at the speed of six post-horses, without seeming to move from one spot. He enjoyed the society of St. Petersburg, and was fortunate enough, before his return, to witness the breaking-up of the ice on the Neva, and see the Czar perform the yearly ceremony of drinking the first glass of water from it. He was absent about three months.

The one active career which would have recommended itself to him in his earlier youth was diplomacy; it was that which he subsequently desired for his son. He would indeed not have been averse to any post of activity and responsibility not unsuited to the training of a gentleman. Soon after his return from Russia he applied for appointment on a mission which was to be despatched to Persia; and the careless wording of the answer which his application received made him think for a moment that it had been granted. He was much disappointed when he learned, through an interview with the 'chief', that the place was otherwise filled.

In 1834 he began a little series of contributions to the 'Monthly Repository', extending into 1835-6, and consisting of five poems. The earliest of these was a sonnet, not contained in any edition of Mr. Browning's works, and which, I believe, first reappeared in Mr. Gosse's article in the 'Century Magazine', December 1881; now part of his 'Personalia'. The second, beginning 'A king lived long ago', was to be published, with alterations and additions, as one of 'Pippa's' songs. 'Porphyria's Lover' and 'Johannes Agricola in Meditation' were reprinted together in 'Bells and Pomegranates' under the heading of 'Madhouse Cells'. The fifth consisted of the Lines beginning 'Still ailing, Wind? wilt be appeased or no?' afterwards introduced into the sixth section of 'James Lee's Wife'. The sonnet is not very striking, though hints of the poet's future psychological subtlety are not wanting in it; but his most essential dramatic quality reveals itself in the last three poems.

This winter of 1834-5 witnessed the birth, perhaps also the extinction, of an amateur periodical, established by some of Mr. Browning's friends; foremost among these the young Dowsons, afterwards connected with Alfred Domett. The magazine was called the 'Trifler', and published in monthly numbers of about ten pages each. It collapsed from lack of pocket-money on the part of the editors; but Mr. Browning had written for it one letter, February 1833, signed with his usual initial Z, and entitled 'Some strictures on a late article in the 'Trifler'.' This boyish production sparkles with fun, while affecting the lengthy quaintnesses of some obsolete modes of speech. The article which it attacks was 'A Dissertation on Debt and Debtors', where the subject was, I imagine, treated in the orthodox way: and he expends all his paradox in showing that indebtedness is a necessary condition of human life, and all his sophistry in confusing it with the abstract sense of obligation. It is, perhaps, scarcely fair to call attention to such a mere argumentative and literary freak; but there is something so comical in a defence of debt, however transparent, proceeding from a man to whom never in his life a bill can have been sent in twice, and who would always have preferred ready-money payment to receiving a bill at all, that I may be forgiven for quoting some passages from it.

For to be man is to be a debtor:—hinting but slightly at the grand and primeval debt implied in the idea of a creation, as matter too hard for ears like thine, for saith not Luther, What hath a cow to do with nutmegs? I must, nevertheless, remind thee that all moralists have concurred in considering this our mortal sojourn as indeed an uninterrupted state of debt, and the world our dwelling-place as represented by nothing so aptly as by an inn, wherein those who lodge most commodiously have in perspective a proportionate score to reduce,* and those who fare least delicately, but an insignificant shot to discharge—or, as the tuneful Quarles well phraseth it—

He's most in debt who lingers out the day, Who dies betimes has less and less to pay.

So far, therefore, from these sagacious ethics holding that

Debt cramps the energies of the soul, &c.

as thou pratest, 'tis plain that they have willed on the very outset to inculcate this truth on the mind of every man,— no barren and inconsequential dogma, but an effectual, ever influencing and productive rule of life,—that he is born a debtor, lives a debtor—aye, friend, and when thou diest, will not some judicious bystander,—no recreant as thou to the bonds of nature, but a good borrower and true—remark, as did his grandsire before him on like occasions, that thou hast 'paid the *debt* of nature'? Ha! I have thee 'beyond the rules', as one a bailiff may say!

* Miss Hickey, on reading this passage, has called my attention to the fact that the sentiment which it parodies is identical with that expressed in these words of 'Prospice', . . . in a minute pay glad life's arrears Of pain, darkness, and cold.

Such performances supplied a distraction to the more serious work of writing 'Paracelsus', which was to be concluded in March 1835, and which occupied the foregoing winter months. We do not know to what extent Mr. Browning had remained in communication with Mr. Fox; but the following letters show that the friend of 'Pauline' gave ready and efficient help in the strangely difficult task of securing a publisher for the new poem.

The first is dated April 2, 1835.

Dear Sir,—I beg to acknowledge the receipt of your letter:—Sardanapalus 'could not go on multiplying kingdoms'—nor I protestations—but I thank you very much.

You will oblige me indeed by forwarding the introduction to Moxon. I merely suggested him in particular, on account of his good name and fame among author-folk, besides he has himself written—as the Americans say—'more poetry 'an you can shake a stick at.' So I hope we shall come to terms.

I also hope my poem will turn out not utterly unworthy your kind interest, and more deserving your favour than anything of mine you have as yet seen; indeed I all along proposed to myself such an endeavour, for it will never do for one so distinguished by past praise to prove nobody after all—'nous verrons'. I am, dear sir, Yours most truly and obliged Robt. Browning.

On April 16 he wrote again as follows:

Dear Sir,

Your communication gladdened the cockles of my heart. I lost no time in presenting myself to Moxon, but no sooner was Mr. Clarke's letter perused than the Moxonian visage loured exceedingly thereat—the Moxonian accent grew dolorous thereupon:—'Artevelde' has not paid expenses by about thirty odd pounds. Tennyson's poetry is 'popular at Cambridge', and yet of 800 copies which were printed of his last, some 300 only have gone off: Mr. M. hardly knows whether he shall ever venture again, &c. &c., and in short begs to decline even inspecting, &c. &c.

I called on Saunders and Otley at once, and, marvel of marvels, do really think there is some chance of our coming to decent terms—I shall know at the beginning of next week, but am not over-sanguine.

You will 'sarve me out'? two words to that; being the man you are, you must need very little telling from me, of the real feeling I have of your criticism's worth, and if I have had no more of it, surely I am hardly to blame, who have in more than one instance bored you sufficiently: but not a particle of your article has been rejected or neglected by your observant humble servant, and very proud shall I be if my new work bear in it the marks of the influence under which it was undertaken—and if I prove not a fit compeer of the potter in Horace who anticipated an amphora and produced a porridge-pot. I purposely keep back the subject until you see my conception of its capabilities—otherwise you would be planning a vase fit to give the go-by to Evander's best crockery, which my cantharus would cut but a sorry figure beside—hardly up to the ansa.

But such as it is, it is very earnest and suggestive—and likely I hope to do good; and though I am rather scared at the thought of a *fresh eye* going over its 4,000 lines—discovering blemishes of all sorts which my one wit cannot avail to detect, fools treated as sages, obscure passages, slipshod verses, and much that worse is,—yet on the whole I am not much afraid of the issue, and I would give something to be allowed to read it some morning to you—for every rap o' the knuckles I should get a clap o' the back, I know.

I have another affair on hand, rather of a more popular nature, I conceive, but not so decisive and explicit on a point or two—so I decide on trying the question with this:—I really shall *need* your notice, on this account; I shall affix my name and stick my arms akimbo; there are a few precious bold bits here and there, and the drift and scope are awfully radical—I am 'off' for ever with the other side, but must by all means be 'on' with yours—a position once gained, worthier works shall follow—therefore a certain writer* who meditated a notice it matters not laudatory or otherwise on 'Pauline' in the 'Examiner', must be benignant or supercilious as he shall choose, but in no case an idle spectator of my first appearance on any stage having previously only dabbled in private theatricals and bawl 'Hats off!' 'Down in front!' &c., as soon as I get to the proscenium; and he may depend that tho' my 'Now is the winter of our discontent' be rather awkward, yet there shall be occasional outbreaks of good stuff—that I shall warm as I get on, and finally wish 'Richmond at the bottom of the seas,' &c. in the best style imaginable.

* Mr. John Stuart Mill.

Excuse all this swagger, I know you will, and

The signature has been cut off; evidently for an autograph.

Mr. Effingham Wilson was induced to publish the poem, but more, we understand, on the ground of radical sympathies in Mr. Fox and the author than on that of its intrinsic worth.

The title-page of 'Paracelsus' introduces us to one of the warmest friendships of Mr. Browning's life. Count de Ripert-Monclar was a young French Royalist, one of those who had accompanied the Duchesse de Berri on her Chouan expedition, and was then, for a few years, spending his summers in England; ostensibly for his pleasure, really—as he confessed to the Browning family—in the character of private agent of communication between the royal exiles and their friends in France. He was four years older than the poet, and of intellectual tastes which created an immediate bond of union between them. In the course of one of their conversations, he suggested the life of Paracelsus as a possible subject for a poem; but on second thoughts pronounced it unsuitable, because it gave no room for the introduction of love: about which, he added, every young man of their age thought he had something quite new to say. Mr. Browning decided, after the necessary study, that he would write a poem on Paracelsus, but treating him in his own way. It was dedicated, in fulfilment of a promise, to the friend to whom its inspiration had been due.

The Count's visits to England entirely ceased, and the two friends did not meet for twenty years. Then, one day, in a street in Rome, Mr. Browning heard a voice behind him crying, 'Robert!' He turned, and there was 'Amedee'. Both were, by that time, married; the Count—then, I believe, Marquis—to an English lady, Miss Jerningham. Mrs. Browning, to whom of course he was introduced, liked him very much.*

* A minor result of the intimacy was that Mr. Browning became member, in 1835, of the Institut Historique, and in 1836 of the Societe Francaise de Statistique Universelle, to both of which learned bodies his friend belonged.

Mr. Browning did treat Paracelsus in his own way; and in so doing produced a character—at all events a history—which, according to recent judgments, approached far nearer to the reality than any conception which had until then been formed of it. He had carefully collected all the known facts of the great discoverer's life, and interpreted them with a sympathy which was no less an intuition of their truth than a reflection of his own genius upon them. We are enabled in some measure to judge of this by a paper entitled 'Paracelsus, the Reformer of Medicine', written by Dr. Edward Berdoe for the Browning Society, and read at its October meeting in 1888; and in the difficulty which exists for most of us of verifying the historical data of Mr. Browning's poem, it becomes a valuable guide to, as well as an interesting comment upon it.

Dr. Berdoe reminds us that we cannot understand the real Paracelsus without reference to the occult sciences so largely cultivated in his day, as also to the mental atmosphere which produced them; and he quotes in illustration a passage from the writings of that Bishop of Spanheim who was the instructor of Paracelsus, and who appears as such in the poem. The passage is a definition of divine magic, which is apparently another term for alchemy; and lays down the great doctrine of all mediaeval occultism, as of all modern theosophy—of a soul-power equally operative in the material and the immaterial, in nature and in the consciousness of man.

The same clue will guide us, as no other can, through what is apparently conflicting in the aims and methods, anomalous in the moral experience, of the Paracelsus of the poem. His feverish pursuit, among the things of Nature, of an ultimate of knowledge, not contained, even in fragments, in her isolated truths; the sense of failure which haunts his most valuable attainments; his tampering with the lower or diabolic magic, when the divine has failed; the ascetic exaltation in which he begins his career; the sudden awakening to the spiritual sterility which has been consequent on it; all these find their place, if not always their counterpart, in the real life.

The language of Mr. Browning's Paracelsus, his attitude towards himself and the world, are not, however, quite consonant with the alleged facts. They are more appropriate to an ardent explorer of the world of abstract thought than to a mystical scientist pursuing the secret of existence. He preserves, in all his mental vicissitudes, a loftiness of tone and a unity of intention, difficult to connect, even in fancy, with the real man, in whom the inherited superstitions and the prognostics of true science must often have clashed with each other. Dr. Berdoe's picture of the 'Reformer' drawn more directly from history, conveys this double impression. Mr. Browning has rendered him more simple by, as it were, recasting him in the atmosphere of a more modern time, and of his own intellectual life. This poem still, therefore, belongs to the same group as 'Pauline', though, as an effort of dramatic creation, superior to it.

We find the Poet with still less of dramatic disguise in the deathbed revelation which forms so beautiful a close to the story. It supplies a fitter comment to the errors of the dramatic Paracelsus, than to those of the historical, whether or not its utterance was within the compass of historical probability, as Dr. Berdoe believes. In any case it was the direct product of Mr. Browning's mind, and expressed what was to be his permanent conviction. It might then have been an echo of German pantheistic philosophies. From the point of view of science—of modern science at least—it was prophetic; although the prophecy of one for whom evolution could never mean less or more than a divine creation operating on this progressive plan.

The more striking, perhaps, for its personal quality are the evidences of imaginative sympathy, even direct human insight, in which the poem abounds. Festus is, indeed, an essentially human creature: the man—it might have been the woman—of unambitious intellect and large intelligence of the heart, in whom so many among us have found comfort and help. We often feel, in reading 'Pauline', that the poet in it was older than the man. The impression is more strongly and more definitely conveyed by this second work, which has none of the intellectual crudeness of 'Pauline', though it still belongs to an early phase of the author's intellectual life. Not only its mental, but its moral maturity, seems so much in advance of his uncompleted twenty-third year.

To the first edition of 'Paracelsus' was affixed a preface, now long discarded, but which acquires fresh interest in a retrospect of the author's completed work; for it lays down the constant principle of dramatic creation by which that work was to be inspired. It also anticipates probable criticism of the artistic form which on this, and so many subsequent occasions, he selected for it.

'I am anxious that the reader should not, at the very outset—mistaking my performance for one of a class with which it has nothing in common—judge it by principles on which it was never moulded, and subject it to a standard to which it was never meant to conform. I therefore anticipate his discovery, that it is an attempt, probably more novel than happy, to reverse the method usually adopted by writers whose aim it is to set forth any phenomenon of the mind or the passions, by the operation of persons and events; and that, instead of having recourse to an external machinery of incidents to create and evolve the crisis I desire to produce, I have ventured to display somewhat minutely the mood itself in its rise and progress, and have suffered the agency by which it is influenced and determined, to be generally discernible in its effects alone, and subordinate throughout, if not altogether excluded: and this for a reason. I have endeavoured to write a poem, not a drama: the canons of the drama are well known, and I cannot but think that, inasmuch as they have immediate regard to stage representation, the peculiar advantages they hold out are really such only so long as the purpose for which they were at first instituted is kept in view. I do not very well understand what is called a Dramatic Poem, wherein all those restrictions only submitted to on account of compensating good in the original scheme are scrupulously retained, as though for some special fitness in themselves—and all new facilities placed at an author's disposal by the vehicle he selects, as pertinaciously rejected. . . .'

Mr. Fox reviewed this also in the 'Monthly Repository'. The article might be obtained through the kindness of Mrs. Bridell-Fox; but it will be sufficient for my purpose to refer to its closing paragraph, as given by her in the 'Argosy' of February 1890. It was a final expression of what the writer regarded as the fitting intellectual attitude towards a rising poet, whose aims and methods lay so far beyond the range of the conventional rules of poetry. The great event in the history of 'Paracelsus' was John Forster's article on it in the 'Examiner'. Mr. Forster had recently come to town. He could barely have heard Mr. Browning's name, and, as he afterwards told him, was perplexed in reading the poem by the question of whether its author was an old or a young man; but he knew that a writer in the 'Athenaeum' had called it rubbish, and he had taken it up as a probable subject for a piece of slashing criticism. What he did write can scarcely be defined as praise. It was the simple, ungrudging admission of the unequivocal power, as well as brilliant promise, which he recognized in the work. This mutual experience was the introduction to a long and, certainly on Mr. Browning's part, a sincere friendship.

Chapter 6

1835-1838

Removal to Hatcham; some Particulars—Renewed Intercourse with the second Family of Robert Browning's Grandfather—Reuben Browning—William Shergold Browning—Visitors at Hatcham—Thomas Carlyle—Social Life—New Friends and Acquaintance—Introduction to Macready—New Year's Eve at Elm Place—Introduction to John Forster—Miss Fanny Haworth—Miss Martineau—Serjeant Talfourd—The 'Ion' Supper—'Strafford'—Relations with Macready—Performance of 'Strafford'—Letters concerning it from Mr. Browning and Miss Flower—Personal Glimpses of Robert Browning—Rival Forms of Dramatic Inspiration—Relation of 'Strafford' to 'Sordello'—Mr. Robertson and the 'Westminster Review'.

It was soon after this time, though the exact date cannot be recalled, that the Browning family moved from Camberwell to Hatcham. Some such change had long been in contemplation, for their house was now too small; and the finding one more suitable, in the latter place, had decided the question. The new home possessed great attractions. The long, low rooms of its upper storey supplied abundant accommodation for the elder Mr. Browning's six thousand books. Mrs. Browning was suffering greatly from her chronic ailment, neuralgia; and the large garden, opening on to the Surrey hills, promised her all the benefits of country air. There were a coach-house and stable, which, by a curious, probably old-fashioned, arrangement, formed part of the house, and were accessible from it. Here the 'good horse', York, was eventually put up; and near this, in the garden, the poet soon had another though humbler friend in the person of a toad, which became so much attached to him that it would follow him as he walked. He visited it daily, where it burrowed under a white rose tree, announcing himself by a pinch of gravel dropped into its hole; and the creature would crawl forth, allow its head to be gently tickled, and reward the act with that loving glance of the soft full eyes which Mr. Browning has recalled in one of the poems of 'Asolando'.

This change of residence brought the grandfather's second family, for the first time, into close as well as friendly contact with the first. Mr. Browning had always remained on outwardly friendly terms with his stepmother; and both he and his children were rewarded for this forbearance by the cordial relations which grew up between themselves and two of her sons. But in the earlier days they lived too far apart for frequent meeting. The old Mrs. Browning was now a widow, and, in order to be near her relations, she also came to Hatcham, and established herself there in close neighbourhood to them. She had then with her only a son and a daughter, those known to the poet's friends as Uncle Reuben and Aunt Jemima; respectively nine years, and one year, older than he. 'Aunt Jemima' married not long afterwards, and is chiefly remembered as having been very amiable, and, in early youth, to use her nephew's words, 'as beautiful as the day;' but kindly, merry 'Uncle Reuben', then clerk in the Rothschilds' London bank,* became a conspicuous member of the family circle. This does not mean that the poet was ever indebted to him for pecuniary help; and it is desirable that this should be understood, since it has been confidently asserted that he was so. So long as he was dependent at all, he depended exclusively on his father. Even the use of his uncle's horse, which might have been accepted as a friendly concession on Mr. Reuben's part, did not really represent one. The animal stood, as I have said, in Mr. Browning's stable, and it was groomed by his gardener. The promise of these conveniences had induced Reuben Browning to buy a horse instead of continuing to hire one. He could only ride it on a few days of the week, and it was rather a gain than a loss to him that so good a horseman as his nephew should exercise it during the interval.

* This uncle's name, and his business relations with the great Jewish firm, have contributed to the mistaken theory of the poet's descent.

Uncle Reuben was not a great appreciator of poetry—at all events of his nephew's; and an irreverent remark on 'Sordello', imputed to a more eminent contemporary, proceeded, under cover of a friend's name, from him. But he had his share of mental endowments. We are told that he was a good linguist, and that he wrote on finance under an assumed name. He was also, apparently, an accomplished classic. Lord Beaconsfield is said to have declared that the inscription on a silver inkstand, presented to the daughter of Lionel Rothschild on her marriage, by the clerks at New Court, 'was the most appropriate thing he had ever come across;' and that whoever had selected it must be one of the first Latin scholars of the day. It was Mr. Reuben Browning.

Another favourite uncle was William Shergold Browning, though less intimate with his nephew and niece than he would have become if he had not married while they were still children, and settled in Paris, where his father's interest had placed him in the Rothschild house. He is known by his 'History of the Huguenots', a work, we are told, 'full of research, with a reference to contemporary literature for almost every occurrence mentioned or referred to.' He also wrote the 'Provost of Paris', and 'Hoel Morven', historical novels, and 'Leisure Hours', a collection of miscellanies; and was a contributor for some years to the 'Gentleman's Magazine'. It was chiefly from this uncle that Miss Browning and her brother heard the now often-repeated stories of their probable ancestors, Micaiah Browning, who distinguished himself at the siege of Derry, and that commander of the ship 'Holy Ghost' who conveyed Henry V. to France before the battle of Agincourt, and received the coat-of-arms, with its emblematic waves, in reward for his service. Robert Browning was also indebted to him for the acquaintance of M. de Ripert-Monclar; for he was on friendly terms with the uncle of the young count, the Marquis de Fortia, a learned man and member of the Institut, and gave a letter of introduction—actually, I believe, to his brother Reuben—at the Marquis's request.*

* A grandson of William Shergold, Robert Jardine Browning, graduated at Lincoln College, was called to the Bar, and is now Crown Prosecutor in New South Wales; where his name first gave rise to a report that he was Mr. Browning's son, while the announcement of his marriage was, for a moment, connected with Mr. Browning himself. He was also intimate with the poet and his sister, who liked him very much.

The friendly relations with Carlyle, which resulted in his high estimate of the poet's mother, also began at Hatcham. On one occasion he took his brother, the doctor, with him to dine there. An earlier and much attached friend of the family was Captain Pritchard, cousin to the noted physician Dr. Blundell. He enabled the young Robert, whom he knew from the age of sixteen, to attend some of Dr. Blundell's lectures; and this aroused in him a considerable interest in the sciences connected with medicine, though, as I shall have occasion to show, no knowledge of either disease or its treatment ever seems to have penetrated into his life. A Captain Lloyd is indirectly associated with 'The Flight of the Duchess'. That poem was not completed according to its original plan; and it was the always welcome occurrence of a visit from this gentleman which arrested its completion. Mr. Browning vividly remembered how the click of the garden gate, and the sight of the familiar figure advancing towards the house, had broken in upon his work and dispelled its first inspiration.

The appearance of 'Paracelsus' did not give the young poet his just place in popular judgment and public esteem. A generation was to pass before this was conceded to him. But it compelled his recognition by the leading or rising literary men of the day; and a fuller and more varied social life now opened before him. The names of Serjeant Talfourd, Horne, Leigh Hunt, Barry Cornwall Procter, Monckton Milnes Lord Houghton, Eliot Warburton, Dickens, Wordsworth, and Walter Savage Landor, represent, with that of Forster, some of the acquaintances made, or the friendships begun, at this period. Prominent among the friends that were to be, was also Archer Gurney, well known in later life as the Rev. Archer

Gurney, and chaplain to the British embassy in Paris. His sympathies were at present largely absorbed by politics. He was contesting the representation of some county, on the Conservative side; but he took a very vivid interest in Mr. Browning's poems; and this perhaps fixes the beginning of the intimacy at a somewhat later date; since a pretty story by which it was illustrated connects itself with the publication of 'Bells and Pomegranates'. He himself wrote dramas and poems. Sir John, afterwards Lord, Hanmer was also much attracted by the young poet, who spent a pleasant week with him at Bettisfield Park. He was the author of a volume entitled 'Fra Cipollo and other Poems', from which the motto of 'Colombe's Birthday' was subsequently taken.

The friends, old and new, met in the informal manner of those days, at afternoon dinners, or later suppers, at the houses of Mr. Fox, Serjeant Talfourd, and, as we shall see, Mr. Macready; and Mr. Fox's daughter, then only a little girl, but intelligent and observant for her years, well remembers the pleasant gatherings at which she was allowed to assist, when first performances of plays, or first readings of plays and poems, had brought some of the younger and more ardent spirits together. Miss Flower, also, takes her place in the literary group. Her sister had married in 1834, and left her free to live for her own pursuits and her own friends; and Mr. Browning must have seen more of her then than was possible in his boyish days.

None, however, of these intimacies were, at the time, so important to him as that formed with the great actor Macready. They were introduced to each other by Mr. Fox early in the winter of 1835-6; the meeting is thus chronicled in Macready's diary, November 27.*

* 'Macready's Reminiscences', edited by Sir Frederick Pollock; 1875.

'Went from chambers to dine with Rev. William Fox, Bayswater. . . . Mr. Robert Browning, the author of 'Paracelsus', came in after dinner; I was very much pleased to meet him. His face is full of intelligence. . . . I took Mr. Browning on, and requested to be allowed to improve my acquaintance with him. He expressed himself warmly, as gratified by the proposal, wished to send me his book; we exchanged cards and parted.'

On December 7 he writes:

'Read 'Paracelsus', a work of great daring, starred with poetry of thought, feeling, and diction, but occasionally obscure; the writer can scarcely fail to be a leading spirit of his time. . . .'

He invited Mr. Browning to his country house, Elm Place, Elstree, for the last evening of the year; and again refers to him under date of December 31.

'. . . Our other guests were Miss Henney, Forster, Cattermole, Browning, and Mr. Munro. Mr. Browning was very popular with the whole party; his simple and enthusiastic manner engaged attention, and won opinions from all present; he looks and speaks more like a youthful poet than any man I ever saw.'

This New-Year's-Eve visit brought Browning and Forster together for the first time. The journey to Elstree was then performed by coach, and the two young men met at the 'Blue Posts', where, with one or more of Mr. Macready's other guests, they waited for the coach to start. They eyed each other with interest, both being striking in their way, and neither knowing who the other was. When the introduction took place at Macready's house, Mr. Forster supplemented it by saying: 'Did you see a little notice of you I wrote in the 'Examiner'?' The two names will now be constantly associated in Macready's diary, which, except for Mr. Browning's own casual utterances, is almost our only record of his literary and social life during the next two years.

It was at Elm Place that Mr. Browning first met Miss Euphrasia Fanny Haworth, then a neighbour of Mr. Macready, residing with her mother at Barham Lodge. Miss Haworth was still a young woman, but her love and talent for art and literature made her a fitting member of the genial circle to which Mr. Browning belonged; and she and the poet soon became fast friends. Her first name appears as 'Eyebright' in 'Sordello'. His letters to her, returned after her death by her brother, Mr. Frederick Haworth, supply valuable records of his experiences and of his feelings at one very interesting, and one deeply sorrowful, period of his history. She was a thoroughly kindly, as well as gifted woman, and much appreciated by those of the poet's friends who knew her as a resident in London during her last years. A portrait which she took of him in 1874 is considered by some persons very good.

At about this time also, and probably through Miss Haworth, he became acquainted with Miss Martineau.

Soon after his introduction to Macready, if not before, Mr. Browning became busy with the thought of writing for the stage. The diary has this entry for February 16, 1836:

'Forster and Browning called, and talked over the plot of a tragedy, which Browning had begun to think of: the subject, Narses. He said that I had *bit* him by my performance of Othello, and I told him I hoped I should make the blood come. It would indeed be some recompense for the miseries, the humiliations, the heart-sickening disgusts which I have endured in my profession, if, by its exercise, I had awakened a spirit of poetry whose influence would elevate, ennoble, and adorn our degraded drama. May it be!'

But Narses was abandoned, and the more serious inspiration and more definite motive were to come later. They connect themselves with one of the pleasant social occurrences which must have lived in the young poet's memory. On May 26 'Ion' had been performed for the first time and with great success, Mr. Macready sustaining the principal part; and the great actor and a number of their common friends had met at supper at Serjeant Talfourd's house to celebrate the occasion. The party included Wordsworth and Landor, both of whom Mr. Browning then met for the first time. Toasts flew right and left. Mr. Browning's health was proposed by Serjeant Talfourd as that of the youngest poet of England, and Wordsworth responded to the appeal with very kindly courtesy. The conversation afterwards turned upon plays, and Macready, who had ignored a half-joking question of Miss Mitford, whether, if she wrote one, he would act in it, overtook Browning as they were leaving the house, and said, 'Write a play, Browning, and keep me from going to America.' The reply was, 'Shall it be historical and English; what do you say to a drama on Strafford?'

This ready response on the poet's part showed that Strafford, as a dramatic subject, had been occupying his thoughts. The subject was in the air, because Forster was then bringing out a life of that statesman, with others belonging to the same period. It was more than in the air, so far as Browning was concerned, because his friend had been disabled, either through sickness or sorrow, from finishing this volume by the appointed time, and he, as well he might, had largely helped him in its completion. It was, however, not till August 3 that Macready wrote in his diary:

'Forster told me that Browning had fixed on Strafford for the subject of a tragedy; he could not have hit upon one that I could have more readily concurred in.'

A previous entry of May 30, the occasion of which is only implied, shows with how high an estimate of Mr. Browning's intellectual importance Macready's professional relations to him began.

'Arriving at chambers, I found a note from Browning. What can I say upon it? It was a tribute which remunerated me for the annoyances and cares of years: it was one of the very highest, may I not say the highest, honour I have through life received.'

The estimate maintained itself in reference to the value of Mr. Browning's work, since he wrote on March 13, 1837:

'Read before dinner a few pages of 'Paracelsus', which raises my wonder the more I read it. . . . Looked over two plays, which it was not possible to read, hardly as I tried. . . . Read some scenes in 'Strafford', which restore one to the world of sense and feeling once again.'

But as the day of the performance drew near, he became at once more anxious and more critical. An entry of April 28 comments somewhat sharply on the dramatic faults of 'Strafford', besides declaring the writer's belief that the only chance for it is in the acting, which, 'by possibility, might carry it to the end without disapprobation,' though he dares not hope without opposition. It is quite conceivable that his first complete study of the play, and first rehearsal of it, brought to light deficiencies which had previously escaped him; but so complete a change of sentiment points also to private causes of uneasiness and irritation; and, perhaps, to the knowledge that its being saved by collective good acting was out of the question.

'Strafford' was performed at Covent Garden Theatre on May 1. Mr. Browning wrote to Mr. Fox after one of the last rehearsals:

May Day, Lincoln's Inn Fields.

Dear Sir,—All my endeavours to procure a copy before this morning have been fruitless. I send the first book of the first bundle. *Pray* look over it—the alterations to-night will be considerable. The complexion of the piece is, I grieve to say, 'perfect gallows' just now—our *King*, Mr. Dale, being . . . but you'll see him, and, I fear, not much applaud. Your unworthy son, in things literary, Robert Browning.

P.S. in pencil.—A most unnecessary desire, but urged on me by Messrs. Longman: no notice on Str. in to-night's True Sun,* lest the other papers be jealous!!!

* Mr. Fox reviewed 'Strafford' in the 'True Sun'.

A second letter, undated, but evidently written a day or two later, refers to the promised notice, which had then appeared.

Tuesday Night.

No words can express my feelings: I happen to be much annoyed and unwell—but your most generous notice has almost made 'my soul well and happy now.'

I thank you, my most kind, most constant friend, from my heart for your goodness—which is brave enough, just now. I am ever and increasingly yours, Robert Browning.

You will be glad to see me on the earliest occasion, will you not? I shall certainly come.

A letter from Miss Flower to Miss Sarah Fox sister to the Rev. William Fox, at Norwich, contains the following passage, which evidently continues a chapter of London news:

'Then 'Strafford'; were you not pleased to hear of the success of one you must, I think, remember a very little boy, years ago. If not, you have often heard us speak of Robert Browning: and it is a great deal to have accomplished a successful tragedy, although he seems a good deal annoyed at the go of things behind the scenes, and declares he will never write a play again, as long as he lives. You have no idea of the ignorance and obstinacy of the whole set, with here and there an exception; think of his having to write out the meaning of the word 'impeachment', as some of them thought it meant 'poaching'.'

On the first night, indeed, the fate of 'Strafford' hung in the balance; it was saved by Macready and Miss Helen Faucit. After this they must have been better supported, as it was received on the second night with enthusiasm by a full house. The catastrophe came after the fifth performance, with the desertion of the actor who had sustained the part of Pym. We cannot now judge whether, even under favourable circumstances, the play would have had as long a run as was intended; but the casting vote in favour of this view is given by the conduct of Mr. Osbaldistone, the manager, when it was submitted to him. The diary says, March 30, that he caught at it with avidity, and agreed to produce it without delay. The terms he offered to the author must also have been considered favourable in those days.

The play was published in April by Longman, this time not at the author's expense; but it brought no return either to him or to his publisher. It was dedicated 'in all affectionate admiration' to William C. Macready.

We gain some personal glimpses of the Browning of 1835-6; one especially through Mrs. Bridell-Fox, who thus describes her first meeting with him:

'I remember . . . when Mr. Browning entered the drawing-room, with a quick light step; and on hearing from me that my father was out, and in fact that nobody was at home but myself, he said: "It's my birthday to-day; I'll wait till they come in," and sitting down to the piano, he added: "If it won't disturb you, I'll play till they do." And as he turned to the instrument, the bells of some neighbouring church suddenly burst out with a frantic merry peal. It seemed, to my childish fancy, as if in response to the remark that it was his birthday. He was then slim and dark, and very handsome; and—may I hint it—just a trifle of a dandy, addicted to lemon-coloured kid-gloves and such things: quite "the glass of fashion and the mould of form." But full of ambition, eager for success, eager for fame, and, what's more, determined to conquer fame and to achieve success.'

I do not think his memory ever taxed him with foppishness, though he may have had the innocent personal vanity of an attractive young man at his first period of much seeing and being seen; but all we know of him at that time bears out the impression Mrs. Fox conveys, of a joyous, artless confidence in himself and in life, easily depressed, but quickly reasserting itself; and in which the eagerness for new experiences had freed itself from the rebellious impatience of boyish days. The self-confidence had its touches of flippancy and conceit; but on this side it must have been constantly counteracted by his gratitude for kindness, and by his enthusiastic appreciation of the merits of other men. His powers of feeling, indeed, greatly expended themselves in this way. He was very attractive to women and, as we have seen, warmly loved by very various types of men; but, except in its poetic sense, his emotional nature was by no means then in the ascendant: a fact difficult to realize when we remember the passion of his childhood's love for mother and home, and the new and deep capabilities of affection to be developed in future days. The poet's soul in him was feeling its wings; the realities of life had not yet begun to weight them.

We see him again at the 'Ion' supper, in the grace and modesty with which he received the honours then adjudged to him. The testimony has been said to come from Miss Mitford, but may easily have been supplied by Miss Haworth, who was also present on this occasion.

Mr. Browning's impulse towards play-writing had not, as we have seen, begun with 'Strafford'. It was still very far from being exhausted. And though he had struck out for himself another line of dramatic activity, his love for the higher theatrical life, and the legitimate inducements of the more lucrative and not necessarily less noble form of composition, might ultimately in some degree have prevailed with him if circumstances had been such as to educate his theatrical capabilities, and to reward them. His first acted drama was, however, an interlude to the production of the important group of poems which was to be completed by 'Sordello'; and he alludes to this later work in an also discarded preface to 'Strafford', as one on which he had for some time been engaged. He even characterizes the Tragedy as an attempt 'to freshen a jaded mind by diverting it to the healthy natures of a grand epoch.' 'Sordello' again occupied him during the remainder of 1837 and the beginning of 1838; and by the spring of this year he must have been thankful to vary the scene and mode of his labours by means of a first visit to Italy. He announces his impending journey, with its immediate plan and purpose, in the following note:

To John Robertson, Esq.

Good Friday, 1838.

Dear Sir,—I was not fortunate enough to find you the day before yesterday—and must tell you very hurriedly that I sail this morning for Venice—intending to finish my poem among the scenes it describes. I shall have your good wishes I know. Believe me, in return, Dear sir, Yours faithfully and obliged, Robert Browning.

Mr. John Robertson had influence with the 'Westminster Review', either as editor, or member of its staff. He had been introduced to Mr. Browning by Miss Martineau; and, being a great admirer of 'Paracelsus', had promised careful attention for 'Sordello'; but, when the time approached, he made conditions of early reading, &c., which Mr. Browning thought so unfair towards other magazines that he refused to fulfil them. He lost his review, and the goodwill of its intending writer; and even Miss Martineau was ever afterwards cooler towards him, though his attitude in the matter had been in some degree prompted by a chivalrous partisanship for her.

Chapter 7

1838-1841

First Italian Journey—Letters to Miss Haworth—Mr. John Kenyon—'Sordello'—Letter to Miss Flower—'Pippa Passes'—'Bells and Pomegranates'.

Mr. Browning sailed from London with Captain Davidson of the 'Norham Castle', a merchant vessel bound for Trieste, on which he found himself the only passenger. A striking experience of the voyage, and some characteristic personal details, are given in the following letter to Miss Haworth. It is dated 1838, and was probably written before that year's summer had closed.

Tuesday Evening.

Dear Miss Haworth,—Do look at a fuchsia in full bloom and notice the clear little honey-drop depending from every flower. I have just found it out to my no small satisfaction,—a bee's breakfast. I only answer for the long-blossomed sort, though,—indeed, for this plant in my room. Taste and be Titania; you can, that is. All this while I forget that you will perhaps never guess the good of the discovery: I have, you are to know, such a love for flowers and leaves—some leaves—that I every now and then, in an impatience at being able to possess myself of them thoroughly, to see them quite, satiate myself with their scent,—bite them to bits—so there will be some sense in that. How I remember the flowers—even grasses—of places I have seen! Some one flower or weed, I should say, that gets some strangehow connected with them.

Snowdrops and Tilsit in Prussia go together; cowslips and Windsor Park, for instance; flowering palm and some place or other in Holland.

Now to answer what can be answered in the letter I was happy to receive last week. I am quite well. I did not expect you would write,—for none of your written reasons, however. You will see 'Sordello' in a trice, if the fagging fit holds. I did not write six lines while absent except a scene in a play, jotted down as we sailed thro' the Straits of Gibraltar—but I did hammer out some four, two of which are addressed to you, two to the Queen*—the whole to go in Book III—perhaps. I called you 'Eyebright'—meaning a simple and sad sort of translation of "Euphrasia" into my own language: folks would know who Euphrasia, or Fanny, was—and I should not know Ianthe or Clemanthe. Not that there is anything in them to care for, good or bad. Shall I say 'Eyebright'?

* I know no lines directly addressed to the Queen.

I was disappointed in one thing, Canova.

What companions should I have?

The story of the ship must have reached you 'with a difference' as Ophelia says; my sister told it to a Mr. Dow, who delivered it to Forster, I suppose, who furnished Macready with it, who made it over &c., &c., &c.—As short as I can tell, this way it happened: the captain woke me one bright Sunday morning to say there was a ship floating keel uppermost half a mile off; they lowered a boat, made ropes fast to some floating canvas, and towed her towards our vessel. Both met halfway, and the little air that had risen an hour or two before, sank at once. Our men made the wreck fast in high glee at having 'new trousers out of the sails,' and quite sure she was a French boat, broken from her moorings at Algiers, close by. Ropes were next hove hang this sea-talk! round her stanchions, and after a quarter of an hour's pushing at the capstan, the vessel righted suddenly, one dead body floating out; five more were in the forecastle, and had probably been there a month under a blazing African sun—don't imagine the wretched state of things. They were, these six, the 'watch below'—I give you the result of the day's observation—the rest, some eight or ten, had been washed overboard at first. One or two were Algerines, the rest Spaniards. The vessel was a smuggler bound for Gibraltar; there were two stupidly disproportionate guns, taking up the whole deck, which was convex and—nay, look you! a rough pen-and-ink sketch of the different parts of the wreck is here introduced these are the gun-rings, and the black square the place where the bodies lay. All the 'bulwarks' or sides of the top, carried away by the waves. Well, the sailors covered up the hatchway, broke up the aft-deck, hauled up tobacco and cigars, such heaps of them, and then bale after bale of prints and chintz, don't you call it, till the captain was half-frightened—he would get at the ship's papers, he said; so these poor fellows were pulled up, piecemeal, and pitched into the sea, the very sailors calling to each other to 'cover the faces',—no papers of importance were found, however, but fifteen swords, powder and ball enough for a dozen such boats, and bundles of cotton, &c., that would have taken a day to get out, but the captain vowed that after five o'clock she should be cut adrift: accordingly she was cast loose, not a third of her cargo having been touched; and you hardly can conceive the strange sight when the battered hulk turned round, actually, and looked at us, and then reeled off, like a mutilated creature from some scoundrel French surgeon's lecture-table, into the most gorgeous and lavish sunset in the world: there; only thank me for not taking you at your word, and giving you the whole 'story'.—'What I did?' I went to Trieste, then Venice—then through Treviso and Bassano to the mountains, delicious Asolo, all my places and castles, you will see. Then to Vicenza, Padua, and Venice again. Then to Verona, Trent, Innspruck the Tyrol, Munich, Salzburg in Franconia, Frankfort and Mayence; down the Rhine to Cologne, then to Aix-la-Chapelle, Liege and Antwerp—then home. Shall you come to town, anywhere near town, soon? I shall be off again as soon as my book is out, whenever that will be.

I never read that book of Miss Martineau's, so can't understand what you mean. Macready is looking well; I just saw him the other day for a minute after the play; his Kitely was Kitely—superb from his flat cap down to his shining shoes. I saw very few Italians, 'to know', that is. Those I did see I liked. Your friend Pepoli has been lecturing here, has he not?

I shall be vexed if you don't write soon, a long Elstree letter. What are you doing, writing—drawing? Ever yours truly R. B. To Miss Haworth, Barham Lodge, Elstree.

Miss Browning's account of this experience, supplied from memory of her brother's letters and conversations, contains some vivid supplementary details. The drifting away of the wreck put probably no effective distance between it and the ship; hence the necessity of 'sailing away' from it.

'Of the dead pirates, one had his hands clasped as if praying; another, a severe gash in his head. The captain burnt disinfectants and blew gunpowder, before venturing on board, but even then, he, a powerful man, turned very sick with the smell and sight. They stayed one whole day by the side, but the sailors, in spite of orders, began to plunder the cigars, &c. The captain said privately to Robert, "I cannot restrain my men, and they will bring the plague into our ship, so I mean quietly in the night to sail away." Robert took two cutlasses and a dagger; they were of the coarsest workmanship, intended for use. At the end of one of the sheaths was a heavy bullet, so that it could be used as a sling. The day after, to their great relief, a heavy rain fell and cleansed the ship. Captain Davidson reported the sight of the wreck and its condition as soon as he arrived at Trieste.'

Miss Browning also relates that the weather was stormy in the Bay of Biscay, and for the first fortnight her brother suffered terribly. The captain supported him on to the deck as they passed through the Straits of Gibraltar, that he might not lose the sight. He recovered, as we know, sufficiently to write 'How they brought the Good News from Ghent to Aix'; but we can imagine in what revulsion of feeling towards firm land and healthy motion this dream of a headlong gallop was born in him. The poem was pencilled on the cover of Bartoli's "De' Simboli trasportati al Morale", a favourite book and constant companion of his; and, in spite of perfect effacement as far as the sense goes, the pencil dints are still visible. The little poem 'Home Thoughts from the Sea' was written at the same time, and in the same manner.

By the time they reached Trieste, the captain, a rough north-countryman, had become so attached to Mr. Browning that he offered him a free passage to Constantinople; and after they had parted, carefully preserved, by way of remembrance, a pair of very old gloves worn by him on deck. Mr. Browning might, on such an occasion, have dispensed with gloves altogether; but it was one of his peculiarities that he could never endure to be out of doors with uncovered hands. The captain also showed his friendly feeling on his return to England by bringing to Miss Browning, whom he had heard of through her brother, a present of six bottles of attar of roses.

The inspirations of Asolo and Venice appear in 'Pippa Passes' and 'In a Gondola'; but the latter poem showed, to Mr. Browning's subsequent vexation, that Venice had been imperfectly seen; and the magnetism which Asolo was to exercise upon him, only fully asserted itself at a much later time.

A second letter to Miss Haworth is undated, but may have been written at any period of this or the ensuing year.

I have received, a couple of weeks since, a present—an album large and gaping, and as Cibber's Richard says of the 'fair Elizabeth': 'My heart is empty—she shall fill it'—so say I impudently? of my grand trouble-table, which holds a sketch or two by my fine fellow Monclar, one lithograph—his own face of faces,—'all the rest was amethyst.' F. H. everywhere! not a soul beside 'in the chrystal silence there,' and it locks, this album; now, don't shower drawings on M., who has so many advantages over me as it is: or at least don't bid *me* of all others say what he is to have.

The 'Master' is somebody you don't know, W. J. Fox, a magnificent and poetical nature, who used to write in reviews when I was a boy, and to whom my verses, a bookful, written at the ripe age of twelve and thirteen, were shown: which verses he praised not a little; which praise comforted me not a little. Then I lost sight of him for years and years; then I published *anonymously* a little poem—which he, to my inexpressible delight, praised and expounded in a gallant article in a magazine of which he was the editor; then I found him out again; he got a publisher for 'Paracelsus' I read it to him in manuscript and is in short 'my literary father'. Pretty nearly the same thing did he for Miss Martineau, as she has said somewhere. God knows I forget what the 'talk', table-talk was about—I think she must have told you the results of the whole day we spent tete-a-tete at Ascot, and that day's, the dinner-day's morning at Elstree and St. Albans. She is to give me advice about my worldly concerns, and not before I need it!

I cannot say or sing the pleasure your way of writing gives me—do go on, and tell me all sorts of things, 'the story' for a beginning; but your moralisings on 'your age' and the rest, are—now what *are* they? not to be reasoned on, disputed, laughed at, grieved about: they are 'Fanny's crotchets'. I thank thee, Jew lia, for teaching me that word.

I don't know that I shall leave town for a month: my friend Monclar looks piteous when I talk of such an event. I can't bear to leave him; he is to take my portrait to-day a famous one he *has* taken! and very like he engages it shall be. I am going to town for the purpose. . . .

Now, then, do something for me, and see if I'll ask Miss M——to help you! I am going to begin the finishing 'Sordello'—and to begin thinking a Tragedy an Historical one, so I shall want heaps of criticisms on 'Strafford' and I want to have *another* tragedy in prospect, I write best so provided: I had chosen a splendid subject for it, when I learned that a magazine for next, this, month, will have a scene founded on my story; vulgarizing or doing no good to it: and I accordingly throw it up. I want a subject of the most wild and passionate love, to contrast with the one I mean to have ready in a short time. I have many half-conceptions, floating fancies: give me your notion of a thorough self-devotement, self-forgetting; should it be a woman who loves thus, or a man? What circumstances will best draw out, set forth this feeling? . . .

The tragedies in question were to be 'King Victor and King Charles', and 'The Return of the Druses'.

This letter affords a curious insight into Mr. Browning's mode of work; it is also very significant of the small place which love had hitherto occupied in his life. It was evident, from his appeal to Miss Haworth's 'notion' on the subject, that he had as yet no experience, even imaginary, of a genuine passion, whether in woman or man. The experience was still distant from him in point of time. In circumstance he was nearer to it than he knew; for it was in 1839 that he became acquainted with Mr. Kenyon.

When dining one day at Serjeant Talfourd's, he was accosted by a pleasant elderly man, who, having, we conclude, heard who he was, asked leave to address to him a few questions: 'Was his father's name Robert? had he gone to school at the Rev. Mr. Bell's at Cheshunt, and was he still alive?' On receiving affirmative answers, he went on to say that Mr. Browning and he had been great chums at school, and though they had lost sight of each other in after-life, he had never forgotten his old playmate, but even alluded to him in a little book which he had published a few years before.*

* The volume is entitled 'Rhymed Plea for Tolerance' 1833, and contains a reference to Mr. Kenyon's schooldays, and to the classic fights which Mr. Browning had instituted.

The next morning the poet asked his father if he remembered a schoolfellow named John Kenyon. He replied, 'Certainly! This is his face,' and sketched a boy's head, in which his son at once recognized that of the grown man. The acquaintance was renewed, and Mr. Kenyon proved ever afterwards a warm friend. Mr. Browning wrote of him, in a letter to Professor Knight of St. Andrews, Jan. 10, 1884: 'He was one of the best of human beings, with a general sympathy for excellence of every kind. He enjoyed the friendship of Wordsworth, of Southey, of Landor, and, in later days, was intimate with most of my contemporaries of eminence.' It was at Mr. Kenyon's house that the poet saw most of Wordsworth, who always stayed there when he came to town.

In 1840 'Sordello' appeared. It was, relatively to its length, by far the slowest in preparation of Mr. Browning's poems. This seemed, indeed, a condition of its peculiar character. It had lain much deeper in the author's mind than the various slighter works which were thrown off in the course of its inception. We know from the preface to 'Strafford' that it must have been begun soon after 'Paracelsus'. Its plan may have belonged to a still earlier date; for it connects itself with 'Pauline' as the history of a poetic soul; with both the earlier poems, as the manifestation of the self-conscious spiritual ambitions which were involved in that history. This first imaginative mood was also outgrowing itself in the very act of self-expression; for the tragedies written before the conclusion of 'Sordello' impress us as the product of a different mental state—as the work of a more balanced imagination and a more mature mind.

It would be interesting to learn how Mr. Browning's typical poet became embodied in this mediaeval form: whether the half-mythical character of the real Sordello presented him as a fitting subject for imaginative psychological treatment, or whether the circumstances among which he moved seemed the best adapted to the development of the intended type. The inspiration may have come through the study of Dante, and his testimony to the creative influence of Sordello on their mother-tongue. That period of Italian history must also have assumed, if it did not already possess, a great charm for Mr. Browning's fancy, since he studied no less than thirty works upon it, which were to contribute little more to his dramatic picture than what he calls 'decoration', or 'background'. But the one guide which he has given us to the reading of the poem is his assertion that its historical circumstance is only to be regarded as background; and the extent to which he identified himself with the figure of Sordello has been proved by his continued belief that its prominence was throughout maintained. He could still declare, so late as 1863, in his preface to the reprint of the work, that his 'stress' in writing it had lain 'on the incidents in the development of a soul, little else' being to his mind 'worth study'. I cannot therefore help thinking that recent investigations of the life and character of the actual poet, however in themselves praiseworthy and interesting, have been often in some degree a mistake; because, directly or indirectly, they referred Mr. Browning's Sordello to an historical reality, which his author had grasped, as far as was then possible, but to which he was never intended to conform.

Sordello's story does exhibit the development of a soul; or rather, the sudden awakening of a self-regarding nature to the claims of other men—the sudden, though slowly prepared, expansion of the narrower into the larger self, the selfish into the sympathetic existence; and this takes place in accordance with Mr. Browning's here expressed belief that poetry is the appointed vehicle for all lasting truths; that the true poet must be their exponent. The work is thus obviously, in point of moral utterance, an advance on 'Pauline'. Its metaphysics are, also, more distinctly formulated than those of either

'Pauline' or 'Paracelsus'; and the frequent use of the term Will in its metaphysical sense so strongly points to German associations that it is difficult to realize their absence, then and always, from Mr. Browning's mind. But he was emphatic in his assurance that he knew neither the German philosophers nor their reflection in Coleridge, who would have seemed a likely medium between them and him. Miss Martineau once said to him that he had no need to study German thought, since his mind was German enough—by which she possibly meant too German—already.

The poem also impresses us by a Gothic richness of detail,* the picturesque counterpart of its intricacy of thought, and, perhaps for this very reason, never so fully displayed in any subsequent work. Mr. Browning's genuinely modest attitude towards it could not preclude the consciousness of the many imaginative beauties which its unpopular character had served to conceal; and he was glad to find, some years ago, that 'Sordello' was represented in a collection of descriptive passages which a friend of his was proposing to make. 'There is a great deal of that in it,' he said, 'and it has always been overlooked.'

* The term Gothic has been applied to Mr. Browning's work, I believe, by Mr. James Thomson, in writing of 'The Ring and the Book', and I do not like to use it without saying so. But it is one of those which must have spontaneously suggested themselves to many other of Mr. Browning's readers.

It was unfortunate that new difficulties of style should have added themselves on this occasion to those of subject and treatment; and the reason of it is not generally known. Mr. John Sterling had made some comments on the wording of 'Paracelsus'; and Miss Caroline Fox, then quite a young woman, repeated them, with additions, to Miss Haworth, who, in her turn, communicated them to Mr. Browning, but without making quite clear to him the source from which they sprang. He took the criticism much more seriously than it deserved, and condensed the language of this his next important publication into what was nearly its present form.

In leaving 'Sordello' we emerge from the self-conscious stage of Mr. Browning's imagination, and his work ceases to be autobiographic in the sense in which, perhaps erroneously, we have hitherto felt it to be. 'Festus' and 'Salinguerra' have already given promise of the world of 'Men and Women' into which he will now conduct us. They will be inspired by every variety of conscious motive, but never again by the old real or imagined self-centred, self-directing Will. We have, indeed, already lost the sense of disparity between the man and the poet; for the Browning of 'Sordello' was growing older, while the defects of the poem were in many respects those of youth. In 'Pippa Passes', published one year later, the poet and the man show themselves full-grown. Each has entered on the inheritance of the other.

Neither the imagination nor the passion of what Mr. Gosse so fitly calls this 'lyrical masque'* gives much scope for tenderness; but the quality of humour is displayed in it for the first time; as also a strongly marked philosophy of life—or more properly, of association—from which its idea and development are derived. In spite, however, of these evidences of general maturity, Mr. Browning was still sometimes boyish in personal intercourse, if we may judge from a letter to Miss Flower written at about the same time.

* These words, and a subsequent paragraph, are quoted from Mr. Gosse's 'Personalia'.

Monday night, March 9 ? 1841.

My dear Miss Flower,—I have this moment received your very kind note—of course, I understand your objections. How else? But they are somewhat lightened already confess—nay 'confess' is vile—you will be rejoiced to holla from the house-top—will go on, or rather go off, lightening, and will be—oh, where *will* they be half a dozen years hence?

Meantime praise what you can praise, do me all the good you can, you and Mr. Fox as if you will not! for I have a head full of projects—mean to song-write, play-write forthwith,—and, believe me, dear Miss Flower, Yours ever faithfully, Robert Browning.

By the way, you speak of 'Pippa'—could we not make some arrangement about it? The lyrics *want* your music—five or six in all—how say you? When these three plays are out I hope to build a huge Ode—but 'all goeth by God's Will.'

The loyal Alfred Domett now appears on the scene with a satirical poem, inspired by an impertinent criticism on his friend. I give its first two verses:

On a Certain Critique on 'Pippa Passes'.

Query—Passes what?—the critic's comprehension.

Ho! everyone that by the nose is led, Automatons of which the world is full, Ye myriad bodies, each without a head, That dangle from a critic's brainless skull, Come, hearken to a deep discovery made, A mighty truth now wondrously displayed. A black squat beetle, vigorous for his size, Pushing tail-first by every road that's wrong The dung-ball of his dirty thoughts along His tiny sphere of grovelling sympathies— Has knocked himself full-butt, with blundering trouble, Against a mountain he can neither double Nor ever hope to scale. So like a free, Pert, self-conceited scarabaeus, he Takes it into his horny head to swear There's no such thing as any mountain there.

The writer lived to do better things from a literary point of view; but these lines have a fine ring of youthful indignation which must have made them a welcome tribute to friendship.

There seems to have been little respectful criticism of 'Pippa Passes'; it is less surprising that there should have been very little of 'Sordello'. Mr. Browning, it is true, retained a limited number of earnest appreciators, foremost of whom was the writer of an admirable notice of these two works, quoted from an 'Eclectic Review' of 1847, in Dr. Furnivall's 'Bibliography'. I am also told that the series of poems which was next to appear was enthusiastically greeted by some poets and painters of the pre-Raphaelite school; but he was now entering on a period of general neglect, which covered nearly twenty years of his life, and much that has since become most deservedly popular in his work.

'Pippa Passes' had appeared as the first instalment of 'Bells and Pomegranates', the history of which I give in Mr. Gosse's words. This poem, and the two tragedies, 'King Victor and King Charles' and 'The Return of the Druses'—first christened 'Mansoor, the Hierophant'—were lying idle in Mr. Browning's desk. He had not found, perhaps not very vigorously sought, a publisher for them.

'One day, as the poet was discussing the matter with Mr. Edward Moxon, the publisher, the latter remarked that at that time he was bringing out some editions of the old Elizabethan dramatists in a comparatively cheap form, and that if Mr. Browning would consent to print his poems as pamphlets, using this cheap type, the expense would be very inconsiderable. The poet jumped at the idea, and it was agreed that each poem should form a separate brochure of just one sheet—sixteen pages in double columns—the entire cost of which should not exceed twelve or fifteen pounds. In this fashion began the celebrated series of 'Bells and Pomegranates', eight numbers of which, a perfect treasury of fine poetry, came out successively between 1841 and 1846. 'Pippa Passes' led the way, and was priced first at sixpence; then, the sale being inconsiderable, at a shilling, which greatly encouraged the sale; and so, slowly, up to half-a-crown, at which the price of each number finally rested.'

Mr. Browning's hopes and intentions with respect to this series are announced in the following preface to 'Pippa Passes', of which, in later editions, only the dedicatory words appear:

'Two or three years ago I wrote a Play, about which the chief matter I care to recollect at present is, that a Pit-full of good-natured people applauded it:—ever since, I have been desirous of doing something in the same way that should better reward their attention. What follows I mean for the first of a series of Dramatical Pieces, to come out at intervals, and I amuse myself by fancying that the cheap mode in which they appear will for once help me to a sort of Pit-audience again. Of course, such a work must go on no longer than it is liked; and to provide against a certain and but too possible contingency, let me hasten to say now—what, if I were sure of success, I would try to say circumstantially enough at the close—that I dedicate my best intentions most admiringly to the author of "Ion"—most affectionately to Serjeant Talfourd.'

A necessary explanation of the general title was reserved for the last number: and does something towards justifying the popular impression that Mr. Browning exacted a large measure of literary insight from his readers.

'Here ends my first series of "Bells and Pomegranates": and I take the opportunity of explaining, in reply to inquiries, that I only meant by that title to indicate an endeavour towards something like an alternation, or mixture, of music with discoursing, sound with sense, poetry with thought; which looks too ambitious, thus expressed, so the symbol was preferred. It is little to the purpose, that such is actually one of the most familiar of the many Rabbinical and Patristic acceptations of the phrase; because I confess that, letting authority alone, I supposed the bare words, in such juxtaposition, would sufficiently convey the desired meaning. "Faith and good works" is another fancy, for instance, and perhaps no easier to arrive at: yet Giotto placed a pomegranate fruit in the hand of Dante, and Raffaelle crowned his Theology in the 'Camera della Segnatura' with blossoms of the same; as if the Bellari and Vasari would be sure to come after, and explain that it was merely "simbolo delle buone opere—il qual Pomogranato fu pero usato nelle vesti del Pontefice appresso gli Ebrei."'

The Dramas and Poems contained in the eight numbers of 'Bells and Pomegranates' were:

I. Pippa Passes. 1841. II. King Victor and King Charles. 1842. III. Dramatic Lyrics. 1842. Cavalier Tunes; I. Marching Along; II. Give a Rouse; III. My Wife Gertrude. ['Boot and Saddle'.] Italy and France; I. Italy; II. France. Camp and Cloister; I. Camp French; II. Cloister Spanish. In a Gondola. Artemis Prologuizes. Waring; I.; II. Queen Worship; I. Rudel and The Lady of Tripoli; II. Cristina. Madhouse Cells; I. [Johannes Agricola.]; II. [Porphyria.] Through the Metidja to Abd-el-Kadr. 1842. The Pied Piper of Hamelin; a Child's Story. IV. The Return of the Druses. A Tragedy, in Five Acts. 1843. V. A Blot in the 'Scutcheon. A Tragedy, in Three Acts. 1843. [Second Edition, same year.] VI. Colombe's Birthday. A Play, in Five Acts. 1844. VII. Dramatic Romances and Lyrics. 1845. 'How they brought the Good News from Ghent to Aix. 16—.' Pictor Ignotus. Florence, 15—. Italy in England. England in Italy. Piano di Sorrento. The Lost Leader. The Lost Mistress. Home Thoughts, from Abroad. The Tomb at St. Praxed's: Rome, 15—. Garden Fancies; I. The Flower's Name; II. Sibrandus Schafnaburgensis. France and Spain; I. The Laboratory Ancien Regime; II. Spain—The Confessional. The Flight of the Duchess. Earth's Immortalities. Song. 'Nay but you, who do not love her.' The Boy and the Angel. Night and Morning; I. Night; II. Morning. Claret and Tokay. Saul. Part I. Time's Revenges. The Glove. Peter Ronsard loquitur. VIII. and last. Luria; and A Soul's Tragedy. 1846.

This publication has seemed entitled to a detailed notice, because it is practically extinct, and because its nature and circumstance confer on it a biographical interest not possessed by any subsequent issue of Mr. Browning's works. The dramas and poems of which it is composed belong to that more mature period of the author's life, in which the analysis of his work ceases to form a necessary part of his history. Some few of them, however, are significant to it; and this is notably the case with 'A Blot in the 'Scutcheon'.

Chapter 8

1841-1844

'A Blot in the 'Scutcheon'—Letters to Mr. Frank Hill; Lady Martin—Charles Dickens—Other Dramas and Minor Poems—Letters to Miss Lee; Miss Haworth; Miss Flower—Second Italian Journey; Naples—E. J. Trelawney—Stendhal.

'A Blot in the 'Scutcheon' was written for Macready, who meant to perform the principal part; and we may conclude that the appeal for it was urgent, since it was composed in the space of four or five days. Macready's journals must have contained a fuller reference to both the play and its performance at Drury Lane, February 1843 than appears in published form; but considerable irritation had arisen between him and Mr. Browning, and he possibly wrote something which his editor, Sir Frederick Pollock, as the friend of both, thought it best to omit. What occurred on this occasion has been told in some detail by Mr. Gosse, and would not need repeating if the question were only of re-telling it on the same authority, in another person's words; but, through the kindness of Mr. and Mrs. Frank Hill, I am able to give Mr. Browning's direct statement of the case, as also his expressed judgment upon it. The statement was made more than forty years later than the events to which it refers, but will, nevertheless, be best given in its direct connection with them.

The merits, or demerits, of 'A Blot in the 'Scutcheon' had been freshly brought under discussion by its performance in London through the action of the Browning Society, and in Washington by Mr. Laurence Barrett; and it became the subject of a paragraph in one of the theatrical articles prepared for the 'Daily News'. Mr. Hill was then editor of the paper, and when the article came to him for revision, he thought it right to submit to Mr. Browning the passages devoted to his tragedy, which embodied some then prevailing, but, he strongly suspected, erroneous impressions concerning it. The results of this kind and courteous proceeding appear in the following letter.

19, Warwick Crescent: December 15, 1884.

My dear Mr. Hill,—It was kind and considerate of you to suppress the paragraph which you send me,—and of which the publication would have been unpleasant for reasons quite other than as regarding my own work,—which exists to defend or accuse itself. You will judge of the true reasons when I tell you the facts—so much of them as contradicts the statements of your critic—who, I suppose, has received a stimulus from the notice, in an American paper which arrived last week, of Mr. Laurence Barrett's intention 'shortly to produce the play' in New York—and subsequently in London: so that 'the failure' of forty-one years ago might be duly influential at present—or two years hence perhaps. The 'mere amateurs' are no high game.

Macready received and accepted the play, while he was engaged at the Haymarket, and retained it for Drury Lane, of which I was ignorant that he was about to become the manager: he accepted it 'at the instigation' of nobody,—and Charles Dickens was not in England when he did so: it was read to him after his return, by Forster—and the glowing letter which contains his opinion of it, although directed by him to be shown to myself, was never heard of nor seen by me till printed in Forster's book some thirty years after. When the Drury Lane season began, Macready informed me that he should act the play when he had brought out two others—'The Patrician's Daughter', and 'Plighted Troth': having done so, he wrote to me that the former had been unsuccessful in money-drawing, and the latter had 'smashed his arrangements altogether': but he would still produce my play. I had—in my ignorance of certain symptoms better understood by Macready's professional acquaintances—I had no notion that it was a proper thing, in such a case, to 'release him from his promise'; on the contrary, I should have fancied that such a proposal was offensive. Soon after, Macready begged that I would call on him: he said the play had been read to the actors the day before, 'and laughed at from beginning to end': on my speaking my mind about this, he explained that the reading had been done by the Prompter, a grotesque person with a red nose and wooden leg, ill at ease in the love scenes, and that he would himself make amends by reading the play next morning— which he did, and very adequately—but apprised me that, in consequence of the state of his mind, harassed by business and various trouble, the principal character must be taken by Mr. Phelps; and again I failed to understand,—what Forster subsequently assured me was plain as the sun at noonday,—that to allow at Macready's Theatre any other than Macready to play the principal part in a new piece was suicidal,—and really believed I was meeting his exigencies by accepting the substitution. At the rehearsal, Macready announced that Mr. Phelps was ill, and that he himself would read the part: on the third rehearsal, Mr. Phelps appeared for the first time, and sat in a chair while Macready more than read, rehearsed the part. The next morning Mr. Phelps waylaid me at the stage-door to say, with much emotion, that it never was intended that *he* should be instrumental in the success of a new tragedy, and that Macready would play Tresham on the ground that himself, Phelps, was unable to do so. He added that he could not expect me to waive such an advantage,—but that, if I were prepared to waive it, 'he would take ether, sit up all night, and have the words in his memory by next day.' I bade him follow me to the green-room, and hear what I decided upon—which was that as Macready had given him the part, he should keep it: this was on a Thursday; he rehearsed on Friday and Saturday,—the play being acted the same evening,—*of the fifth day after the 'reading' by MacReady*. Macready at once wished to reduce the importance of the 'play',—as he styled it in the bills,—tried to leave out so much of the text, that I baffled him by getting it printed in four-and-twenty hours, by Moxon's assistance. He wanted me to call it 'The Sister'!—and I have before me, while I write, the stage-acting copy, with two lines of his own insertion to avoid the tragical ending—Tresham was to announce his intention of going into a monastery! all this, to keep up the belief that Macready, and Macready alone, could produce a veritable 'tragedy', unproduced before. Not a shilling was spent on scenery or dresses—and a striking scene which had been used for the 'Patrician's Daughter', did duty a second time. If your critic considers this treatment of the play an instance of 'the failure of powerful and experienced actors' to ensure its success,—I can only say that my own opinion was shown by at once breaking off a friendship of many years—a friendship which had a right to be plainly and simply told that the play I had contributed as a proof of it, would through a change of circumstances, no longer be to my friend's advantage,—all I could possibly care for. Only recently, when by the publication of Macready's journals the extent of his pecuniary embarrassments at that time was made known, could I in a measure understand his motives for such conduct—and less than ever understand why he so strangely disguised and disfigured them. If 'applause' means success, the play thus maimed and maltreated was successful enough: it 'made way' for Macready's own Benefit, and the Theatre closed a fortnight after.

Having kept silence for all these years, in spite of repeated explanations, in the style of your critic's, that the play 'failed in spite of the best endeavours' &c. I hardly wish to revive a very painful matter: on the other hand,—as I have said; my play subsists, and is as open to praise or blame as it was forty-one years ago: is it necessary to search out what somebody or other,—not improbably a jealous adherent of Macready, 'the only organizer of theatrical victories', chose to say on the subject? If the characters are 'abhorrent' and 'inscrutable'—and the language conformable,—they were so when Dickens pronounced upon them, and will be so whenever the critic pleases to re-consider them—which, if he ever has an opportunity of doing, apart from the printed copy, I can assure you is through no motion of mine. This particular experience was sufficient: but the Play is out of my power now; though amateurs and actors may do what they please.

Of course, this being the true story, I should desire that it were told *thus* and no otherwise, if it must be told at all: but *not* as a statement of mine,—the substance of it has been partly stated already by more than one qualified person, and if I have been willing to let the poor matter drop, surely there is no need that it should be gone into now when Macready and his Athenaeum upholder are no longer able to speak for themselves: this is just a word to you, dear Mr. Hill, and may be brought under the notice of your critic if you think proper—but only for the facts—not as a communication for the public.

Yes, thank you, I am in full health, as you wish—and I wish you and Mrs. Hill, I assure you, all the good appropriate to the season. My sister has completely recovered from her illness, and is grateful for your enquiries.

With best regards to Mrs. Hill, and an apology for this long letter, which however,—when once induced to write it,—I could not well shorten,—believe me, Yours truly ever Robert Browning.

I well remember Mr. Browning's telling me how, when he returned to the green-room, on that critical day, he drove his hat more firmly on to his head, and said to Macready, 'I beg pardon, sir, but you have given the part to Mr. Phelps, and I am satisfied that he should act it;' and how Macready, on hearing this, crushed up the MS., and flung it on to the ground. He also admitted that his own manner had been provocative; but he was indignant at what he deemed the unjust treatment which Mr. Phelps had received. The occasion of the next letter speaks for itself.

December 21, 1884.

My dear Mr. Hill,—Your goodness must extend to letting me have the last word—one of sincere thanks. You cannot suppose I doubted for a moment of a good-will which I have had abundant proof of. I only took the occasion your considerate letter gave me, to tell the simple truth which my forty years' silence is a sign I would only tell on compulsion. I never thought your critic had any less generous motive for alluding to the performance as he did than that which he professes: he doubtless heard the account of the matter which Macready and his intimates gave currency to at the time; and which, being confined for a while to their limited number, I never chose to notice. But of late years I have got to *read*,—not merely *hear*,—of the play's failure 'which all the efforts of my friend the great actor could not avert;' and the nonsense of this untruth gets hard to bear. I told you the principal facts in the letter I very hastily wrote: I could, had it been worth while, corroborate them by others in plenty, and refer to the living witnesses—Lady Martin, Mrs. Stirling, and I believe Mr. Anderson: it was solely through the admirable loyalty of the two former that . . . a play . . . deprived of every advantage, in the way of scenery, dresses, and rehearsing—proved—what Macready himself declared it to be—'a complete success'. *So* he sent a servant to tell me, 'in case there was a call for the author at the end of the act'—to which I replied that the author had been too sick and sorry at the whole treatment of his play to do any such thing. Such a call there truly *was*, and Mr. Anderson had to come forward and 'beg the author to come forward if he were in the house—a circumstance of which he was not aware:' whereat the author laughed at him from a box just opposite. . . . I would submit to anybody drawing a conclusion from one or two facts past contradiction, whether that play could have thoroughly failed which was not only not withdrawn at once but acted three nights in the same week, and years afterwards, reproduced at his own theatre, during my absence in Italy, by Mr. Phelps—the person most completely aware of the untoward circumstances which stood originally in the way of success. Why not enquire how it happens that, this second time, there was no doubt of the play's doing as well as plays ordinarily do? for those were not the days of a 'run'.

. . . . .

. . . This 'last word' has indeed been an Aristophanic one of fifty syllables: but I have spoken it, relieved myself, and commend all that concerns me to the approved and valued friend of whom I am proud to account myself in corresponding friendship, His truly ever Robert Browning.

Mr. Browning also alludes to Mr. Phelps's acting as not only not having been detrimental to the play, but having helped to save it, in the conspiracy of circumstances which seemed to invoke its failure. This was a mistake, since Macready had been anxious to resume the part, and would have saved it, to say the least, more thoroughly. It must, however, be remembered that the irritation which these letters express was due much less to the nature of the facts recorded in them than to the manner in which they had been brought before Mr. Browning's mind. Writing on the subject to Lady Martin in February 1881, he had spoken very temperately of Macready's treatment of his play, while deprecating the injustice towards his own friendship which its want of frankness involved: and many years before this, the touch of a common sorrow had caused the old feeling, at least momentarily, to well up again. The two met for the first time after these occurrences when Mr. Browning had returned, a widower, from Italy. Mr. Macready, too, had recently lost his wife; and Mr. Browning could only start forward, grasp the hand of his old friend, and in a voice choked with emotion say, 'O Macready!'

Lady Martin has spoken to me of the poet's attitude on the occasion of this performance as being full of generous sympathy for those who were working with him, as well as of the natural anxiety of a young author for his own success. She also remains convinced that this sympathy led him rather to over-than to under-rate the support he received. She wrote concerning it in 'Blackwood's Magazine', March 1881:

'It seems but yesterday that I sat by his [Mr. Elton's] side in the green-room at the reading of Robert Browning's beautiful drama, 'A Blot in the 'Scutcheon'. As a rule Mr. Macready always read the new plays. But owing, I suppose, to some press of business, the task was entrusted on this occasion to the head prompter,—a clever man in his way, but wholly unfitted to bring out, or even to understand, Mr. Browning's meaning. Consequently, the delicate, subtle lines were twisted, perverted, and sometimes even made ridiculous in his hands. My "cruel father" [Mr. Elton] was a warm admirer of the poet. He sat writhing and indignant, and tried by gentle asides to make me see the real meaning of the verse. But somehow the mischief proved irreparable, for a few of the actors during the rehearsals chose to continue to misunderstand the text, and never took the interest in the play which they would have done had Mr. Macready read it.'

Looking back on the first appearance of his tragedy through the widening perspectives of nearly forty years, Mr. Browning might well declare as he did in the letter to Lady Martin to which I have just referred, that her '*perfect* behaviour as a woman' and her 'admirable playing as an actress' had been or at all events were to him 'the one gratifying circumstance connected with it.'

He also felt it a just cause of bitterness that the letter from Charles Dickens,* which conveyed his almost passionate admiration of 'A Blot in the 'Scutcheon', and was clearly written to Mr. Forster in order that it might be seen, was withheld for thirty years from his knowledge, and that of the public whose judgment it might so largely have influenced. Nor was this the only time in the poet's life that fairly earned honours escaped him.

* See Forster's 'Life of Dickens'.

'Colombe's Birthday' was produced in 1853 at the Haymarket;* and afterwards in the provinces, under the direction of Miss Helen Faucit, who created the principal part. It was again performed for the Browning Society in 1885,** and although Miss Alma Murray, as Colombe, was almost entirely supported by amateurs, the result fully justified Miss Mary Robinson now Madame James Darmesteter in writing immediately afterwards in the Boston 'Literary World':***

* Also in 1853 or 1854 at Boston. ** It had been played by amateurs, members of the Browning Society, and their friends, at the house of Mr. Joseph King, in January 1882. *** December 12, 1885; quoted in Mr. Arthur Symons' 'Introduction to the Study of Browning'.

'"Colombe's Birthday" is charming on the boards, clearer, more direct in action, more full of delicate surprises than one imagines it in print. With a very little cutting it could be made an excellent acting play.'

Mr. Gosse has seen a first edition copy of it marked for acting, and alludes in his 'Personalia' to the greatly increased knowledge of the stage which its minute directions displayed. They told also of sad experience in the sacrifice of the poet which the play-writer so often exacts: since they included the proviso that unless a very good Valence could be found, a certain speech of his should be left out. That speech is very important to the poetic, and not less to the moral, purpose of the play: the triumph of unworldly affections. It is that in which Valence defies the platitudes so often launched against rank and power, and shows that these may be very beautiful things—in which he pleads for his rival, and against his own heart. He is the better man of the two, and Colombe has fallen genuinely in love with him. But the instincts of sovereignty are not outgrown in one day however eventful, and the young duchess has shown herself amply endowed with them. The Prince's offer promised much, and it held still more. The time may come when she will need that crowning memory of her husband's unselfishness and truth, not to regret what she has done.

'King Victor and King Charles' and 'The Return of the Druses' are both admitted by competent judges to have good qualifications for the stage; and Mr. Browning would have preferred seeing one of these acted to witnessing the revival of 'Strafford' or 'A Blot in the 'Scutcheon', from neither of which the best amateur performance could remove the stigma of past, real or reputed, failure; and when once a friend belonging to the Browning Society told him she had been seriously occupied with the possibility of producing the Eastern play, he assented to the idea with a simplicity that was almost touching, 'It *was* written for the stage,' he said, 'and has only one scene.' He knew, however, that the single scene was far from obviating all the difficulties of the case, and that the Society, with its limited means, did the best it could.

I seldom hear any allusion to a passage in 'King Victor and King Charles' which I think more than rivals the famous utterance of Valence, revealing as it does the same grasp of non-conventional truth, while its occasion lends itself to a far deeper recognition of the mystery, the frequent hopeless dilemma of our moral life. It is that in which Polixena, the wife of Charles, entreats him for *duty's* sake to retain the crown, though he will earn, by so doing, neither the credit of a virtuous deed nor the sure, persistent consciousness of having performed one.

Four poems of the 'Dramatic Lyrics' had appeared, as I have said, in the 'Monthly Repository'. Six of those included in the 'Dramatic Lyrics and Romances' were first published in 'Hood's Magazine' from June 1844 to April 1845, a month before Hood's death. These poems were, 'The Laboratory', 'Claret and Tokay', 'Garden Fancies', 'The Boy and the Angel', 'The Tomb at St. Praxed's', and 'The Flight of the Duchess'. Mr. Hood's health had given way under stress of work, and Mr. Browning with other friends thus came forward to help him. The fact deserves remembering in connection with his subsequent unbroken rule never to write for magazines. He might always have made exceptions for friendly or philanthropic objects; the appearance of 'Herve Riel' in the 'Cornhill Magazine', 1870, indeed proves that it was so. But the offer of a blank cheque would not have tempted him, for his own sake, to this concession, as he would have deemed it, of his integrity of literary purpose.

'In a Gondola' grew out of a single verse extemporized for a picture by Maclise, in what circumstances we shall hear in the poet's own words.

The first proof of 'Artemis Prologuizes' had the following note:

'I had better say perhaps that the above is nearly all retained of a tragedy I composed, much against my endeavour, while in bed with a fever two years ago—it went farther into the story of Hippolytus and Aricia; but when I got well, putting only thus much down at once, I soon forgot the remainder.'*

* When Mr. Browning gave me these supplementary details for the 'Handbook', he spoke as if his illness had interrupted the work, not preceded its conception. The real fact is, I think, the more striking.

Mr. Browning would have been very angry with himself if he had known he ever wrote 'I *had* better'; and the punctuation of this note, as well as of every other unrevised specimen which we possess of his early writing, helps to show by what careful study of the literary art he must have acquired his subsequent mastery of it.

'Cristina' was addressed in fancy to the Spanish queen. It is to be regretted that the poem did not remain under its original heading of 'Queen Worship': as this gave a practical clue to the nature of the love described, and the special remoteness of its object.

'The Pied Piper of Hamelin' and another poem were written in May 1842 for Mr. Macready's little eldest son, Willy, who was confined to the house by illness, and who was to amuse himself by illustrating the poems as well as reading them;* and the first of these, though not intended for publication, was added to the 'Dramatic Lyrics', because some columns of that number of 'Bells and Pomegranates' still required filling. It is perhaps not known that the second was 'Crescentius, the Pope's Legate': now included in 'Asolando'.

* Miss Browning has lately found some of the illustrations, and the touching childish letter together with which her brother received them.

Mr. Browning's father had himself begun a rhymed story on the subject of 'The Pied Piper'; but left it unfinished when he discovered that his son was writing one. The fragment survives as part of a letter addressed to Mr. Thomas Powell, and which I have referred to as in the possession of Mr. Dykes Campbell.

'The Lost Leader' has given rise to periodical questionings continued until the present day, as to the person indicated in its title. Mr. Browning answered or anticipated them fifteen years ago in a letter to Miss Lee, of West Peckham, Maidstone. It was his reply to an application in verse made to him in their very young days by herself and two other members of her family, the manner of which seems to have unusually pleased him.

Villers-sur-mer, Calvados, France: September 7, '75.

Dear Friends,—Your letter has made a round to reach me—hence the delay in replying to it—which you will therefore pardon. I have been asked the question you put to me—tho' never asked so poetically and so pleasantly—I suppose a score of times: and I can only answer, with something of shame and contrition, that I undoubtedly had

Wordsworth in my mind—but simply as 'a model'; you know, an artist takes one or two striking traits in the features of his 'model', and uses them to start his fancy on a flight which may end far enough from the good man or woman who happens to be 'sitting' for nose and eye.

I thought of the great Poet's abandonment of liberalism, at an unlucky juncture, and no repaying consequence that I could ever see. But—once call my fancy-portrait 'Wordsworth'—and how much more ought one to say,—how much more would not I have attempted to say!

There is my apology, dear friends, and your acceptance of it will confirm me Truly yours, Robert Browning.

Some fragments of correspondence, not all very interesting, and his own allusion to an attack of illness, are our only record of the poet's general life during the interval which separated the publication of 'Pippa Passes' from his second Italian journey.

An undated letter to Miss Haworth probably refers to the close of 1841.

'. . . I am getting to love painting as I did once. Do you know I was a young wonder as are eleven out of the dozen of us at drawing? My father had faith in me, and over yonder in a drawer of mine lies, I well know, a certain cottage and rocks in lead pencil and black currant jam-juice paint being rank poison, as they said when I sucked my brushes with his my father's note in one corner, "R. B., aetat. two years three months." "How fast, alas, our days we spend—How vain they be, how soon they end!" I am going to print "Victor", however, by February, and there is one thing not so badly painted in there—oh, let me tell you. I chanced to call on Forster the other day, and he pressed me into committing verse on the instant, not the minute, in Maclise's behalf, who has wrought a divine Venetian work, it seems, for the British Institution. Forster described it well—but I could do nothing better, than this wooden ware—all the "properties", as we say, were given, and the problem was how to catalogue them in rhyme and unreason.

I send my heart up to thee, all my heart In this my singing! For the stars help me, and the sea bears part; The very night is clinging Closer to Venice' streets to leave me space Above me, whence thy face May light my joyous heart to thee its dwelling-place.

Singing and stars and night and Venice streets and joyous heart, are properties, do you please to see. And now tell me, is this below the average of catalogue original poetry? Tell me—for to that end of being told, I write. . . . I dined with dear Carlyle and his wife catch me calling people "dear" in a hurry, except in letter-beginnings! yesterday. I don't know any people like them. There was a son of Burns there, Major Burns whom Macready knows—he sung "Of all the airts", "John Anderson", and another song of his father's. . . .'

In the course of 1842 he wrote the following note to Miss Flower, evidently relating to the publication of her 'Hymns and Anthems'.

New Cross, Hatcham, Surrey: Tuesday morning.

Dear Miss Flower,—I am sorry for what must grieve Mr. Fox; for myself, I beg him earnestly not to see me till his entire convenience, however pleased I shall be to receive the letter you promise on his part.

And how can I thank you enough for this good news—all this music I shall be so thoroughly gratified to hear? Ever yours faithfully, Robert Browning.

His last letter to her was written in 1845; the subject being a concert of her own sacred music which she was about to give; and again, although more slightly, I anticipate the course of events, in order to give it in its natural connection with the present one. Mr. Browning was now engaged to be married, and the last ring of youthful levity had disappeared from his tone; but neither the new happiness nor the new responsibility had weakened his interest in his boyhood's friend. Miss Flower must then have been slowly dying, and the closing words of the letter have the solemnity of a last farewell.

Sunday.

Dear Miss Flower,—I was very foolishly surprized at the sorrowful finical notice you mention: foolishly; for, God help us, how else is it with all critics of everything—don't I hear them talk and see them write? I dare-say he admires you as he said.

For me, I never had another feeling than entire admiration for your music—entire admiration—I put it apart from all other English music I know, and fully believe in it as *the* music we all waited for.

Of your health I shall not trust myself to speak: you must know what is unspoken. I should have been most happy to see you if but for a minute—and if next Wednesday, I might take your hand for a moment.—

But you would concede that, if it were right, remembering what is now very old friendship. May God bless you for ever The signature has been cut off.

In the autumn of 1844 Mr. Browning set forth for Italy, taking ship, it is believed, direct to Naples. Here he made the acquaintance of a young Neapolitan gentleman who had spent most of his life in Paris; and they became such good friends that they proceeded to Rome together. Mr. Scotti was an invaluable travelling companion, for he engaged their conveyance, and did all such bargaining in their joint interest as the habits of his country required. 'As I write,' Mr. Browning said in a letter to his sister, 'I hear him disputing our bill in the next room. He does not see why we should pay for six wax candles when we have used only two.' At Rome they spent most of their evenings with an old acquaintance of

Mr. Browning's, then Countess Carducci, and she pronounced Mr. Scotti the handsomest man she had ever seen. He certainly bore no appearance of being the least prosperous. But he blew out his brains soon after he and his new friend had parted; and I do not think the act was ever fully accounted for.

It must have been on his return journey that Mr. Browning went to Leghorn to see Edward John Trelawney, to whom he carried a letter of introduction. He described the interview long afterwards to Mr. Val Prinsep, but chiefly in his impressions of the cool courage which Mr. Trelawney had displayed during its course. A surgeon was occupied all the time in probing his leg for a bullet which had been lodged there some years before, and had lately made itself felt; and he showed himself absolutely indifferent to the pain of the operation. Mr. Browning's main object in paying the visit had been, naturally, to speak with one who had known Byron and been the last to see Shelley alive; but we only hear of the two poets that they formed in part the subject of their conversation. He reached England, again, we suppose, through Germany—since he avoided Paris as before.

It has been asserted by persons otherwise well informed, that on this, if not on his previous Italian journey, Mr. Browning became acquainted with Stendhal, then French Consul at Civita Vecchia, and that he imbibed from the great novelist a taste for curiosities of Italian family history, which ultimately led him in the direction of the Franceschini case. It is certain that he profoundly admired this writer, and if he was not, at some time or other, introduced to him it was because the opportunity did not occur. But there is abundant evidence that no introduction took place, and quite sufficient proof that none was possible. Stendhal died in Paris in March 1842; and granting that he was at Civita Vecchia when the poet made his earlier voyage—no certainty even while he held the appointment—the ship cannot have touched there on its way to Trieste. It is also a mistake to suppose that Mr. Browning was specially interested in ancient chronicles, as such. This was one of the points on which he distinctly differed from his father. He took his dramatic subjects wherever he found them, and any historical research which they ultimately involved was undertaken for purposes of verification. 'Sordello' alone may have been conceived on a rather different plan, and I have no authority whatever for admitting that it was so. The discovery of the record of the Franceschini case was, as its author has everywhere declared, an accident.

A single relic exists for us of this visit to the South—a shell picked up, according to its inscription, on one of the Syren Isles, October 4, 1844; but many of its reminiscences are embodied in that vivid and charming picture 'The Englishman in Italy', which appeared in the 'Bells and Pomegranates' number for the following year. Naples always remained a bright spot in the poet's memory; and if it had been, like Asolo, his first experience of Italy, it must have drawn him in later years the more powerfully of the two. At one period, indeed, he dreamed of it as a home for his declining days.

Chapter 9

1844-1849

Introduction to Miss Barrett—Engagement—Motives for Secrecy—Marriage—Journey to Italy—Extract of Letter from Mr. Fox—Mrs. Browning's Letters to Miss Mitford—Life at Pisa—Vallombrosa—Florence; Mr. Powers; Miss Boyle—Proposed British Mission to the Vatican—Father Prout—Palazzo Guidi—Fano; Ancona—'A Blot in the 'Scutcheon' at Sadler's Wells.

During his recent intercourse with the Browning family Mr. Kenyon had often spoken of his invalid cousin, Elizabeth Barrett,* and had given them copies of her works; and when the poet returned to England, late in 1844, he saw the volume containing 'Lady Geraldine's Courtship', which had appeared during his absence. On hearing him express his admiration of it, Mr. Kenyon begged him to write to Miss Barrett, and himself tell her how the poems had impressed him; 'for,' he added, 'my cousin is a great invalid, and sees no one, but great souls jump at sympathy.' Mr. Browning did write, and, a few months, probably, after the correspondence had been established, begged to be allowed to visit her. She at first refused this, on the score of her delicate health and habitual seclusion, emphasizing the refusal by words of such touching humility and resignation that I cannot refrain from quoting them. 'There is nothing to see in me, nothing to hear in me. I am a weed fit for the ground and darkness.' But her objections were overcome, and their first interview sealed Mr. Browning's fate.

* Properly E. Barrett Moulton-Barrett. The first of these surnames was that originally borne by the family, but dropped on the annexation of the second. It has now for some years been resumed.

There is no cause for surprize in the passionate admiration with which Miss Barrett so instantly inspired him. To begin with, he was heart-whole. It would be too much to affirm that, in the course of his thirty-two years, he had never met with a woman whom he could entirely love; but if he had, it was not under circumstances which favoured the growth of such a feeling. She whom he now saw for the first time had long been to him one of the greatest of living poets; she was learned as women seldom were in those days. It must have been apparent, in the most fugitive contact, that her moral nature was as exquisite as her mind was exceptional. She looked much younger than her age, which he only recently knew to have been six years beyond his own; and her face was filled with beauty by the large, expressive eyes. The imprisoned love within her must unconsciously have leapt to meet his own. It would have been only natural that he should grow into the determination to devote his life to hers, or be swept into an offer of marriage by a sudden impulse which his after-judgment would condemn. Neither of these things occurred. The offer was indeed made under a sudden and overmastering impulse. But it was persistently repeated, till it had obtained a conditional assent. No sane man in Mr. Browning's position could have been ignorant of the responsibilities he was incurring. He had, it is true, no experience of illness. Of its nature, its treatment, its symptoms direct and indirect, he remained pathetically ignorant to his dying day. He did not know what disqualifications for active existence might reside in the fragile, recumbent form, nor in the long years lived without change of air or scene beyond the passage, not always even allowed, from bed-room to sitting-room, from sofa to bed again. But he did know that Miss Barrett received him lying down, and that his very ignorance of her condition left him without security for her ever being able to stand. A strong sense of sympathy and pity could alone entirely justify or explain his act—a strong desire to bring sunshine into that darkened life. We might be sure that these motives had been present with him if we had no direct authority for believing it; and we have this authority in his own comparatively recent words: 'She had so much need of care and protection. There was so much pity in what I felt for her!' The pity was, it need hardly be said, at no time a substitute for love, though the love in its full force only developed itself later; but it supplied an additional incentive.

Miss Barrett had made her acceptance of Mr. Browning's proposal contingent on her improving in health. The outlook was therefore vague. But under the influence of this great new happiness she did gain some degree of strength. They saw each other three times a week; they exchanged letters constantly, and a very deep and perfect understanding established itself between them. Mr. Browning never mentioned his visits except to his own family, because it was naturally feared that if Miss Barrett were known to receive one person, other friends, or even acquaintances, would claim admittance to her; and Mr. Kenyon, who was greatly pleased by the result of his introduction, kept silence for the same reason.

In this way the months slipped by till the summer of 1846 was drawing to its close, and Miss Barrett's doctor then announced that her only chance of even comparative recovery lay in spending the coming winter in the South. There was no rational obstacle to her acting on this advice, since more than one of her brothers was willing to escort her; but Mr. Barrett, while surrounding his daughter with every possible comfort, had resigned himself to her invalid condition and expected her also to acquiesce in it. He probably did not believe that she would benefit by the proposed change. At any rate he refused his consent to it. There remained to her only one alternative—to break with the old home and travel southwards as Mr. Browning's wife.

When she had finally assented to this course, she took a preparatory step which, in so far as it was known, must itself have been sufficiently startling to those about her: she drove to Regent's Park, and when there, stepped out of the carriage and on to the grass. I do not know how long she stood—probably only for a moment; but I well remember hearing that when, after so long an interval, she felt earth under her feet and air about her, the sensation was almost bewilderingly strange.

They were married, with strict privacy, on September 12, 1846, at St. Pancras Church.

The engaged pair had not only not obtained Mr. Barrett's sanction to their marriage; they had not even invoked it; and the doubly clandestine character thus forced upon the union could not be otherwise than repugnant to Mr. Browning's pride; but it was dictated by the deepest filial affection on the part of his intended wife. There could be no question in so enlightened a mind of sacrificing her own happiness with that of the man she loved; she was determined to give herself to him. But she knew that her father would never consent to her doing so; and she preferred marrying without his knowledge to acting in defiance of a prohibition which, once issued, he would never have revoked, and which would have weighed like a portent of evil upon her. She even kept the secret of her engagement from her intimate friend Miss Mitford, and her second father, Mr. Kenyon, that they might not be involved in its responsibility. And Mr. Kenyon, who, probably of all her circle, best understood the case, was grateful to her for this consideration.

Mr. Barrett was one of those men who will not part with their children; who will do anything for them except allow them to leave the parental home. We have all known fathers of this type. He had nothing to urge against Robert Browning. When Mr. Kenyon, later, said to him that he could not understand his hostility to the marriage, since there was no man in the world to whom he would more gladly have given his daughter if he had been so fortunate as to possess one,[*] he replied: 'I have no objection to the young man, but my daughter should have been thinking of another world;' and, given his conviction that Miss Barrett's state was hopeless, some allowance must be made for the angered sense of fitness which her elopement was calculated to arouse in him. But his attitude was the same, under the varying circumstances, with all his daughters and sons alike. There was no possible husband or wife whom he would cordially have accepted for one of them.

* Mr. Kenyon had been twice married, but he had no children.

Mr. Browning had been willing, even at that somewhat late age, to study for the Bar, or accept, if he could obtain it, any other employment which might render him less ineligible from a pecuniary point of view. But Miss Barrett refused to hear of such a course; and the subsequent necessity for her leaving England would have rendered it useless.

For some days after their marriage Mr. and Mrs. Browning returned to their old life. He justly thought that the agitation of the ceremony had been, for the moment, as much as she could endure, and had therefore fixed for it a day prior by one week to that of their intended departure from England. The only difference in their habits was that he did not see her; he recoiled from the hypocrisy of asking for her under her maiden name; and during this passive interval, fortunately short, he carried a weight of anxiety and of depression which placed it among the most painful periods of his existence.

In the late afternoon or evening of September 19, Mrs. Browning, attended by her maid and her dog, stole away from her father's house. The family were at dinner, at which meal she was not in the habit of joining them; her sisters Henrietta and Arabel had been throughout in the secret of her attachment and in full sympathy with it; in the case of the servants, she was also sure of friendly connivance. There was no difficulty in her escape, but that created by the dog, which might be expected to bark its consciousness of the unusual situation. She took him into her confidence. She said: 'O Flush, if you make a sound, I am lost.' And Flush understood, as what good dog would not?—and crept after his mistress in silence. I do not remember where her husband joined her; we may be sure it was as near her home as possible. That night they took the boat to Havre, on their way to Paris.

Only a short time elapsed before Mr. Barrett became aware of what had happened. It is not necessary to dwell on his indignation, which at that moment, I believe, was shared by all his sons. Nor were they the only persons to be agitated by the occurrence. If there was wrath in the Barrett family, there was consternation in that of Mr. Browning. He had committed a crime in the eyes of his wife's father; but he had been guilty, in the judgment of his own parents, of one of those errors which are worse. A hundred times the possible advantages of marrying a Miss Barrett could never have balanced for them the risks and dangers he had incurred in wresting to himself the guardianship of that frail life which might perish in his hands, leaving him to be accused of having destroyed it; and they must have awaited the event with feelings never to be forgotten.

It was soon to be apparent that in breaking the chains which bound her to a sick room, Mr. Browning had not killed his wife, but was giving her a new lease of existence. His parents and sister soon loved her dearly, for her own sake as well as her husband's; and those who, if in a mistaken manner, had hitherto cherished her, gradually learned, with one exception, to value him for hers. It would, however, be useless to deny that the marriage was a hazardous experiment, involving risks of suffering quite other than those connected with Mrs. Browning's safety: the latent practical disparities of an essentially vigorous and an essentially fragile existence; and the time came when these were to make themselves felt. Mrs. Browning had been a delicate infant. She had also outgrown this delicacy and developed into a merry, and, in the harmless sense, mischief-loving child. The accident which subsequently undermined her life could only have befallen a very active and healthy girl.* Her condition justified hope and, to a great extent, fulfilled it. She rallied surprisingly and almost suddenly in the sunshine of her new life, and remained for several years at the higher physical level: her natural and now revived spirits sometimes, I imagine, lifting her beyond it. But her ailments were too radical for permanent cure, as the weak voice and shrunken form never ceased to attest. They renewed themselves, though in slightly different conditions; and she gradually relapsed, during the winters at least, into something like the home-bound condition of her earlier days. It became impossible that she should share the more active side of her husband's existence. It had to be alternately suppressed and carried on without her. The deep heart-love, the many-sided intellectual sympathy, preserved their union in rare beauty to the end. But to say that it thus maintained itself as if by magic, without effort of self-sacrifice on his part or of resignation on hers, would be as unjust to the noble qualities of both, as it would be false to assert that its compensating happiness had ever failed them.

* Her family at that time lived in the country. She was a constant rider, and fond of saddling her pony; and one day, when she was about fourteen, she overbalanced herself in lifting the saddle, and fell backward, inflicting injuries on her head, or rather spine, which caused her great suffering, but of which the nature remained for some time undiscovered.

Mr. Browning's troubles did not, even for the present, exhaust themselves in that week of apprehension. They assumed a deeper reality when his delicate wife first gave herself into his keeping, and the long hours on steamboat and in diligence were before them. What she suffered in body, and he in mind, during the first days of that wedding-journey is better imagined than told. In Paris they either met, or were joined by, a friend, Mrs. Anna Jameson then also en route for Italy, and Mrs. Browning was doubly cared for till she and her husband could once more put themselves on their way. At Genoa came the long-needed rest in southern land. From thence, in a few days, they went on to Pisa, and settled there for the winter.

Even so great a friend as John Forster was not in the secret of Mr. Browning's marriage; we learn this through an amusing paragraph in a letter from Mr. Fox, written soon after it had taken place:

'Forster never heard of the Browning marriage till the proof of the newspaper 'Examiner' notice was sent; when he went into one of his great passions at the supposed hoax, ordered up the compositor to have a swear at him, and demanded to see the MS. from which it was taken: so it was brought, and he instantly recognised the hand of Browning's sister. Next day came a letter from R. B., saying he had often meant to tell him or write of it, but hesitated between the two, and neglected both.

'She was better, and a winter in Italy had been recommended some months ago.

'It seems as if made up by their poetry rather than themselves.'

Many interesting external details of Mr. Browning's married life must have been lost to us through the wholesale destruction of his letters to his family, of which mention has been already made, and which he carried out before leaving Warwick Crescent about four years ago; and Mrs. Browning's part in the correspondence, though still preserved, cannot fill the gap, since for a long time it chiefly consisted of little personal outpourings, inclosed in her husband's letters and supplementary to them. But she also wrote constantly to Miss Mitford; and, from the letters addressed to her, now fortunately in Mr. Barrett Browning's hands, it has been possible to extract many passages of a sufficiently great, and not too private, interest for our purpose. These extracts—in some cases almost entire letters—indeed constitute a fairly complete record of Mr. and Mrs. Browning's joint life till the summer of 1854, when Miss Mitford's death was drawing near, and the correspondence ceased. Their chronological order is not always certain, because Mrs. Browning never gave the year in which her letters were written, and in some cases the postmark is obliterated; but the missing date can almost always be gathered from their contents. The first letter is probably written from Paris.

Oct. 2 '46.

'. . . and he, as you say, had done everything for me—he loved me for reasons which had helped to weary me of myself—loved me heart to heart persistently—in spite of my own will . . . drawn me back to life and hope again when I had done with both. My life seemed to belong to him and to none other, at last, and I had no power to speak a word. Have faith in me, my dearest friend, till you know him. The intellect is so little in comparison to all the rest—to the womanly tenderness, the inexhaustible goodness, the high and noble aspiration of every hour. Temper, spirits, manners—there is not a flaw anywhere. I shut my eyes sometimes and fancy it all a dream of my guardian angel. Only, if it had been a dream, the pain of some parts of it would have wakened me before now—it is not a dream. . . .'

The three next speak for themselves.

Pisa: '46.

'. . . For Pisa, we both like it extremely. The city is full of beauty and repose,—and the purple mountains gloriously seem to beckon us on deeper into the vine land. We have rooms close to the Duomo, and leaning down on the great Collegio built by Facini. Three excellent bed-rooms and a sitting-room matted and carpeted, looking comfortable even for England. For the last fortnight, except the last few sunny days, we have had rain; but the climate is as mild as possible, no cold with all the damp. Delightful weather we had for the travelling. Mrs. Jameson says she won't call me improved but transformed rather. . . . I mean to know something about pictures some day. Robert does, and I shall get him to open my eyes for me with a little instruction—in this place are to be seen the first steps of Art. . . .'

Pisa: Dec. 19 '46.

'. . . Within these three or four days we have had frost—yes, and a little snow—for the first time, say the Pisans, within five years. Robert says the mountains are powdered towards Lucca. . . .'

Feb. 3 '47.

'. . . Robert is a warm admirer of Balzac and has read most of his books, but certainly he does not in a general way appreciate our French people quite with my warmth. He takes too high a standard, I tell him, and won't listen to a story for a story's sake—I can bear, you know, to be amused without a strong pull on my admiration. So we have great wars sometimes—I put up Dumas' flag or Soulie's or Eugene Sue's yet he was properly impressed by the 'Mysteres de Paris', and carry it till my arms ache. The plays and vaudevilles he knows far more of than I do, and always maintains they are the happiest growth of the French school. Setting aside the 'masters', observe; for Balzac and George Sand hold all their honours. Then we read together the other day 'Rouge et Noir', that powerful work of Stendhal's, and he observed that it was exactly like Balzac 'in the raw'—in the material and undeveloped conception . . . We leave Pisa in April, and pass through Florence towards the north of Italy . . .'

She writes out a long list of the 'Comedie Humaine' for Miss Mitford.

Mr. and Mrs. Browning must have remained in Florence, instead of merely passing through it; this is proved by the contents of the two following letters:

Aug. 20 '47.

'. . . We have spent one of the most delightful of summers notwithstanding the heat, and I begin to comprehend the possibility of St. Lawrence's ecstasies on the gridiron. Very hot certainly it has been and is, yet there have been cool intermissions, and as we have spacious and airy rooms, as Robert lets me sit all day in my white dressing-gown without a single masculine criticism, and as we can step out of the window on a sort of balcony terrace which is quite private, and swims over with moonlight in the evenings, and as we live upon water-melons and iced water and figs and all manner of fruit, we bear the heat with an angelic patience.

We tried to make the monks of Vallombrosa let us stay with them for two months, but the new abbot said or implied that Wilson and I stank in his nostrils, being women. So we were sent away at the end of five days. So provoking! Such scenery, such hills, such a sea of hills looking alive among the clouds—which rolled, it was difficult to discern. Such fine woods, supernaturally silent, with the ground black as ink. There were eagles there too, and there was no road. Robert went on horseback, and Wilson and I were drawn on a sledge—i.e. an old hamper, a basket wine-hamper—without a wheel by two white bullocks, up the precipitous mountains. Think of my travelling in those wild places at four o'clock in the morning! a little frightened, dreadfully tired, but in an ecstasy of admiration. It was a sight to see before one died and went away into another world. But being expelled ignominiously at the end of five days, we had to come back to Florence to find a new apartment cooler than the old, and wait for dear Mr. Kenyon, and dear Mr. Kenyon does not come after all. And on the 20th of September we take up our knapsacks and turn our faces towards Rome, creeping slowly along, with a pause at Arezzo, and a longer pause at Perugia, and another perhaps at Terni. Then we plan to take an apartment we have heard of, over the Tarpeian rock, and enjoy Rome as we have enjoyed Florence. More can scarcely be. This Florence is unspeakably beautiful . . .'

Oct. '47.

'. . . Very few acquaintances have we made in Florence, and very quietly lived out our days. Mr. Powers, the sculptor, is our chief friend and favourite. A most charming, simple, straightforward, genial American—as simple as the man of genius he has proved himself to be. He sometimes comes to talk and take coffee with us, and we like him much. The sculptor has eyes like a wild Indian's, so black and full of light—you would scarcely marvel if they clove the marble without the help of his hands. We have seen, besides, the Hoppners, Lord Byron's friends at Venice; and Miss Boyle, a niece of the Earl of Cork, an authoress and poetess on her own account, having been introduced to Robert in London at Lady Morgan's, has hunted us out, and paid us a visit. A very vivacious little person, with sparkling talk enough . . .'

In this year, 1847, the question arose of a British mission to the Vatican; and Mr. Browning wrote to Mr. Monckton Milnes begging him to signify to the Foreign Office his more than willingness to take part in it. He would be glad and proud, he said, to be secretary to such an embassy, and to work like a horse in his vocation. The letter is given in the lately published biography of Lord Houghton, and I am obliged to confess that it has been my first intimation of the fact recorded there. When once his 'Paracelsus' had appeared, and Mr. Browning had taken rank as a poet, he renounced all idea of more active work; and the tone and habits of his early married life would have seemed scarcely consistent with a renewed impulse towards it. But the fact was in some sense due to the very circumstances of that life: among them, his wife's probable incitement to, and certain sympathy with, the proceeding.

The projected winter in Rome had been given up, I believe against the doctor's advice, on the strength of the greater attractions of Florence. Our next extract is dated from thence, Dec. 8, 1847.

'. . . Think what we have done since I last wrote to you. Taken two houses, that is, two apartments, each for six months, presigning the contract. You will set it down to excellent poet's work in the way of domestic economy, but the fault was altogether mine, as usual. My husband, to please me, took rooms which I could not be pleased with three days through the absence of sunshine and warmth. The consequence was that we had to pay heaps of guineas away, for leave to go away ourselves—any alternative being preferable to a return of illness—and I am sure I should have been ill if we had persisted in staying there. You can scarcely fancy the wonderful difference which the sun makes in Italy. So away we came into the blaze of him in the Piazza Pitti; precisely opposite the Grand Duke's palace; I with my remorse, and poor Robert without a single reproach. Any other man, a little lower than the angels, would have stamped and sworn a little for the mere relief of the thing—but as to *his* being angry with *me* for any cause except not eating enough dinner, the said sun would turn the wrong way first. So here we are in the Pitti till April, in small rooms yellow with sunshine from morning till evening, and most days I am able to get out into the piazza and walk up and down for twenty minutes without feeling a breath of the actual winter . . . and Miss Boyle, ever and anon, comes at night, at nine o'clock, to catch us at hot chestnuts and mulled wine, and warm her feet at our fire—and a kinder, more cordial little creature, full of talent and accomplishment never had the world's polish on it. Very amusing she is too, and original; and a good deal of laughing she and Robert make between them. And this is nearly all we see of the Face Divine—I can't make Robert go out a single evening. . . .'

We have five extracts for 1848. One of these, not otherwise dated, describes an attack of sore-throat which was fortunately Mr. Browning's last; and the letter containing it must have been written in the course of the summer.

'. . . My husband was laid up for nearly a month with fever and relaxed sore-throat. Quite unhappy I have been over those burning hands and languid eyes—the only unhappiness I ever had by him. And then he wouldn't see a physician, and if it had not been that just at the right moment Mr. Mahoney, the celebrated Jesuit, and "Father Prout" of Fraser, knowing everything as those Jesuits are apt to do, came in to us on his way to Rome, pointed out to us that the fever got ahead through weakness, and mixed up with his own kind hand a potion of eggs and port wine; to the horror of our Italian servant, who lifted up his eyes at such a prescription for fever, crying, "O Inglesi! Inglesi!" the case would have been far worse, I have no kind of doubt, for the eccentric prescription gave the power of sleeping, and the pulse grew quieter directly. I shall always be grateful to Father Prout—always.'*

* It had not been merely a case of relaxed sore-throat. There was an abscess, which burst during this first night of sleep.

May 28.

'... And now I must tell you what we have done since I wrote last, little thinking of doing so. You see our problem was, to get to England as much in summer as possible, the expense of the intermediate journeys making it difficult of solution. On examination of the whole case, it appeared manifest that we were throwing money into the Arno, by our way of taking furnished rooms, while to take an apartment and furnish it would leave us a clear return of the furniture at the end of the first year in exchange for our outlay, and all but a free residence afterwards, the cheapness of furniture being quite fabulous at the present crisis. ... In fact we have really done it magnificently, and planted ourselves in the Guidi Palace in the favourite suite of the last Count his arms are in scagliola on the floor of my bedroom. Though we have six beautiful rooms and a kitchen, three of them quite palace rooms and opening on a terrace, and though such furniture as comes by slow degrees into them is antique and worthy of the place, we yet shall have saved money by the end of this year. ... Now I tell you all this lest you should hear dreadful rumours of our having forsaken our native land, venerable institutions and all, whereas we remember it so well it's a dear land in many senses, that we have done this thing chiefly in order to make sure of getting back comfortably, ... a stone's throw, too, it is from the Pitti, and really in my present mind I would hardly exchange with the Grand Duke himself. By the bye, as to street, we have no spectators in windows in just the grey wall of a church called San Felice for good omen.

'Now, have you heard enough of us? What I claimed first, in way of privilege, was a spring-sofa to loll upon, and a supply of rain water to wash in, and you shall see what a picturesque oil-jar they have given us for the latter purpose; it would just hold the Captain of the Forty Thieves. As for the chairs and tables, I yield the more especial interest in them to Robert; only you would laugh to hear us correct one another sometimes. "Dear, you get too many drawers, and not enough washing-stands. Pray don't let us have any more drawers when we've nothing more to put in them." There was no division on the necessity of having six spoons—some questions passed themselves. ...'

July.

'... I am quite well again and strong. Robert and I go out often after tea in a wandering walk to sit in the Loggia and look at the Perseus, or, better still, at the divine sunsets on the Arno, turning it to pure gold under the bridges. After more than twenty months of marriage, we are happier than ever. ...'

Aug.

'... As for ourselves we have hardly done so well—yet well—having enjoyed a great deal in spite of drawbacks. Murray, the traitor, sent us to Fano as "a delightful summer residence for an English family," and we found it uninhabitable from the heat, vegetation scorched into paleness, the very air swooning in the sun, and the gloomy looks of the inhabitants sufficiently corroborative of their words that no drop of rain or dew ever falls there during the summer. A "circulating library" which "does not give out books," and "a refined and intellectual Italian society" I quote Murray for that phrase which "never reads a book through" I quote Mrs. Wiseman, Dr. Wiseman's mother, who has lived in Fano seven years complete the advantages of the place. Yet the churches are very beautiful, and a divine picture of Guercino's is worth going all that way to see. ... We fled from Fano after three days, and finding ourselves cheated out of our dream of summer coolness, resolved on substituting for it what the Italians call "un bel giro". So we went to Ancona—a striking sea city, holding up against the brown rocks, and elbowing out the purple tides—beautiful to look upon. An exfoliation of the rock itself you would call the houses that seem to grow there—so identical is the colour and character. I should like to visit Ancona again when there is a little air and shadow. We stayed a week, as it was, living upon fish and cold water. ...'

The one dated Florence, December 16, is interesting with reference to Mr. Browning's attitude when he wrote the letters to Mr. Frank Hill which I have recently quoted.

'We have been, at least I have been, a little anxious lately about the fate of the 'Blot in the 'Scutcheon' which Mr. Phelps applied for my husband's permission to revive at Sadler's. Of course putting the request was mere form, as he had every right to act the play—only it made ME anxious till we heard the result—and we both of us are very grateful to dear Mr. Chorley, who not only made it his business to be at the theatre the first night, but, before he slept, sat down like a true friend to give us the story of the result, and never, he says, was a more legitimate success. The play went straight to the hearts of the audience, it seems, and we hear of its continuance on the stage, from the papers. You may remember, or may not have heard, how Macready brought it out and put his foot on it, in the flush of a quarrel between manager and author; and Phelps, knowing the whole secret and feeling the power of the play, determined on making a revival of it in his own theatre. Mr. Chorley called his acting "fine". ...'

Chapter 10

1849-1852

Death of Mr. Browning's Mother—Birth of his Son—Mrs. Browning's Letters continued—Baths of Lucca—Florence again—Venice—Margaret Fuller Ossoli—Visit to England—Winter in Paris—Carlyle—George Sand—Alfred de Musset.

On March 9, 1849, Mr. Browning's son was born. With the joy of his wife's deliverance from the dangers of such an event came also his first great sorrow. His mother did not live to receive the news of her grandchild's birth. The letter which conveyed it found her still breathing, but in the unconsciousness of approaching death. There had been no time for warning. The sister could only break the suddenness of the shock. A letter of Mrs. Browning's tells what was to be told.

Florence: April 30 '49.

'. . . This is the first packet of letters, except one to Wimpole Street, which I have written since my confinement. You will have heard how our joy turned suddenly into deep sorrow by the death of my husband's mother. An unsuspected disease ossification of the heart terminated in a fatal way—and she lay in the insensibility precursive of the grave's when the letter written with such gladness by my poor husband and announcing the birth of his child, reached her address. "It would have made her heart bound," said her daughter to us. Poor tender heart—the last throb was too near. The medical men would not allow the news to be communicated. The next joy she felt was to be in heaven itself. My husband has been in the deepest anguish, and indeed, except for the courageous consideration of his sister who wrote two letters of preparation, saying "She was not well" and she "was very ill" when in fact all was over, I am frightened to think what the result would have been to him. He has loved his mother as such passionate natures only can love, and I never saw a man so bowed down in an extremity of sorrow—never. Even now, the depression is great—and sometimes when I leave him alone a little and return to the room, I find him in tears. I do earnestly wish to change the scene and air—but where to go? England looks terrible now. He says it would break his heart to see his mother's roses over the wall and the place where she used to lay her scissors and gloves—which I understand so thoroughly that I can't say "Let us go to England." We must wait and see what his father and sister will choose to do, or choose us to do—for of course a duty plainly seen would draw us anywhere. My own dearest sisters will be painfully disappointed by any change of plan—only they are too good and kind not to understand the difficulty—not to see the motive. So do you, I am certain. It has been very, very painful altogether, this drawing together of life and death. Robert was too enraptured at my safety and with his little son, and the sudden reaction was terrible. . . .'

Bagni di Lucca.

'. . . We have been wandering in search of cool air and a cool bough among all the olive trees to build our summer nest on. My husband has been suffering beyond what one could shut one's eyes to, in consequence of the great mental shock of last March—loss of appetite, loss of sleep—looks quite worn and altered. His spirits never rallied except with an effort, and every letter from New Cross threw him back into deep depression. I was very anxious, and feared much that the end of it all would be the intense heat of Florence assisting nervous fever or something similar; and I had the greatest difficulty in persuading him to leave Florence for a month or two. He who generally delights in travelling, had no mind for change or movement. I had to say and swear that Baby and I couldn't bear the heat, and that we must and would go away. "Ce que femme veut, *homme* veut," if the latter is at all amiable, or the former persevering. At last I gained the victory. It was agreed that we two should go on an exploring journey, to find out where we could have most shadow at least expense; and we left our child with his nurse and Wilson, while we were absent. We went along the coast to Spezzia, saw Carrara with the white marble mountains, passed through the olive-forests and the vineyards, avenues of acacia trees, chestnut woods, glorious surprises of the most exquisite scenery. I say olive-forests advisedly—the olive grows like a forest-tree in those regions, shading the ground with tints of silvery network. The olive near Florence is but a shrub in comparison, and I have learnt to despise a little too the Florentine vine, which does not swing such portcullises of massive dewy green from one tree to another as along the whole road where we travelled. Beautiful indeed it was. Spezzia wheels the blue sea into the arms of the wooded mountains; and we had a glance at Shelley's house at Lerici. It was melancholy to me, of course. I was not sorry that the lodgings we inquired about were far above our means. We returned on our steps after two days in the dirtiest of possible inns, saw Seravezza, a village in the mountains, where rock river and wood enticed us to stay, and the inhabitants drove us off by their unreasonable prices. It is curious—but just in proportion to the want of civilization the prices rise in Italy. If you haven't cups and saucers, you are made to pay for plate. Well—so finding no rest for the soles of our feet, I persuaded Robert to go to the Baths of Lucca, only to see them. We were to proceed afterwards to San Marcello, or some safer wilderness. We had both of us, but he chiefly, the strongest prejudice against the Baths of Lucca; taking them for a sort of wasp's nest of scandal and gaming, and expecting to find everything trodden flat by the continental English—yet, I wanted to see the place, because it is a place to see, after all. So we came, and were so charmed by the exquisite beauty of the scenery, by the coolness of the climate, and the absence of our countrymen—political troubles serving admirably our private requirements, that we made an offer for rooms on the spot, and returned to Florence for Baby and the rest of our establishment without further delay. Here we are then. We have been here more than a fortnight. We have taken an apartment for the season—four months, paying twelve pounds for the whole term, and hoping to be able to stay till the end of October. The living is cheaper than even in Florence, so that there has been no extravagance in coming here. In fact Florence is scarcely tenable during the summer from the excessive heat by day and night, even if there were no particular motive for leaving it. We have taken a sort of eagle's nest in this place—the highest house of the highest of the three villages which are called the Bagni di Lucca, and which lie at the heart of a hundred mountains sung to continually by a rushing mountain stream. The sound of the river and of the cicale is all the noise we hear. Austrian drums and carriage-wheels cannot vex us, God be thanked for it! The silence is full of joy and consolation. I think my husband's spirits are better already, and his appetite improved. Certainly little Babe's great cheeks are growing rosier and rosier. He is out all day when the sun is not too strong, and Wilson will have it that he is prettier than the whole population of babies here. . . . Then my whole strength has wonderfully improved—just as my medical friends prophesied,—and it seems like a dream when I find myself able to climb the hills with Robert, and help him to lose himself in the forests. Ever since my confinement I have been growing stronger and stronger, and where it is to stop I can't tell really. I can do as much or more than at any point of my life since I arrived at woman's estate. The air of the place seems to penetrate the heart, and not the lungs only: it draws you, raises you, excites you. Mountain air without its keenness—sheathed in Italian sunshine—think what that must be! And the beauty and the solitude—for with a few paces we get free of the habitations of men—all is delightful to me. What is peculiarly beautiful and wonderful, is the variety of the shapes of the mountains. They are a multitude—and yet there is no likeness. None, except where the golden mist comes and transfigures them into one glory. For the rest, the mountain there wrapt in the chestnut forest is not like that bare peak which tilts against the sky—nor like the serpent-twine of another which seems to move and coil in the moving coiling shadow. . . .'

She writes again:
Bagni di Lucca: Oct. 2 '49.
'. . . I have performed a great exploit—ridden on a donkey five miles deep into the mountain, to an almost inaccessible volcanic ground not far from the stars. Robert on horseback, and Wilson and the nurse with Baby on other donkies,—guides of course. We set off at eight in the morning, and returned at six P.M. after dining on the mountain pinnacle, I dreadfully tired, but the child laughing as usual, burnt brick colour for all bad effect. No horse or ass untrained for the mountains could have kept foot a moment where we penetrated, and even as it was, one could not help the natural thrill. No road except the bed of exhausted torrents—above and through the chestnut forests precipitous beyond what you would think possible for ascent or descent. Ravines tearing the ground to pieces under your feet. The scenery, sublime and wonderful, satisfied us wholly, as we looked round on the world of innumerable mountains, bound faintly with the grey sea—and not a human habitation. . . .'

The following fragment, which I have received quite without date, might refer to this or to a somewhat later period.
'If he is vain about anything in the world it is about my improved health, and I say to him, "But you needn't talk so much to people, of how your wife walked here with you, and there with you, as if a wife with a pair of feet was a miracle of nature."'

Florence: Feb. 18 '50.
'. . . You can scarcely imagine to yourself the retired life we live, and how we have retreated from the kind advances of the English society here. Now people seem to understand that we are to be left alone. . . .'

Florence: April 1 '50.
'. . . We drive day by day through the lovely Cascine, just sweeping through the city. Just such a window where Bianca Capello looked out to see the Duke go by—and just such a door where Tasso stood and where Dante drew his chair out to sit. Strange to have all that old world life about us, and the blue sky so bright. . . .'

Venice: June 4 probably '50.
'. . . I have been between Heaven and Earth since our arrival at Venice. The Heaven of it is ineffable—never had I touched the skirts of so celestial a place. The beauty of the architecture, the silver trails of water up between all that gorgeous colour and carving, the enchanting silence, the music, the gondolas—I mix it all up together and maintain that nothing is like it, nothing equal to it, not a second Venice in the world.

'Do you know when I came first I felt as if I never could go away. But now comes the earth-side.

'Robert, after sharing the ecstasy, grows uncomfortable and nervous, unable to eat or sleep, and poor Wilson still worse, in a miserable condition of sickness and headache. Alas for these mortal Venices, so exquisite and so bilious. Therefore I am constrained away from my joys by sympathy, and am forced to be glad that we are going away on Friday. For myself, it did not affect me at all. Take the mild, soft, relaxing climate—even the scirocco does not touch me. And the baby grows gloriously fatter in spite of everything. . . . As for Venice, you can't get even a "Times", much less an

"Athenaeum". We comfort ourselves by taking a box at the opera a whole box on the grand tier, mind for two shillings and eightpence, English. Also, every evening at half-past eight, Robert and I are sitting under the moon in the great piazza of St. Mark, taking excellent coffee and reading the French papers.'

If it were possible to draw more largely on Mrs. Browning's correspondence for this year, it would certainly supply the record of her intimacy, and that of her husband, with Margaret Fuller Ossoli. A warm attachment sprang up between them during that lady's residence in Florence. Its last evenings were all spent at their house; and, soon after she had bidden them farewell, she availed herself of a two days' delay in the departure of the ship to return from Leghorn and be with them one evening more. She had what seemed a prophetic dread of the voyage to America, though she attached no superstitious importance to the prediction once made to her husband that he would be drowned; and learned when it was too late to change her plans that her presence there was, after all, unnecessary. Mr. Browning was deeply affected by the news of her death by shipwreck, which took place on July 16, 1850; and wrote an account of his acquaintance with her, for publication by her friends. This also, unfortunately, was lost. Her son was of the same age as his, little more than a year old; but she left a token of the friendship which might some day have united them, in a small Bible inscribed to the baby Robert, 'In memory of Angelo Ossoli.'

The intended journey to England was delayed for Mr. Browning by the painful associations connected with his mother's death; but in the summer of 1851 he found courage to go there: and then, as on each succeeding visit paid to London with his wife, he commemorated his marriage in a manner all his own. He went to the church in which it had been solemnized, and kissed the paving-stones in front of the door. It needed all this love to comfort Mrs. Browning in the estrangement from her father which was henceforth to be accepted as final. He had held no communication with her since her marriage, and she knew that it was not forgiven; but she had cherished a hope that he would so far relent towards her as to kiss her child, even if he would not see her. Her prayer to this effect remained, however, unanswered.

In the autumn they proceeded to Paris; whence Mrs. Browning wrote, October 22 and November 12.

138, Avenue des Champs Elysees.

'... It was a long time before we could settle ourselves in a private apartment.... At last we came off to these Champs Elysees, to a very pleasant apartment, the window looking over a large terrace almost large enough to serve the purpose of a garden to the great drive and promenade of the Parisians when they come out of the streets to sun and shade and show themselves off among the trees. A pretty little dining-room, a writing and dressing-room for Robert beside it, a drawing-room beyond that, with two excellent bedrooms, and third bedroom for a "femme de menage", kitchen, &c.... So this answers all requirements, and the sun suns us loyally as in duty bound considering the southern aspect, and we are glad to find ourselves settled for six months. We have had lovely weather, and have seen a fire only yesterday for the first time since we left England.... We have seen nothing in Paris, except the shell of it. Yet, two evenings ago we hazarded going to a reception at Lady Elgin's, in the Faubourg St. Germain, and saw some French, but nobody of distinction.

'It is a good house, I believe, and she has an earnest face which must mean something. We were invited to go every Monday between eight and twelve. We go on Friday to Madame Mohl's, where we are to have some of the "celebrities".... Carlyle, for instance, I liked infinitely more in his personality than I expected to like him, and I saw a great deal of him, for he travelled with us to Paris, and spent several evenings with us, we three together. He is one of the most interesting men I could imagine, even deeply interesting to me; and you come to understand perfectly when you know him, that his bitterness is only melancholy, and his scorn, sensibility. Highly picturesque, too, he is in conversation; the talk of writing men is very seldom so good.

'And, do you know, I was much taken, in London, with a young authoress, Geraldine Jewsbury. You have read her books.... She herself is quiet and simple, and drew my heart out of me a good deal. I felt inclined to love her in our half-hour's intercourse....'

138, Avenue des Champs Elysees: Nov. 12.

'... Robert's father and sister have been paying us a visit during the last three weeks. They are very affectionate to me, and I love them for his sake and their own, and am very sorry at the thought of losing them, as we are on the point of doing. We hope, however, to establish them in Paris, if we can stay, and if no other obstacle should arise before the spring, when they must leave Hatcham. Little Wiedemann 'draws', as you may suppose ... he is adored by his grandfather, and then, Robert! They are an affectionate family, and not easy when removed one from another....'

On their journey from London to Paris, Mr. and Mrs. Browning had been joined by Carlyle; and it afterwards struck Mr. Browning as strange that, in the 'Life' of Carlyle, their companionship on this occasion should be spoken of as the result of a chance meeting. Carlyle not only went to Paris with the Brownings, but had begged permission to do so; and Mrs. Browning had hesitated to grant this because she was afraid her little boy would be tiresome to him. Her fear, however, proved mistaken. The child's prattle amused the philosopher, and led him on one occasion to say: 'Why, sir, you have as many aspirations as Napoleon!' At Paris he would have been miserable without Mr. Browning's help, in his ignorance of the language, and impatience of the discomforts which this created for him. He couldn't ask for anything, he complained, but they brought him the opposite.

On one occasion Mr. Carlyle made a singular remark. He was walking with Mr. Browning, either in Paris or the neighbouring country, when they passed an image of the Crucifixion; and glancing towards the figure of Christ, he said, with his deliberate Scotch utterance, 'Ah, poor fellow, *your* part is played out!'

Two especially interesting letters are dated from the same address, February 15 and April 7, 1852.

'. . . Beranger lives close to us, and Robert has seen him in his white hat, wandering along the asphalte. I had a notion, somehow, that he was very old, but he is only elderly—not much above sixty which is the prime of life, nowadays and he lives quietly and keeps out of scrapes poetical and political, and if Robert and I had a little less modesty we are assured that we should find access to him easy. But we can't make up our minds to go to his door and introduce ourselves as vagrant minstrels, when he may probably not know our names. We could never follow the fashion of certain authors, who send their books about with intimations of their being likely to be acceptable or not—of which practice poor Tennyson knows too much for his peace. If, indeed, a letter of introduction to Beranger were vouchsafed to us from any benign quarter, we should both be delighted, but we must wait patiently for the influence of the stars. Meanwhile, we have at last sent our letter [Mazzini's] to George Sand, accompanied with a little note signed by both of us, though written by me, as seemed right, being the woman. We half-despaired in doing this—for it is most difficult, it appears, to get at her, she having taken vows against seeing strangers, in consequence of various annoyances and persecutions, in and out of print, which it's the mere instinct of a woman to avoid—I can understand it perfectly. Also, she is in Paris for only a few days, and under a new name, to escape from the plague of her notoriety. People said, "She will never see you—you have no chance, I am afraid." But we determined to try. At least I pricked Robert up to the leap—for he was really inclined to sit in his chair and be proud a little. "No," said I, "you *sha'n't* be proud, and I *won't* be proud, and we *will* see her—I won't die, if I can help it, without seeing George Sand." So we gave our letter to a friend, who was to give it to a friend who was to place it in her hands—her abode being a mystery, and the name she used unknown. The next day came by the post this answer:

'"Madame, j'aurai l'honneur de vous recevoir Dimanche prochain, rue Racine, 3. C'est le seul jour que je puisse passer chez moi; et encore je n'en suis pas absolument certaine—mais je ferai tellement mon possible, que ma bonne etoile m'y aidera peut-etre un peu. Agreez mille remerciments de coeur ainsi que Monsieur Browning, que j'espere voir avec vous, pour la sympathie que vous m'accordez. George Sand. Paris: 12 fevrier '52."

'This is graceful and kind, is it not?—and we are going to-morrow—I, rather at the risk of my life, but I shall roll myself up head and all in a thick shawl, and we shall go in a close carriage, and I hope I shall be able to tell you the result before shutting up this letter.

'Monday.—I have seen G. S. She received us in a room with a bed in it, the only room she has to occupy, I suppose, during her short stay in Paris. She received us very cordially with her hand held out, which I, in the emotion of the moment, stooped and kissed—upon which she exclaimed, "Mais non! je ne veux pas," and kissed me. I don't think she is a great deal taller than I am,—yes, taller, but not a great deal—and a little over-stout for that height. The upper part of the face is fine, the forehead, eyebrows and eyes—dark glowing eyes as they should be; the lower part not so good. The beautiful teeth project a little, flashing out the smile of the large characteristic mouth, and the chin recedes. It never could have been a beautiful face Robert and I agree, but noble and expressive it has been and is. The complexion is olive, quite without colour; the hair, black and glossy, divided with evident care and twisted back into a knot behind the head, and she wore no covering to it. Some of the portraits represent her in ringlets, and ringlets would be much more becoming to the style of face, I fancy, for the cheeks are rather over-full. She was dressed in a sort of woollen grey gown, with a jacket of the same material according to the ruling fashion, the gown fastened up to the throat, with a small linen collarette, and plain white muslin sleeves buttoned round the wrists. The hands offered to me were small and well-shaped. Her manners were quite as simple as her costume. I never saw a simpler woman. Not a shade of affectation or consciousness, even—not a suffusion of coquetry, not a cigarette to be seen! Two or three young men were sitting with her, and I observed the profound respect with which they listened to every word she said. She spoke rapidly, with a low, unemphatic voice. Repose of manner is much more her characteristic than animation is—only, under all the quietness, and perhaps by means of it, you are aware of an intense burning soul. She kissed me again when we went away. . . .'

'April 7.—George Sand we came to know a great deal more of. I think Robert saw her six times. Once he met her near the Tuileries, offered her his arm and walked with her the whole length of the gardens. She was not on that occasion looking as well as usual, being a little too much "endimanchee" in terrestrial lavenders and super-celestial blues—not, in fact, dressed with the remarkable taste which he has seen in her at other times. Her usual costume is both pretty and quiet, and the fashionable waistcoat and jacket which are respectable in all the "Ladies' Companions" of the day make the only approach to masculine wearings to be observed in her.

'She has great nicety and refinement in her personal ways, I think—and the cigarette is really a feminine weapon if properly understood.

'Ah! but I didn't see her smoke. I was unfortunate. I could only go with Robert three times to her house, and once she was out. He was really very good and kind to let me go at all after he found the sort of society rampant around her. He didn't like it extremely, but being the prince of husbands, he was lenient to my desires, and yielded the point. She seems to live in the abomination of desolation, as far as regards society—crowds of ill-bred men who adore her, 'a genoux bas', betwixt a puff of smoke and an ejection of saliva—society of the ragged red, diluted with the low theatrical. She herself so different, so apart, so alone in her melancholy disdain. I was deeply interested in that poor woman. I felt a profound compassion for her. I did not mind much even the Greek, in Greek costume, who 'tutoyed' her, and kissed her I believe, so Robert said—or the other vulgar man of the theatre, who went down on his knees and called her "sublime". "Caprice d'amitie," said she with her quiet, gentle scorn. A noble woman under the mud, be certain. *I* would kneel down to her, too, if she would leave it all, throw it off, and be herself as God made her. But she would not care for my kneeling—she does not care for me. Perhaps she doesn't care much for anybody by this time, who knows? She wrote one or two or three kind notes to me, and promised to 'venir m'embrasser' before she left Paris, but she did not come. We both tried hard to please her, and she told a friend of ours that she "liked us". Only we always felt that we couldn't penetrate—couldn't really *touch* her—it was all vain.

'Alfred de Musset was to have been at M. Buloz' where Robert was a week ago, on purpose to meet him, but he was prevented in some way. His brother, Paul de Musset, a very different person, was there instead, but we hope to have Alfred on another occasion. Do you know his poems? He is not capable of large grasps, but he has poet's life and blood in him, I assure you. . . . We are expecting a visit from Lamartine, who does a great deal of honour to both of us in the way of appreciation, and was kind enough to propose to come. I will tell you all about it.'

Mr. Browning fully shared his wife's impression of a want of frank cordiality on George Sand's part; and was especially struck by it in reference to himself, with whom it seemed more natural that she should feel at ease. He could only imagine that his studied courtesy towards her was felt by her as a rebuke to the latitude which she granted to other men.

Another eminent French writer whom he much wished to know was Victor Hugo, and I am told that for years he carried about him a letter of introduction from Lord Houghton, always hoping for an opportunity of presenting it. The hope was not fulfilled, though, in 1866, Mr. Browning crossed to Saint Malo by the Channel Islands and spent three days in Jersey.

Chapter II

1852-1855

M. Joseph Milsand—His close Friendship with Mr. Browning; Mrs. Browning's Impression of him—New Edition of Mr. Browning's Poems—'Christmas Eve and Easter Day'—'Essay' on Shelley—Summer in London—Dante Gabriel Rossetti—Florence; secluded Life—Letters from Mr. and Mrs. Browning—'Colombe's Birthday'—Baths of Lucca—Mrs. Browning's Letters—Winter in Rome—Mr. and Mrs. Story—Mrs. Sartoris—Mrs. Fanny Kemble—Summer in London—Tennyson—Ruskin.

It was during this winter in Paris that Mr. Browning became acquainted with M. Joseph Milsand, the second Frenchman with whom he was to be united by ties of deep friendship and affection. M. Milsand was at that time, and for long afterwards, a frequent contributor to the 'Revue des Deux Mondes'; his range of subjects being enlarged by his, for a Frenchman, exceptional knowledge of English life, language, and literature. He wrote an article on Quakerism, which was much approved by Mr. William Forster, and a little volume on Ruskin called 'L'Esthetique Anglaise', which was published in the 'Bibliotheque de Philosophie Contemporaine'.* Shortly before the arrival of Mr. and Mrs. Browning in Paris, he had accidentally seen an extract from 'Paracelsus'. This struck him so much that he procured the two volumes of the works and 'Christmas Eve', and discussed the whole in the 'Revue' as the second part of an essay entitled 'La Poesie Anglaise depuis Byron'. Mr. Browning saw the article, and was naturally touched at finding his poems the object of serious study in a foreign country, while still so little regarded in his own. It was no less natural that this should lead to a friendship which, the opening once given, would have grown up unassisted, at least on Mr. Browning's side; for M. Milsand united the qualities of a critical intellect with a tenderness, a loyalty, and a simplicity of nature seldom found in combination with them.

* He published also an admirable little work on the requirements of secondary education in France, equally applicable in many respects to any country and to any time.

The introduction was brought about by the daughter of William Browning, Mrs. Jebb-Dyke, or more directly by Mr. and Mrs. Fraser Corkran, who were among the earliest friends of the Browning family in Paris. M. Milsand was soon an 'habitue' of Mr. Browning's house, as somewhat later of that of his father and sister; and when, many years afterwards, Miss Browning had taken up her abode in England, he spent some weeks of the early summer in Warwick Crescent, whenever his home duties or personal occupations allowed him to do so. Several times also the poet and his sister joined him at Saint-Aubin, the seaside village in Normandy which was his special resort, and where they enjoyed the good offices of Madame Milsand, a home-staying, genuine French wife and mother, well acquainted with the resources of its very primitive life. M. Milsand died, in 1886, of apoplexy, the consequence, I believe, of heart-disease brought on by excessive cold-bathing. The first reprint of 'Sordello', in 1863, had been, as is well known, dedicated to him. The 'Parleyings', published within a year of his death, were inscribed to his memory. Mr. Browning's affection for him finds utterance in a few strong words which I shall have occasion to quote. An undated fragment concerning him from Mrs. Browning to her sister-in-law, points to a later date than the present, but may as well be inserted here.

'. . . I quite love M. Milsand for being interested in Penini. What a perfect creature he is, to be sure! He always stands in the top place among our gods—Give him my cordial regards, always, mind. . . . He wants, I think—the only want of that noble nature—the sense of spiritual relation; and also he puts under his feet too much the worth of impulse and passion, in considering the powers of human nature. For the rest, I don't know such a man. He has intellectual conscience—or say—the conscience of the intellect, in a higher degree than I ever saw in any man of any country—and this is no less Robert's belief than mine. When we hear the brilliant talkers and noisy thinkers here and there and everywhere, we go back to Milsand with a real reverence. Also, I never shall forget his delicacy to me personally, nor his tenderness of heart about my child. . . .'

The criticism was inevitable from the point of view of Mrs. Browning's nature and experience; but I think she would have revoked part of it if she had known M. Milsand in later years. He would never have agreed with her as to the authority of 'impulse and passion', but I am sure he did not underrate their importance as factors in human life.

M. Milsand was one of the few readers of Browning with whom I have talked about him, who had studied his work from the beginning, and had realized the ambition of his first imaginative flights. He was more perplexed by the poet's utterance in later years. 'Quel homme extraordinaire!' he once said to me; 'son centre n'est pas au milieu.' The usual criticism would have been that, while his own centre was in the middle, he did not seek it in the middle for the things of which he wrote; but I remember that, at the moment in which the words were spoken, they impressed me as full of penetration. Mr. Browning had so much confidence in M. Milsand's linguistic powers that he invariably sent him his proof-sheets for final revision, and was exceedingly pleased with such few corrections as his friend was able to suggest.

With the name of Milsand connects itself in the poet's life that of a younger, but very genuine friend of both, M. Gustave Dourlans: a man of fine critical and intellectual powers, unfortunately neutralized by bad health. M. Dourlans also became a visitor at Warwick Crescent, and a frequent correspondent of Mr. or rather of Miss Browning. He came from Paris once more, to witness the last sad scene in Westminster Abbey.

The first three years of Mr. Browning's married life had been unproductive from a literary point of view. The realization and enjoyment of the new companionship, the duties as well as interests of the dual existence, and, lastly, the shock and pain of his mother's death, had absorbed his mental energies for the time being. But by the close of 1848 he had prepared for publication in the following year a new edition of 'Paracelsus' and the 'Bells and Pomegranates' poems. The reprint was in two volumes, and the publishers were Messrs. Chapman and Hall; the system, maintained through Mr. Moxon, of publication at the author's expense, being abandoned by Mr. Browning when he left home. Mrs. Browning writes of him on this occasion that he is paying 'peculiar attention to the objections made against certain obscurities.' He himself prefaced the edition by these words: 'Many of these pieces were out of print, the rest had been withdrawn from circulation, when the corrected edition, now submitted to the reader, was prepared. The various Poems and Dramas have received the author's most careful revision. December 1848.'

In 1850, in Florence, he wrote 'Christmas Eve and Easter Day'; and in December 1851, in Paris, the essay on Shelley, to be prefixed to twenty-five supposed letters of that poet, published by Moxon in 1852.*

* They were discovered, not long afterwards, to be spurious, and the book suppressed.

The reading of this Essay might serve to correct the frequent misapprehension of Mr. Browning's religious views which has been based on the literal evidence of 'Christmas Eve', were it not that its companion poem has failed to do so; though the tendency of 'Easter Day' is as different from that of its precursor as their common Christianity admits. The balance of argument in 'Christmas Eve' is in favour of direct revelation of religious truth and prosaic certainty regarding it; while the 'Easter Day' vision makes a tentative and unresting attitude the first condition of the religious life; and if Mr. Browning has meant to say—as he so often did say—that religious certainties are required for the undeveloped mind, but that the growing religious intelligence walks best by a receding light, he denies the positive basis of Christian belief, and is no more orthodox in the one set of reflections than in the other. The spirit, however, of both poems is ascetic: for the first divorces religious worship from every appeal to the poetic sense; the second refuses to recognize, in poetry or art, or the attainments of the intellect, or even in the best human love, any practical correspondence with religion. The dissertation on Shelley is, what 'Sordello' was, what its author's treatment of poets and poetry always must be—an indirect vindication of the conceptions of human life which 'Christmas Eve and Easter Day' condemns. This double poem stands indeed so much alone in Mr. Browning's work that we are tempted to ask ourselves to what circumstance or impulse, external or internal, it has been due; and we can only conjecture that the prolonged communion with a mind so spiritual as that of his wife, the special sympathies and differences which were elicited by it, may have quickened his religious imagination, while directing it towards doctrinal or controversial issues which it had not previously embraced.

The 'Essay' is a tribute to the genius of Shelley; it is also a justification of his life and character, as the balance of evidence then presented them to Mr. Browning's mind. It rests on a definition of the respective qualities of the objective and the subjective poet. . . . While both, he says, are gifted with the fuller perception of nature and man, the one endeavours to

'reproduce things external whether the phenomena of the scenic universe, or the manifested action of the human heart and brain with an immediate reference, in every case, to the common eye and apprehension of his fellow-men, assumed capable of receiving and profiting by this reproduction'—the other 'is impelled to embody the thing he perceives, not so much with reference to the many below, as to the One above him, the supreme Intelligence which apprehends all things in their absolute truth,—an ultimate view ever aspired to, if but partially attained, by the poet's own soul. Not what man sees, but what God sees—the 'Ideas' of Plato, seeds of creation lying burningly on the Divine Hand—it is toward these that he struggles. Not with the combination of humanity in action, but with the primal elements of humanity he has to do; and he digs where he stands,—preferring to seek them in his own soul as the nearest reflex of that absolute Mind, according to the intuitions of which he desires to perceive and speak.'

The objective poet is therefore a fashioner, the subjective is best described as a seer. The distinction repeats itself in the interest with which we study their respective lives. We are glad of the biography of the objective poet because it reveals to us the power by which he works; we desire still more that of the subjective poet, because it presents us with another aspect of the work itself. The poetry of such a one is an effluence much more than a production; it is

'the very radiance and aroma of his personality, projected from it but not separated. Therefore, in our approach to the poetry, we necessarily approach the personality of the poet; in apprehending it we apprehend him, and certainly we cannot love it without loving him.'

The reason of Mr. Browning's prolonged and instinctive reverence for Shelley is thus set forth in the opening pages of the Essay: he recognized in his writings the quality of a 'subjective' poet; hence, as he understands the word, the evidence of a divinely inspired man.

Mr. Browning goes on to say that we need the recorded life in order quite to determine to which class of inspiration a given work belongs; and though he regards the work of Shelley as carrying its warrant within itself, his position leaves ample room for a withdrawal of faith, a reversal of judgment, if the ascertained facts of the poet's life should at any future time bear decided witness against him. He is also careful to avoid drawing too hard and fast a line between the two opposite kinds of poet. He admits that a pure instance of either is seldom to be found; he sees no reason why

'these two modes of poetic faculty may not issue hereafter from the same poet in successive perfect works. . . . A mere running-in of the one faculty upon the other' being, meanwhile, 'the ordinary circumstance.'

I venture, however, to think, that in his various and necessary concessions, he lets slip the main point; and for the simple reason that it is untenable. The terms 'subjective' and 'objective' denote a real and very important difference on the ground of judgment, but one which tends more and more to efface itself in the sphere of the higher creative imagination. Mr. Browning might as briefly, and I think more fully, have expressed the salient quality of his poet, even while he could describe it in these emphatic words:

'I pass at once, therefore, from Shelley's minor excellencies to his noblest and predominating characteristic.

'This I call his simultaneous perception of Power and Love in the absolute, and of Beauty and Good in the concrete, while he throws, from his poet's station between both, swifter, subtler, and more numerous films for the connexion of each with each, than have been thrown by any modern artificer of whom I have knowledge . . . I would rather consider Shelley's poetry as a sublime fragmentary essay towards a presentment of the correspondency of the universe to Deity, of the natural to the spiritual, and of the actual to the ideal than . . .'

This essay has, in common with the poems of the preceding years, the one quality of a largely religious and, in a certain sense, Christian spirit, and in this respect it falls naturally into the general series of its author's works. The assertion of Platonic ideas suggests, however, a mood of spiritual thought for which the reference in 'Pauline' has been our only, and a scarcely sufficient preparation; nor could the most definite theism to be extracted from Platonic beliefs ever satisfy the human aspirations which, in a nature like that of Robert Browning, culminate in the idea of God. The metaphysical aspect of the poet's genius here distinctly reappears for the first time since 'Sordello', and also for the last. It becomes merged in the simpler forms of the religious imagination.

The justification of the man Shelley, to which great part of the Essay is devoted, contains little that would seem new to his more recent apologists; little also which to the writer's later judgments continued to recommend itself as true. It was as a great poetic artist, not as a great poet, that the author of 'Prometheus' and 'The Cenci', of 'Julian and Maddalo', and 'Epipsychidion' was finally to rank in Mr. Browning's mind. The whole remains nevertheless a memorial of a very touching affection; and whatever intrinsic value the Essay may possess, its main interest must always be biographical. Its motive and inspiration are set forth in the closing lines:

'It is because I have long held these opinions in assurance and gratitude, that I catch at the opportunity offered to me of expressing them here; knowing that the alacrity to fulfil an humble office conveys more love than the acceptance of the honour of a higher one, and that better, therefore, than the signal service it was the dream of my boyhood to render to his fame and memory, may be the saying of a few, inadequate words upon these scarcely more important supplementary letters of *Shelley*.'

If Mr. Browning had seen reason to doubt the genuineness of the letters in question, his Introduction could not have been written. That, while receiving them as genuine, he thought them unimportant, gave it, as he justly discerned, its full significance.

Mr. and Mrs. Browning returned to London for the summer of 1852, and we have a glimpse of them there in a letter from Mr. Fox to his daughter.

July 16, '52.

'. . . I had a charming hour with the Brownings yesterday; more fascinated with her than ever. She talked lots of George Sand, and so beautifully. Moreover she silver-electroplated Louis Napoleon!! They are lodging at 58 Welbeck Street; the house has a queer name on the door, and belongs to some Belgian family.

'They came in late one night, and R. B. says that in the morning twilight he saw three portraits on the bedroom wall, and speculated who they might be. Light gradually showed the first, Beatrice Cenci, "Good!" said he; "in a poetic region." More light: the second, Lord Byron! Who can the third be? And what think you it was, but your sketch engraved chalk portrait of me? He made quite a poem and picture of the affair.

'She seems much better; did not put her hand before her mouth, which I took as a compliment: and the young Florentine was gracious . . .'

It need hardly be said that this valued friend was one of the first whom Mr. Browning introduced to his wife, and that she responded with ready warmth to his claims on her gratitude and regard. More than one joint letter from herself and her husband commemorates this new phase of the intimacy; one especially interesting was written from Florence in 1858, in answer to the announcement by Mr. Fox of his election for Oldham; and Mr. Browning's contribution, which is very characteristic, will appear in due course.

Either this or the preceding summer brought Mr. Browning for the first time into personal contact with an early lover of his works: Mr. D. G. Rossetti. They had exchanged letters a year or two before, on the subject of 'Pauline', which Rossetti as I have already mentioned had read in ignorance of its origin, but with the conviction that only the author of 'Paracelsus' could have produced it. He wrote to Mr. Browning to ascertain the fact, and to tell him he had admired the poem so much as to transcribe it whole from the British Museum copy. He now called on him with Mr. William Allingham; and doubly recommended himself to the poet's interest by telling him that he was a painter. When Mr. Browning was again in London, in 1855, Rossetti began painting his portrait, which he finished in Paris in the ensuing winter.

The winter of 1852-3 saw the family once more in Florence, and at Casa Guidi, where the routine of quiet days was resumed. Mrs. Browning has spoken in more than one of her letters of the comparative social seclusion in which she and her husband had elected to live. This seclusion was much modified in later years, and many well-known English and American names become associated with their daily life. It referred indeed almost entirely to their residence in Florence, where they found less inducement to enter into society than in London, Paris, and Rome. But it is on record that during the fifteen years of his married life, Mr. Browning never dined away from home, except on one occasion—an exception proving the rule; and we cannot therefore be surprised that he should subsequently have carried into the experience of an unshackled and very interesting social intercourse, a kind of freshness which a man of fifty has not generally preserved.

The one excitement which presented itself in the early months of 1853 was the production of 'Colombe's Birthday'. The first allusion to this comes to us in a letter from the poet to Lady, then Mrs. Theodore, Martin, from which I quote a few passages.

Florence: Jan. 31, '53.

'My dear Mrs. Martin,—. . . be assured that I, for my part, have been in no danger of forgetting my promises any more than your performances—which were admirable of all kinds. I shall be delighted if you can do anything for "Colombe"—do what you think best with it, and for me—it will be pleasant to be in such hands—only, pray follow the corrections in the last edition—Chapman and Hall will give you a copy—as they are important to the sense. As for the condensation into three acts—I shall leave that, and all cuttings and the like, to your own judgment—and, come what will, I shall have to be grateful to you, as before. For the rest, you will play the part to heart's content, I *know*. . . . And how good it will be to see you again, and make my wife see you too—she who "never saw a great actress" she says—unless it was Dejazet! . . .'

Mrs. Browning writes about the performance, April 12:

'. . . I am beginning to be anxious about 'Colombe's Birthday'. I care much more about it than Robert does. He says that no one will mistake it for his speculation; it's Mr. Buckstone's affair altogether. True—but I should like it to succeed, being Robert's play, notwithstanding. But the play is subtle and refined for pits and galleries. I am nervous about it. On the other hand, those theatrical people ought to know,—and what in the world made them select it, if it is not likely to answer their purpose? By the way, a dreadful rumour reaches us of its having been "prepared for the stage by the author." Don't believe a word of it. Robert just said "yes" when they wrote to ask him, and not a line of communication has passed since. He has prepared nothing at all, suggested nothing, modified nothing. He referred them to his new edition, and that was the whole. . . .'

She communicates the result in May:

'. . . Yes, Robert's play succeeded, but there could be no "run" for a play of that kind. It was a "succes d'estime" and something more, which is surprising perhaps, considering the miserable acting of the men. Miss Faucit was alone in doing us justice. . . .'

Mrs. Browning did see 'Miss Faucit' on her next visit to England. She agreeably surprised that lady by presenting herself alone, one morning, at her house, and remaining with her for an hour and a half. The only person who had 'done justice' to 'Colombe' besides contributing to whatever success her husband's earlier plays had obtained, was much more than 'a great actress' to Mrs. Browning's mind; and we may imagine it would have gone hard with her before she renounced the pleasure of making her acquaintance.

Two letters, dated from the Baths of Lucca, July 15 and August 20, '53, tell how and where the ensuing summer was passed, besides introducing us, for the first time, to Mr. and Mrs. William Story, between whose family and that of Mr. Browning so friendly an intimacy was ever afterwards to subsist.

July 15.

'. . . We have taken a villa at the Baths of Lucca after a little holy fear of the company there—but the scenery, and the coolness, and convenience altogether prevail, and we have taken our villa for three months or rather more, and go to it next week with a stiff resolve of not calling nor being called upon. You remember perhaps that we were there four years ago just after the birth of our child. The mountains are wonderful in beauty, and we mean to buy our holiday by doing some work.

'Oh yes! I confess to loving Florence, and to having associated with it the idea of home. . . .'

Casa Tolomei, Alta Villa, Bagni di Lucca: Aug. 20.

'. . . We are enjoying the mountains here—riding the donkeys in the footsteps of the sheep, and eating strawberries and milk by basinsful. The strawberries succeed one another throughout the summer, through growing on different aspects of the hills. If a tree is felled in the forests, strawberries spring up, just as mushrooms might, and the peasants sell them for just nothing. . . . Then our friends Mr. and Mrs. Story help the mountains to please us a good deal. He is the son of Judge Story, the biographer of his father, and for himself, sculptor and poet—and she a sympathetic graceful woman, fresh and innocent in face and thought. We go backwards and forwards to tea and talk at one another's houses.

'. . . Since I began this letter we have had a grand donkey excursion to a village called Benabbia, and the cross above it on the mountain-peak. We returned in the dark, and were in some danger of tumbling down various precipices—but the scenery was exquisite—past speaking of for beauty. Oh, those jagged mountains, rolled together like pre-Adamite beasts and setting their teeth against the sky—it was wonderful. . . .'

Mr. Browning's share of the work referred to was 'In a Balcony'; also, probably, some of the 'Men and Women'; the scene of the declaration in 'By the Fireside' was laid in a little adjacent mountain-gorge to which he walked or rode. A fortnight's visit from Mr., now Lord, Lytton, was also an incident of this summer.

The next three letters from which I am able to quote, describe the impressions of Mrs. Browning's first winter in Rome.

Rome: 43 Via Bocca di Leone, 30 piano. Jan. 18, 54.

'. . . Well, we are all well to begin with—and have been well—our troubles came to us through sympathy entirely. A most exquisite journey of eight days we had from Florence to Rome, seeing the great monastery and triple church of Assisi and the wonderful Terni by the way—that passion of the waters which makes the human heart seem so still. In the highest spirits we entered Rome, Robert and Penini singing actually—for the child was radiant and flushed with the continual change of air and scene. . . . You remember my telling you of our friends the Storys—how they and their two children helped to make the summer go pleasantly at the Baths of Lucca. They had taken an apartment for us in Rome, so that we arrived in comfort to lighted fires and lamps as if coming home,—and we had a glimpse of their smiling faces that evening. In the morning before breakfast, little Edith was brought over to us by the manservant with a message, "the boy was in convulsions—there was danger." We hurried to the house, of course, leaving Edith with Wilson. Too true! All that first day we spent beside a death-bed; for the child never rallied—never opened his eyes in consciousness—and by eight in the evening he was gone. In the meanwhile, Edith was taken ill at our house—could not be moved, said the physicians . . . gastric fever, with a tendency to the brain—and within two days her life was almost despaired of—exactly the same malady as her brother's. . . . Also the English nurse was apparently dying at the Story's house, and Emma Page, the artist's youngest daughter, sickened with the same disease.

'... To pass over the dreary time, I will tell you at once that the three patients recovered—only in poor little Edith's case Roman fever followed the gastric, and has persisted ever since in periodical recurrence. She is very pale and thin. Roman fever is not dangerous to life, but it is exhausting.... Now you will understand what ghostly flakes of death have changed the sense of Rome to me. The first day by a death-bed, the first drive-out, to the cemetery, where poor little Joe is laid close to Shelley's heart "Cor cordium" says the epitaph and where the mother insisted on going when she and I went out in the carriage together—I am horribly weak about such things—I can't look on the earth-side of death—I flinch from corpses and graves, and never meet a common funeral without a sort of horror. When I look deathwards I look *over* death, and upwards, or I can't look that way at all. So that it was a struggle with me to sit upright in that carriage in which the poor stricken mother sat so calmly—not to drop from the seat. Well—all this has blackened Rome to me. I can't think about the Caesars in the old strain of thought—the antique words get muddled and blurred with warm dashes of modern, everyday tears and fresh grave-clay. Rome is spoilt to me—there's the truth. Still, one lives through one's associations when not too strong, and I have arrived at almost enjoying some things—the climate, for instance, which, though pernicious to the general health, agrees particularly with me, and the sight of the blue sky floating like a sea-tide through the great gaps and rifts of ruins.... We are very comfortably settled in rooms turned to the sun, and do work and play by turns, having almost too many visitors, hear excellent music at Mrs. Sartoris's A. K. once or twice a week, and have Fanny Kemble to come and talk to us with the doors shut, we three together. This is pleasant. I like her decidedly.

'If anybody wants small talk by handfuls, of glittering dust swept out of salons, here's Mr. Thackeray besides!...'
Rome: March 29.

'... We see a good deal of the Kembles here, and like them both, especially Fanny, who is looking magnificent still, with her black hair and radiant smile. A very noble creature indeed. Somewhat unelastic, unpliant to the age, attached to the old modes of thought and convention—but noble in qualities and defects. I like her much. She thinks me credulous and full of dreams—but does not despise me for that reason—which is good and tolerant of her, and pleasant too, for I should not be quite easy under her contempt. Mrs. Sartoris is genial and generous—her milk has had time to stand to cream in her happy family relations, which poor Fanny Kemble's has not had. Mrs. Sartoris' house has the best society in Rome—and exquisite music of course. We met Lockhart there, and my husband sees a good deal of him—more than I do—because of the access of cold weather lately which has kept me at home chiefly. Robert went down to the seaside, on a day's excursion with him and the Sartorises—and I hear found favour in his sight. Said the critic, "I like Browning—he isn't at all like a damned literary man." That's a compliment, I believe, according to your dictionary. It made me laugh and think of you directly.... Robert has been sitting for his picture to Mr. Fisher, the English artist who painted Mr. Kenyon and Landor. You remember those pictures in Mr. Kenyon's house in London. Well, he has painted Robert's, and it is an admirable likeness. The expression is an exceptional expression, but highly characteristic....'
May 19.

'... To leave Rome will fill me with barbarian complacency. I don't pretend to have a ray of sentiment about Rome. It's a palimpsest Rome, a watering-place written over the antique, and I haven't taken to it as a poet should I suppose. And let us speak the truth above all things. I am strongly a creature of association, and the associations of the place have not been personally favourable to me. Among the rest, my child, the light of my eyes, has been more unwell than I ever saw him.... The pleasantest days in Rome we have spent with the Kembles, the two sisters, who are charming and excellent both of them, in different ways, and certainly they have given us some excellent hours in the Campagna, upon picnic excursions—they, and certain of their friends; for instance, M. Ampere, the member of the French Institute, who is witty and agreeable, M. Goltz, the Austrian minister, who is an agreeable man, and Mr. Lyons, the son of Sir Edmund, &c. The talk was almost too brilliant for the sentiment of the scenery, but it harmonized entirely with the mayonnaise and champagne....'

It must have been on one of the excursions here described that an incident took place, which Mr. Browning relates with characteristic comments in a letter to Mrs. Fitz-Gerald, of July 15, 1882. The picnic party had strolled away to some distant spot. Mrs. Browning was not strong enough to join them, and her husband, as a matter of course, stayed with her; which act of consideration prompted Mrs. Kemble to exclaim that he was the only man she had ever known who behaved like a Christian to his wife. She was, when he wrote this letter, reading his works for the first time, and had expressed admiration for them; but, he continued, none of the kind things she said to him on that subject could move him as did those words in the Campagna. Mrs. Kemble would have modified her statement in later years, for the sake of one English and one American husband now closely related to her. Even then, perhaps, she did not make it without inward reserve. But she will forgive me, I am sure, for having repeated it.

Mr. Browning also refers to her Memoirs, which he had just read, and says: 'I saw her in those [I conclude earlier] days much oftener than is set down, but she scarcely noticed me; though I always liked her extremely.'

Another of Mrs. Browning's letters is written from Florence, June 6 '54:

'... We mean to stay at Florence a week or two longer and then go northward. I love Florence—the place looks exquisitely beautiful in its garden ground of vineyards and olive trees, sung round by the nightingales day and night.... If you take one thing with another, there is no place in the world like Florence, I am persuaded, for a place to live in—cheap, tranquil, cheerful, beautiful, within the limits of civilization yet out of the crush of it. . . . We have spent two delicious evenings at villas outside the gates, one with young Lytton, Sir Edward's son, of whom I have told you, I think. I like him . . . we both do . . . from the bottom of our hearts. Then, our friend, Frederick Tennyson, the new poet, we are delighted to see again.

. . . . .

'. . . Mrs. Sartoris has been here on her way to Rome, spending most of her time with us . . . singing passionately and talking eloquently. She is really charming. . . .'

I have no record of that northward journey or of the experiences of the winter of 1854-5. In all probability Mr. and Mrs. Browning remained in, or as near as possible to, Florence, since their income was still too limited for continuous travelling. They possibly talked of going to England, but postponed it till the following year; we know that they went there in 1855, taking his sister with them as they passed through Paris. They did not this time take lodgings for the summer months, but hired a house at 13 Dorset Street, Portman Square; and there, on September 27, Tennyson read his new poem, 'Maud', to Mrs. Browning, while Rossetti, the only other person present besides the family, privately drew his likeness in pen and ink. The likeness has become well known; the unconscious sitter must also, by this time, be acquainted with it; but Miss Browning thinks no one except herself, who was near Rossetti at the table, was at the moment aware of its being made. All eyes must have been turned towards Tennyson, seated by his hostess on the sofa. Miss Arabel Barrett was also of the party.

Some interesting words of Mrs. Browning's carry their date in the allusion to Mr. Ruskin; but I cannot ascertain it more precisely:

'We went to Denmark Hill yesterday to have luncheon with them, and see the Turners, which, by the way, are divine. I like Mr. Ruskin much, and so does Robert. Very gentle, yet earnest,—refined and truthful. I like him very much. We count him one among the valuable acquaintances made this year in England.'

Chapter 12

1855-1858

'Men and Women'—'Karshook'—'Two in the Campagna'—Winter in Paris; Lady Elgin—'Aurora Leigh'—Death of Mr. Kenyon and Mr. Barrett—Penini—Mrs. Browning's Letters to Miss Browning—The Florentine Carnival—Baths of Lucca—Spiritualism—Mr. Kirkup; Count Ginnasi—Letter from Mr. Browning to Mr. Fox—Havre.

The beautiful 'One Word More' was dated from London in September; and the fifty poems gathered together under the title of 'Men and Women' were published before the close of the year, in two volumes, by Messrs. Chapman and Hall.* They are all familiar friends to Mr. Browning's readers, in their first arrangement and appearance, as in later redistributions and reprints; but one curious little fact concerning them is perhaps not generally known. In the eighth line of the fourteenth section of 'One Word More' they were made to include 'Karshook Ben Karshook's Wisdom', which never was placed amongst them. It was written in April 1854; and the dedication of the volume must have been, as it so easily might be, in existence, before the author decided to omit it. The wrong name, once given, was retained, I have no doubt, from preference for its terminal sound; and 'Karshook' only became 'Karshish' in the Tauchnitz copy of 1872, and in the English edition of 1889.

* The date is given in the edition of 1868 as London 185-; in the Tauchnitz selection of 1872, London and Florence 184- and 185-; in the new English edition 184-and 185-.

'Karshook' appeared in 1856 in 'The Keepsake', edited by Miss Power; but, as we are told on good authority, has been printed in no edition or selection of the Poet's works. I am therefore justified in inserting it here.

I 'Would a man 'scape the rod?' Rabbi Ben Karshook saith, 'See that he turn to God The day before his death.' 'Ay, could a man inquire When it shall come!' I say. The Rabbi's eye shoots fire— 'Then let him turn to-day!'

II Quoth a young Sadducee: 'Reader of many rolls, Is it so certain we Have, as they tell us, souls?' 'Son, there is no reply!' The Rabbi bit his beard: 'Certain, a soul have I— We may have none,' he sneer'd. Thus Karshook, the Hiram's-Hammer, The Right-hand Temple-column, Taught babes in grace their grammar, And struck the simple, solemn.

Among this first collection of 'Men and Women' was the poem called 'Two in the Campagna'. It is a vivid, yet enigmatical little study of a restless spirit tantalized by glimpses of repose in love, saddened and perplexed by the manner in which this eludes it. Nothing that should impress one as more purely dramatic ever fell from Mr. Browning's pen. We are told, nevertheless, in Mr. Sharp's 'Life', that a personal character no less actual than that of the 'Guardian Angel' has been claimed for it. The writer, with characteristic delicacy, evades all discussion of the question; but he concedes a great deal in his manner of doing so. The poem, he says, conveys a sense of that necessary isolation of the individual soul which resists the fusing power of the deepest love; and its meaning cannot be personally—because it is universally—true. I do not think Mr. Browning meant to emphasize this aspect of the mystery of individual life, though the poem, in a certain sense, expresses it. We have no reason to believe that he ever accepted it as constant; and in no case could he have intended to refer its conditions to himself. He was often isolated by the processes of his mind; but there was in him no barrier to that larger emotional sympathy which we think of as sympathy of the soul. If this poem were true, 'One Word More' would be false, quite otherwise than in that approach to exaggeration which is incidental to the poetic form. The true keynote of 'Two in the Campagna' is the pain of perpetual change, and of the conscious, though unexplained, predestination to it. Mr. Browning could have still less in common with such a state, since one of the qualities for which he was most conspicuous was the enormous power of anchorage which his affections possessed. Only length of time and variety of experience could fully test this power or fully display it; but the signs of it had not been absent from even his earliest life. He loved fewer people in youth than in advancing age: nature and circumstance combined to widen the range, and vary the character of his human interests; but where once love or friendship had struck a root, only a moral convulsion could avail to dislodge it. I make no deduction from this statement when I admit that the last and most emphatic words of the poem in question,

Only I discern— Infinite passion, and the pain Of finite hearts that yearn,

did probably come from the poet's heart, as they also found a deep echo in that of his wife, who much loved them.

From London they returned to Paris for the winter of 1855-6. The younger of the Kemble sisters, Mrs. Sartoris, was also there with her family; and the pleasant meetings of the Campagna renewed themselves for Mr. Browning, though in a different form. He was also, with his sister, a constant visitor at Lady Elgin's. Both they and Mrs. Browning were greatly attached to her, and she warmly reciprocated the feeling. As Mr. Locker's letter has told us, Mr. Browning was in the habit of reading poetry to her, and when his sister had to announce his arrival from Italy or England, she would say: 'Robert is coming to nurse you, and read to you.' Lady Elgin was by this time almost completely paralyzed. She had lost the power of speech, and could only acknowledge the little attentions which were paid to her by some graceful pathetic gesture of the left hand; but she retained her sensibilities to the last; and Miss Browning received on one occasion a serious lesson in the risk of ever assuming that the appearance of unconsciousness guarantees its reality. Lady Augusta Bruce had asked her, in her mother's presence, how Mrs. Browning was; and, imagining that Lady Elgin was unable to hear or understand, she had answered with incautious distinctness, 'I am afraid she is very ill,' when a little sob from the invalid warned her of her mistake. Lady Augusta quickly repaired it by rejoining, 'but she is better than she was, is she not?' Miss Browning of course assented.

There were other friends, old and new, whom Mr. Browning occasionally saw, including, I need hardly say, the celebrated Madame Mohl. In the main, however, he led a quiet life, putting aside many inducements to leave his home.

Mrs. Browning was then writing 'Aurora Leigh', and her husband must have been more than ever impressed by her power of work, as displayed by her manner of working. To him, as to most creative writers, perfect quiet was indispensable to literary production. She wrote in pencil, on scraps of paper, as she lay on the sofa in her sitting-room, open to interruption from chance visitors, or from her little omnipresent son; simply hiding the paper beside her if anyone came in, and taking it up again when she was free. And if this process was conceivable in the large, comparatively silent spaces of their Italian home, and amidst habits of life which reserved social intercourse for the close of the working day, it baffles belief when one thinks of it as carried on in the conditions of a Parisian winter, and the little 'salon' of the apartment in the Rue du Colisee in which those months were spent. The poem was completed in the ensuing summer, in Mr. Kenyon's London house, and dedicated, October 17, in deeply pathetic words to that faithful friend, whom the writer was never to see again.

The news of his death, which took place in December 1856, reached Mr. and Mrs. Browning in Florence, to be followed in the spring by that of Mrs. Browning's father. Husband and wife had both determined to forego any pecuniary benefit which might accrue to them from this event; but they were not called upon to exercise their powers of renunciation. By Mr. Kenyon's will they were the richer, as is now, I think, generally known, the one by six thousand, the other by four thousand guineas.* Of that cousin's long kindness Mrs. Browning could scarcely in after-days trust herself to speak. It was difficult to her, she said, even to write his name without tears.

* Mr. Kenyon had considerable wealth, derived, like Mr. Barrett's, from West Indian estates.

I have alluded, perhaps tardily, to Mr. Browning's son, a sociable little being who must for some time have been playing a prominent part in his parents' lives. I saw him for the first time in this winter of 1855-6, and remember the grave expression of the little round face, the outline of which was common, at all events in childhood, to all the members of his mother's family, and was conspicuous in her, if we may trust an early portrait which has recently come to light. He wore the curling hair to which she refers in a later letter, and pretty frocks and frills, in which she delighted to clothe him. It is on record that, on one of the journeys of this year, a trunk was temporarily lost which contained Peni's embroidered trousers, and the MS., whole or in part, of 'Aurora Leigh'; and that Mrs. Browning had scarcely a thought to spare for her poem, in face of the damage to her little boy's appearance which the accident involved.

How he came by his familiar name of Penini—hence Peni, and Pen—neither signifies in itself, nor has much bearing on his father's family history; but I cannot refrain from a word of comment on Mr. Hawthorne's fantastic conjecture, which has been asserted and reasserted in opposition to Mr. Browning's own statement of the case. According to Mr. Hawthorne, the name was derived from Apennino, and bestowed on the child in babyhood, because Apennino was a colossal statue, and he was so very small. It would be strange indeed that any joke connecting 'Baby' with a given colossal statue should have found its way into the family without father, mother, or nurse being aware of it; or that any joke should have been accepted there which implied that the little boy was not of normal size. But the fact is still more unanswerable that Apennino could by no process congenial to the Italian language be converted into Penini. Its inevitable abbreviation would be Pennino with a distinct separate sounding of the central n's, or Nino. The accentuation of Penini is also distinctly German.

During this winter in Paris, little Wiedemann, as his parents tried to call him—his full name was Robert Wiedemann Barrett—had developed a decided turn for blank verse. He would extemporize short poems, singing them to his mother, who wrote them down as he sang. There is no less proof of his having possessed a talent for music, though it first naturally showed itself in the love of a cheerful noise. His father had once sat down to the piano, for a serious study of some piece, when the little boy appeared, with the evident intention of joining in the performance. Mr. Browning rose precipitately, and was about to leave the room. 'Oh!' exclaimed the hurt mother, 'you are going away, and he has brought his three drums to accompany you upon.' She herself would undoubtedly have endured the mixed melody for a little time, though her husband did not think she seriously wished him to do so. But if he did not play the piano to the accompaniment of Pen's drums, he played piano duets with him as soon as the boy was old enough to take part in them; and devoted himself to his instruction in this, as in other and more important branches of knowledge.

Peni had also his dumb companions, as his father had had before him. Tortoises lived at one end of the famous balcony at Casa Guidi; and when the family were at the Baths of Lucca, Mr. Browning would stow away little snakes in his bosom, and produce them for the child's amusement. As the child grew into a man, the love of animals which he had inherited became conspicuous in him; and it gave rise to many amusing and some pathetic little episodes of his artist life. The creatures which he gathered about him were generally, I think, more highly organized than those which elicited his father's peculiar tenderness; it was natural that he should exact more pictorial or more companionable qualities from them. But father and son concurred in the fondness for snakes, and in a singular predilection for owls; and they had not been long established in Warwick Crescent, when a bird of that family was domesticated there. We shall hear of it in a letter from Mr. Browning.

Of his son's moral quality as quite a little child his father has told me pretty and very distinctive stories, but they would be out of place here.*

* I am induced, on second thoughts, to subjoin one of these, for its testimony to the moral atmosphere into which the child had been born. He was sometimes allowed to play with a little boy not of his own class—perhaps the son of a 'contadino'. The child was unobjectionable, or neither Penini nor his parents would have endured the association; but the servants once thought themselves justified in treating him cavalierly, and Pen flew indignant to his mother, to complain of their behaviour. Mrs. Browning at once sought little Alessandro, with kind words and a large piece of cake; but this, in Pen's eyes, only aggravated the offence; it was a direct reflection on his visitor's quality. 'He doesn't tome for take,' he burst forth; 'he tomes because he is my friend.' How often, since I heard this first, have we repeated the words, 'he doesn't tome for take,' in half-serious definition of a disinterested person or act! They became a standing joke.

Mrs. Browning seems now to have adopted the plan of writing independent letters to her sister-in-law; and those available for our purpose are especially interesting. The buoyancy of tone which has habitually marked her communications, but which failed during the winter in Rome, reasserts itself in the following extract. Her maternal comments on Peni and his perfections have hitherto been so carefully excluded, that a brief allusion to him may be allowed on the present occasion.

1857.

'My dearest Sarianna, . . . Here is Penini's letter, which takes up so much room that I must be sparing of mine—and, by the way, if you consider him improved in his writing, give the praise to Robert, who has been taking most patient pains with him indeed. You will see how the little curly head is turned with carnival doings. So gay a carnival never was in our experience, for until last year when we were absent all masks had been prohibited, and now everybody has eaten of the tree of good and evil till not an apple is left. Peni persecuted me to let him have a domino—with tears and embraces—he "*almost never* in all his life had had a domino," and he would like it so. Not a black domino! no—he hated black—but a blue domino, trimmed with pink! that was his taste. The pink trimming I coaxed him out of, but for the rest, I let him have his way. . . . For my part, the universal madness reached me sitting by the fire whence I had not stirred for three months, and you will open your eyes when I tell you that I went in domino and masked to the great opera-ball. Yes! I did, really. Robert, who had been invited two or three times to other people's boxes, had proposed to return their kindness by taking a box himself at the opera this night, and entertaining two or three friends with galantine and champagne. Just as he and I were lamenting the impossibility of my going, on that very morning the wind changed, the air grew soft and mild, and he maintained that I might and should go. There was no time to get a domino of my own Robert himself had a beautiful one made, and I am having it metamorphosed into a black silk gown for myself! so I sent out and hired one, buying the mask. And very much amused I was. I like to see these characteristic things. I shall never rest, Sarianna, till I risk my reputation at the 'bal de l'opera' at Paris. Do you think I was satisfied with staying in the box? No, indeed. Down I went, and Robert and I elbowed our way through the crowd to the remotest corner of the ball below. Somebody smote me on the shoulder and cried "Bella Mascherina!" and I answered as impudently as one feels under a mask. At two o'clock in the morning, however, I had to give up and come away being overcome by the heavy air and ingloriously left Robert and our friends to follow at half-past four. Think of the refinement and gentleness—yes, I must call it *superiority* of this people—when no excess, no quarrelling, no rudeness nor coarseness can be observed in the course of such wild masked liberty; not a touch of licence anywhere, and perfect social equality! Our servant Ferdinando side by side in the same ball-room with the Grand Duke, and no class's delicacy offended against! For the Grand Duke went down into the ball-room for a short time. . . .'

The summer of 1857 saw the family once more at the Baths of Lucca, and again in company with Mr. Lytton. He had fallen ill at the house of their common friend, Miss Blagden, also a visitor there; and Mr. Browning shared in the nursing, of which she refused to entrust any part to less friendly hands. He sat up with the invalid for four nights; and would doubtless have done so for as many more as seemed necessary, but that Mrs. Browning protested against this trifling with his own health.

The only serious difference which ever arose between Mr. Browning and his wife referred to the subject of spiritualism. Mrs. Browning held doctrines which prepared her to accept any real or imagined phenomena betokening intercourse with the spirits of the dead; nor could she be repelled by anything grotesque or trivial in the manner of this intercourse, because it was no part of her belief that a spirit still inhabiting the atmosphere of our earth, should exhibit any dignity or solemnity not belonging to him while he lived upon it. The question must have been discussed by them on its general grounds at a very early stage of their intimacy; but it only assumed practical importance when Mr. Home came to Florence in 1857 or 1858. Mr. Browning found himself compelled to witness some of the 'manifestations'. He was keenly alive to their generally prosaic and irreverent character, and to the appearance of jugglery which was then involved in them. He absolutely denied the good faith of all the persons concerned. Mrs. Browning as absolutely believed it; and no compromise between them was attainable, because, strangely enough, neither of them admitted as possible that mediums or witnesses should deceive themselves. The personal aspect which the question thus received brought it into closer and more painful contact with their daily life. They might agree to differ as to the abstract merits of spiritualism; but Mr. Browning could not resign himself to his wife's trustful attitude towards some of the individuals who at that moment represented it. He may have had no substantial fear of her doing anything that could place her in their power, though a vague dread of this seems to have haunted him; but he chafed against the public association of her name with theirs. Both his love for and his pride in her resented it.

He had subsided into a more judicial frame of mind when he wrote 'Sludge the Medium', in which he says everything which can excuse the liar and, what is still more remarkable, modify the lie. So far back as the autumn of 1860 I heard him discuss the trickery which he believed himself to have witnessed, as dispassionately as any other non-credulous person might have done so. The experience must even before that have passed out of the foreground of his conjugal life. He remained, nevertheless, subject, for many years, to gusts of uncontrollable emotion which would sweep over him whenever the question of 'spirits' or 'spiritualism' was revived; and we can only understand this in connection with the peculiar circumstances of the case. With all his faith in the future, with all his constancy to the past, the memory of pain was stronger in him than any other. A single discordant note in the harmony of that married love, though merged in its actual existence, would send intolerable vibrations through his remembrance of it. And the pain had not been, in this instance, that of simple disagreement. It was complicated by Mrs. Browning's refusal to admit that disagreement was possible. She never believed in her husband's disbelief; and he had been not unreasonably annoyed by her always assuming it to be feigned. But his doubt of spiritualistic sincerity was not feigned. She cannot have thought, and scarcely can have meant to say so. She may have meant to say, 'You believe that these are tricks, but you know that there is something real behind them;' and so far, if no farther, she may have been in the right. Mr. Browning never denied the abstract possibility of spiritual communication with either living or dead; he only denied that such communication had ever been proved, or that any useful end could be subserved by it. The tremendous potentialities of hypnotism and thought-reading, now passing into the region of science, were not then so remote but that an imagination like his must have foreshadowed them. The natural basis of the seemingly supernatural had not yet entered into discussion. He may, from the first, have suspected the existence of some mysterious force, dangerous because not understood, and for this reason doubly liable to fall into dangerous hands. And if this was so, he would necessarily regard the whole system of manifestations with an apprehensive hostility, which was not entire negation, but which rebelled against any effort on the part of others, above all of those he loved, to interpret it into assent. The pain and anger which could be aroused in him by an indication on the part of a valued friend of even an impartial interest in the subject points especially to the latter conclusion.

He often gave an instance of the tricks played in the name of spiritualism on credulous persons, which may amuse those who have not yet heard it. I give the story as it survives in the fresher memory of Mr. Val Prinsep, who also received it from Mr. Browning.

'At Florence lived a curious old savant who in his day was well known to all who cared for art or history. I fear now few live who recollect Kirkup. He was quite a mine of information on all kinds of forgotten lore. It was he who discovered Giotto's portrait of Dante in the Bargello. Speaking of some friend, he said, "He is a most ignorant fellow! Why, he does not know how to cast a horoscope!" Of him Browning told me the following story. Kirkup was much taken up with spiritualism, in which he firmly believed. One day Browning called on him to borrow a book. He rang loudly at the storey, for he knew Kirkup, like Landor, was quite deaf. To his astonishment the door opened at once and Kirkup appeared.

'"Come in," he cried; "the spirits told me there was some one at the door. Ah! I know you do not believe! Come and see. Mariana is in a trance!"

'Browning entered. In the middle room, full of all kinds of curious objects of "vertu", stood a handsome peasant girl, with her eyes fixed as though she were in a trance.

'"You see, Browning," said Kirkup, "she is quite insensible, and has no will of her own. Mariana, hold up your arm."

'The woman slowly did as she was bid.

'"She cannot take it down till I tell her," cried Kirkup.

'"Very curious," observed Browning. "Meanwhile I have come to ask you to lend me a book."

'Kirkup, as soon as he was made to hear what book was wanted, said he should be delighted.

'"Wait a bit. It is in the next room."

'The old man shuffled out at the door. No sooner had he disappeared than the woman turned to Browning, winked, and putting down her arm leaned it on his shoulder. When Kirkup returned she resumed her position and rigid look.

'"Here is the book," said Kirkup. "Isn't it wonderful?" he added, pointing to the woman.

'"Wonderful," agreed Browning as he left the room.

'The woman and her family made a good thing of poor Kirkup's spiritualism.'

Something much more remarkable in reference to this subject happened to the poet himself during his residence in Florence. It is related in a letter to the 'Spectator', dated January 30, 1869, and signed J. S. K.

'Mr. Robert Browning tells me that when he was in Florence some years since, an Italian nobleman a Count Ginnasi of Ravenna, visiting at Florence, was brought to his house without previous introduction, by an intimate friend. The Count professed to have great mesmeric and clairvoyant faculties, and declared, in reply to Mr. Browning's avowed scepticism, that he would undertake to convince him somehow or other of his powers. He then asked Mr. Browning whether he had anything about him then and there, which he could hand to him, and which was in any way a relic or memento. This Mr. Browning thought was perhaps because he habitually wore no sort of trinket or ornament, not even a watchguard, and might therefore turn out to be a safe challenge. But it so happened that, by a curious accident, he was then wearing under his coat-sleeves some gold wrist-studs which he had quite recently taken into wear, in the absence by mistake of a sempstress of his ordinary wrist-buttons. He had never before worn them in Florence or elsewhere, and had found them in some old drawer where they had lain forgotten for years. One of these studs he took out and handed to the Count, who held it in his hand a while, looking earnestly in Mr. Browning's face, and then he said, as if much impressed, "C'equalche cosa che mi grida nell' orecchio 'Uccisione! uccisione!'" "There is something here which cries out in my ear, 'Murder! murder!'"

'"And truly," says Mr. Browning, "those very studs were taken from the dead body of a great uncle of mine who was violently killed on his estate in St. Kitt's, nearly eighty years ago. . . . The occurrence of my great uncle's murder was known only to myself of all men in Florence, as certainly was also my possession of the studs."'

A letter from the poet, of July 21, 1883, affirms that the account is correct in every particular, adding, 'My own explanation of the matter has been that the shrewd Italian felt his way by the involuntary help of my own eyes and face.' The story has been reprinted in the Reports of the Psychical Society.

A pleasant piece of news came to brighten the January of 1858. Mr. Fox was returned for Oldham, and at once wrote to announce the fact. He was answered in a joint letter from Mr. and Mrs. Browning, interesting throughout, but of which only the second part is quite suited for present insertion.

Mrs. Browning, who writes first and at most length, ends by saying she must leave a space for Robert, that Mr. Fox may be compensated for reading all she has had to say. The husband continues as follows:

. . . 'A space for Robert' who has taken a breathing space—hardly more than enough—to recover from his delight; he won't say surprise, at your letter, dear Mr. Fox. But it is all right and, like you, I wish from my heart we could get close together again, as in those old days, and what times we would have here in Italy! The realization of the children's prayer of angels at the corner of your bed i.e. sofa, one to read and one my wife to write,* and both to guard you through the night of lodging-keeper's extortions, abominable charges for firing, and so on. Observe, to call oneself 'an angel' in this land is rather humble, where they are apt to be painted as plumed cutthroats or celestial police—you say of Gabriel at his best and blithesomest, 'Shouldn't admire meeting *him* in a narrow lane!'

* Mr. Fox much liked to be read to, and was in the habit of writing his articles by dictation.

I say this foolishly just because I can't trust myself to be earnest about it. I would, you know, I would, always would, choose you out of the whole English world to judge and correct what I write myself; my wife shall read this and let it stand if I have told her so these twelve years—and certainly I have not grown intellectually an inch over the good and kind hand you extended over my head how many years ago! Now it goes over my wife's too.

How was it Tottie never came here as she promised? Is it to be some other time? Do think of Florence, if ever you feel chilly, and hear quantities about the Princess Royal's marriage, and want a change. I hate the thought of leaving Italy for one day more than I can help—and satisfy my English predilections by newspapers and a book or two. One gets nothing of that kind here, but the stuff out of which books grow,—it lies about one's feet indeed. Yet for me, there would be one book better than any now to be got here or elsewhere, and all out of a great English head and heart,—those 'Memoirs' you engaged to give us. Will you give us them?

Goodbye now—if ever the whim strikes you to 'make beggars happy' remember us.

Love to Tottie, and love and gratitude to you, dear Mr. Fox, From yours ever affectionately, Robert Browning.

In the summer of this year, the poet with his wife and child joined his father and sister at Havre. It was the last time they were all to be together.

Chapter 13

1858-1861

Mrs. Browning's Illness—Siena—Letter from Mr. Browning to Mr. Leighton —Mrs. Browning's Letters continued—Walter Savage Landor—Winter in Rome—Mr. Val Prinsep—Friends in Rome: Mr. and Mrs. Cartwright—Multiplying Social Relations—Massimo d'Azeglio—Siena again—Illness and Death of Mrs. Browning's Sister—Mr. Browning's Occupations—Madame du Quaire—Mrs. Browning's last Illness and Death.

I cannot quite ascertain, though it might seem easy to do so, whether Mr. and Mrs. Browning remained in Florence again till the summer of 1859, or whether the intervening months were divided between Florence and Rome; but some words in their letters favour the latter supposition. We hear of them in September from Mr. Val Prinsep, in Siena or its neighbourhood; with Mr. and Mrs. Story in an adjacent villa, and Walter Savage Landor in a 'cottage' close by. How Mr. Landor found himself of the party belongs to a little chapter in Mr. Browning's history for which I quote Mr. Colvin's words.* He was then living at Fiesole with his family, very unhappily, as we all know; and Mr. Colvin relates how he had thrice left his villa there, determined to live in Florence alone; and each time been brought back to the nominal home where so little kindness awaited him.

* 'Life of Landor', p. 209.

'. . . The fourth time he presented himself in the house of Mr. Browning with only a few pauls in his pocket, declaring that nothing should ever induce him to return.

'Mr. Browning, an interview with the family at the villa having satisfied him that reconciliation or return was indeed past question, put himself at once in communication with Mr. Forster and with Landor's brothers in England. The latter instantly undertook to supply the needs of their eldest brother during the remainder of his life. Thenceforth an income sufficient for his frugal wants was forwarded regularly for his use through the friend who had thus come forward at his need. To Mr. Browning's respectful and judicious guidance Landor showed himself docile from the first. Removed from the inflictions, real and imaginary, of his life at Fiesole, he became another man, and at times still seemed to those about him like the old Landor at his best. It was in July, 1859, that the new arrangements for his life were made. The remainder of that summer he spent at Siena, first as the guest of Mr. Story, the American sculptor and poet, next in a cottage rented for him by Mr. Browning near his own. In the autumn of the same year Landor removed to a set of apartments in the Via Nunziatina in Florence, close to the Casa Guidi, in a house kept by a former servant of Mrs. Browning's, an Englishwoman married to an Italian.* Here he continued to live during the five years that yet remained to him.'

* Wilson, Mrs. Browning's devoted maid, and another most faithful servant of hers and her husband's, Ferdinando Romagnoli.

Mr. Landor's presence is also referred to, with the more important circumstance of a recent illness of Mrs. Browning's, in two characteristic and interesting letters of this period, one written by Mr. Browning to Frederic Leighton, the other by his wife to her sister-in-law. Mr.— now Sir F.— Leighton had been studying art during the previous winter in Italy.

Kingdom of Piedmont, Siena: Oct. 9, '59.

'My dear Leighton—I hope—and think—you know what delight it gave me to hear from you two months ago. I was in great trouble at the time about my wife who was seriously ill. As soon as she could bear removal we brought her to a villa here. She slowly recovered and is at last *well* —I believe—but weak still and requiring more attention than usual. We shall be obliged to return to Rome for the winter—not choosing to risk losing what we have regained with some difficulty. Now you know why I did not write at once—and may imagine why, having waited so long, I put off telling you for a week or two till I could say certainly what we do with ourselves. If any amount of endeavour could induce you to join us there— Cartwright, Russell, the Vatican and all—and if such a step were not inconsistent with your true interests—you should have it: but I know very well that you love Italy too much not to have had weighty reasons for renouncing her at present— and I want your own good and not my own contentment in the matter. Wherever you are, be sure I shall follow your proceedings with deep and true interest. I heard of your successes—and am now anxious to know how you get on with the great picture, the 'Ex voto'—if it does not prove full of beauty and power, two of us will be shamed, that's all! But *I* don't fear, mind! Do keep me informed of your progress, from time to time—a few lines will serve—and then I shall slip some day into your studio, and buffet the piano, without having grown a stranger. Another thing—do take proper care of your health, and exercise yourself; give those vile indigestions no chance against you; keep up your spirits, and be as distinguished and happy as God meant you should. Can I do anything for you at Rome—not to say, Florence? We go thither i.e. to Florence to-morrow, stay there a month, probably, and then take the Siena road again.'

The next paragraph refers to some orders for photographs, and is not specially interesting.

Cartwright arrived here a fortnight ago—very pleasant it was to see him: he left for Florence, stayed a day or two and returned to Mrs. Cartwright who remained at the Inn and they all departed prosperously yesterday for Rome. Odo Russell spent two days here on his way thither—we liked him much. Prinsep and Jones—do you know them?—are in the town. The Storys have passed the summer in the villa opposite,—and no less a lion than dear old Landor is in a house a few steps off. I take care of him—his amiable family having clawed him a little too sharply: so strangely do things come about! I mean his Fiesole 'family'—a trifle of wife, sons and daughter—not his English relatives, who are generous and good in every way.

Take any opportunity of telling dear Mrs. Sartoris however unnecessarily that I and my wife remember her with the old feeling—I trust she is well and happy to heart's content. Pen is quite well and rejoicing just now in a Sardinian pony on which he gallops like Puck on a dragon-fly's back. My wife's kind regard and best wishes go with those of, Dear Leighton, yours affectionately ever, R. Browning.

October 1859.

Mrs. to Miss Browning.

'. . . After all, it is not a cruel punishment to have to go to Rome again this winter, though it will be an undesirable expense, and we did wish to keep quiet this winter,—the taste for constant wanderings having passed away as much for me as for Robert. We begin to see that by no possible means can one spend as much money to so small an end—and then we don't work so well, don't live to as much use either for ourselves or others. Isa Blagden bids us observe that we pretend to live at Florence, and are not there much above two months in the year, what with going away for the summer and going away for the winter. It's too true. It's the drawback of Italy. To live in one place there is impossible for us, almost just as to live out of Italy at all, is impossible for us. It isn't caprice on our part. Siena pleases us very much—the silence and repose have been heavenly things to me, and the country is very pretty—though no more than pretty—nothing marked or romantic—no mountains, except so far off as to be like a cloud only on clear days—and no water. Pretty dimpled ground, covered with low vineyards, purple hills, not high, with the sunsets clothing them. . . . We shall not leave Florence till November—Robert must see Mr. Landor his adopted son, Sarianna settled in his new apartments with Wilson for a duenna. It's an excellent plan for him and not a bad one for Wilson. . . . Forgive me if Robert has told you this already. Dear darling Robert amuses me by talking of his "gentleness and sweetness". A most courteous and refined gentleman he is, of course, and very affectionate to Robert as he ought to be, but of self-restraint, he has not a grain, and of suspiciousness, many grains. Wilson will run many risks, and I, for one, would rather not run them. What do you say to dashing down a plate on the floor when you don't like what's on it? And the contadini at whose house he is lodging now have been already accused of opening desks. Still upon that occasion though there was talk of the probability of Mr. Landor's "throat being cut in his sleep"— as on other occasions, Robert succeeded in soothing him—and the poor old lion is very quiet on the whole, roaring softly, to beguile the time, in Latin alcaics against his wife and Louis Napoleon. He laughs carnivorously when I tell him that one of these days he will have to write an ode in honour of the Emperor, to please me.'

Mrs. Browning writes, somewhat later, from Rome:

'... We left Mr. Landor in great comfort. I went to see his apartment before it was furnished. Rooms small, but with a look-out into a little garden, quiet and cheerful, and he doesn't mind a situation rather out of the way. He pays four pounds ten English the month. Wilson has thirty pounds a year for taking care of him—which sounds a good deal, but it is a difficult position. He has excellent, generous, affectionate impulses—but the impulses of the tiger, every now and then. Nothing coheres in him—either in his opinions, or, I fear, his affections. It isn't age—he is precisely the man of his youth, I must believe. Still, his genius gives him the right of gratitude on all artists at least, and I must say that my Robert has generously paid the debt. Robert always said that he owed more as a writer to Landor than to any contemporary. At present Landor is very fond of him—but I am quite prepared for his turning against us as he has turned against Forster, who has been so devoted for years and years. Only one isn't kind for what one gets by it, or there wouldn't be much kindness in this world....'

Mr. Browning always declared that his wife could impute evil to no one, that she was a living denial of that doctrine of original sin to which her Christianity pledged her; and the great breadth and perfect charity of her views habitually justified the assertion; but she evidently possessed a keen insight into character, which made her complete suspension of judgment on the subject of Spiritualism very difficult to understand.

The spiritualistic coterie had found a satisfactory way of explaining Mr. Browning's antagonistic attitude towards it. He was jealous, it was said, because the Spirits on one occasion had dropped a crown on to his wife's head and none on to his own. The first instalment of his long answer to this grotesque accusation appears in a letter of Mrs. Browning's, probably written in the course of the winter of 1859-60.

'... My brother George sent me a number of the "National Magazine" with my face in it, after Marshall Wood's medallion. My comfort is that my greatest enemy will not take it to be like me, only that does not go far with the indifferent public: the portrait I suppose will have its due weight in arresting the sale of "Aurora Leigh" from henceforth. You never saw a more determined visage of a strong-minded woman with the neck of a vicious bull.... Still, I am surprised, I own, at the amount of success, and that golden-hearted Robert is in ecstasies about it, far more than if it all related to a book of his own. The form of the story, and also, something in the philosophy, seem to have caught the crowd. As to the poetry by itself, anything good in that repels rather. I am not so blind as Romney, not to perceive this ... Give Peni's and my love to the dearest 'nonno' grandfather whose sublime unselfishness and want of common egotism presents such a contrast to what is here. Tell him I often think of him, and always with touched feeling. When *he* is eighty-six or ninety-six, nobody will be pained or humbled by the spectacle of an insane self-love resulting from a long life's ungoverned will. May God bless him!—... Robert has made his third bust copied from the antique. He breaks them all up as they are finished—it's only matter of education. When the power of execution is achieved, he will try at something original. Then reading hurts him; as long as I have known him he has not been able to read long at a time—he can do it now better than at the beginning. The consequence of which is that an active occupation is salvation to him.... Nobody exactly understands him except me, who am in the inside of him and hear him breathe. For the peculiarity of our relation is, that he thinks aloud with me and can't stop himself.... I wanted his poems done this winter very much, and here was a bright room with three windows consecrated to his use. But he had a room all last summer, and did nothing. Then, he worked himself out by riding for three or four hours together—there has been little poetry done since last winter, when he did much. He was not inclined to write this winter. The modelling combines body-work and soul-work, and the more tired he has been, and the more his back ached, poor fellow, the more he has exulted and been happy. So I couldn't be much in opposition against the sculpture—I couldn't in fact at all. He has material for a volume, and will work at it this summer, he says.

'His power is much in advance of "Strafford", which is his poorest work of art. Ah, the brain stratifies and matures, even in the pauses of the pen.

'At the same time, his treatment in England affects him, naturally, and for my part I set it down as an infamy of that public—no other word. He says he has told you some things you had not heard, and which I acknowledge I always try to prevent him from repeating to anyone. I wonder if he has told you besides no, I fancy not that an English lady of rank, an acquaintance of ours, observe that! asked, the other day, the American minister, whether "Robert was not an American." The minister answered—"is it possible that *you* ask me this? Why, there is not so poor a village in the United States, where they would not tell you that Robert Browning was an Englishman, and that they were sorry he was not an American." Very pretty of the American minister, was it not?—and literally true, besides.... Ah, dear Sarianna—I don't complain for myself of an unappreciating public. I *have no reason*. But, just for *that* reason, I complain more about Robert—only he does not hear me complain—to *you* I may say, that the blindness, deafness and stupidity of the English public to Robert are amazing. Of course Milsand had heard his name—well the contrary would have been strange. Robert *is*. All England can't prevent his existence, I suppose. But nobody there, except a small knot of pre-Raffaellite men, pretend to do him justice. Mr. Forster has done the best,—in the press. As a sort of lion, Robert has his range in society—and—for the rest, you should see Chapman's returns!—While, in America he is a power, a writer, a poet—he is read—he lives in the hearts of the people.

'"Browning readings" here in Boston—"Browning evenings" there. For the rest, the English hunt lions, too, Sarianna, but their lions are chiefly chosen among lords and railway kings. . . .'

We cannot be surprised at Mrs. Browning's desire for a more sustained literary activity on her husband's part. We learn from his own subsequent correspondence that he too regarded the persevering exercise of his poetic faculty as almost a religious obligation. But it becomes the more apparent that the restlessness under which he was now labouring was its own excuse; and that its causes can have been no mystery even to those 'outside' him. The life and climate of Italy were beginning to undermine his strength. We owe it perhaps to the great and sorrowful change, which was then drawing near, that the full power of work returned to him.

During the winter of 1859-60, Mr. Val Prinsep was in Rome. He had gone to Siena with Mr. Burne Jones, bearing an introduction from Rossetti to Mr. Browning and his wife; and the acquaintance with them was renewed in the ensuing months. Mr. Prinsep had acquired much knowledge of the popular, hence picturesque aspects of Roman life, through a French artist long resident in the city; and by the help of the two young men Mr. Browning was also introduced to them. The assertion that during his married life he never dined away from home must be so far modified, that he sometimes joined Mr. Prinsep and his friend in a Bohemian meal, at an inn near the Porta Pinciana which they much frequented; and he gained in this manner some distinctive experiences which he liked long afterwards to recall. I am again indebted to Mr. Prinsep for a description of some of these.

'The first time he honoured us was on an evening when the poet of the quarter of the "Monte" had announced his intention of coming to challenge a rival poet to a poetical contest. Such contests are, or were, common in Rome. In old times the Monte and the Trastevere, the two great quarters of the eternal city, held their meetings on the Ponte Rotto. The contests were not confined to the effusions of the poetical muse. Sometimes it was a strife between two lute-players, sometimes guitarists would engage, and sometimes mere wrestlers. The rivalry was so keen that the adverse parties finished up with a general fight. So the Papal Government had forbidden the meetings on the old bridge. But still each quarter had its pet champions, who were wont to meet in private before an appreciative, but less excitable audience, than in olden times.

'Gigi the host had furnished a first-rate dinner, and his usual tap of excellent wine. 'Vino del Popolo' he called it. The 'Osteria' had filled; the combatants were placed opposite each other on either side of a small table on which stood two 'mezzi'—long glass bottles holding about a quart apiece. For a moment the two poets eyed each other like two cocks seeking an opportunity to engage. Then through the crowd a stalwart carpenter, a constant attendant of Gigi's, elbowed his way. He leaned over the table with a hand on each shoulder, and in a neatly turned couplet he then addressed the rival bards.

'"You two," he said, "for the honour of Rome, must do your best, for there is now listening to you a great Poet from England."

'Having said this, he bowed to Browning, and swaggered back to his place in the crowd, amid the applause of the on-lookers.

'It is not necessary to recount how the two Improvisatori poetized, even if I remembered, which I do not.

'On another occasion, when Browning and Story were dining with us, we had a little orchestra mandolins, two guitars, and a lute, to play to us. The music consisted chiefly of well-known popular airs. While they were playing with great fervour the Hymn to Garibaldi—an air strictly forbidden by the Papal Government, three blows at the door resounded through the 'Osteria'. The music stopped in a moment. I saw Gigi was very pale as he walked down the room. There was a short parley at the door. It opened, and a sergeant and two Papal gendarmes marched solemnly up to the counter from which drink was supplied. There was a dead silence while Gigi supplied them with large measures of wine, which the gendarmes leisurely imbibed. Then as solemnly they marched out again, with their heads well in the air, looking neither to the right nor the left. Most discreet if not incorruptible guardians of the peace! When the door was shut the music began again; but Gigi was so earnest in his protestations, that my friend Browning suggested we should get into carriages and drive to see the Coliseum by moonlight. And so we sallied forth, to the great relief of poor Gigi, to whom it meant, if reported, several months of imprisonment, and complete ruin.

'In after-years Browning frequently recounted with delight this night march.

'"We drove down the Corso in two carriages," he would say. "In one were our musicians, in the other we sat. Yes! and the people all asked, 'who are these who make all this parade?' At last some one said, 'Without doubt these are the fellows who won the lottery,' and everybody cried, 'Of course these are the lucky men who have won.'"'

The two persons whom Mr. Browning saw most, and most intimately, during this and the ensuing winter, were probably Mr. and Mrs. Story. Allusion has already been made to the opening of the acquaintance at the Baths of Lucca in 1853, to its continuance in Rome in '53 and '54, and to the artistic pursuits which then brought the two men into close and frequent contact with each other. These friendly relations were cemented by their children, who were of about the same age; and after Mrs. Browning's death, Miss Browning took her place in the pleasant intercourse which renewed itself whenever their respective visits to Italy and to England again brought the two families together. A no less lasting and truly affectionate intimacy was now also growing up with Mr. Cartwright and his wife—the Cartwrights of Aynhoe of whom mention was made in the Siena letter to F. Leighton; and this too was subsequently to include their daughter, now Mrs. Guy Le Strange, and Mr. Browning's sister. I cannot quite ascertain when the poet first knew Mr. Odo Russell, and his mother, Lady William Russell, who was also during this, or at all events the following winter, in Rome; and whom afterwards in London he regularly visited until her death; but the acquaintance was already entering on the stage in which it would spread as a matter of course through every branch of the family. His first country visit, when he had returned to England, was paid with his son to Woburn Abbey.

We are now indeed fully confronted with one of the great difficulties of Mr. Browning's biography: that of giving a sufficient idea of the growing extent and growing variety of his social relations. It is evident from the fragments of his wife's correspondence that during, as well as after, his married life, he always and everywhere knew everyone whom it could interest him to know. These acquaintances constantly ripened into friendliness, friendliness into friendship. They were necessarily often marked by interesting circumstances or distinctive character. To follow them one by one, would add not chapters, but volumes, to our history. The time has not yet come at which this could even be undertaken; and any attempt at systematic selection would create a false impression of the whole. I must therefore be still content to touch upon such passages of Mr. Browning's social experience as lie in the course of a comparatively brief record; leaving all such as are not directly included in it to speak indirectly for themselves.

Mrs. Browning writes again, in 1859:

'Massimo d'Azeglio came to see us, and talked nobly, with that noble head of his. I was far prouder of his coming than of another personal distinction you will guess at,* though I don't pretend to have been insensible to that.'

* An invitation to Mr. Browning to dine in company with the young Prince of Wales.

Dr.—afterwards Cardinal—Manning was also among the distinguished or interesting persons whom they knew in Rome.

Another, undated extract might refer to the early summer of 1859 or 1860, when a meeting with the father and sister must have been once more in contemplation.

Casa Guidi.

'My dearest Sarianna,—I am delighted to say that we have arrived, and see our dear Florence—the Queen of Italy, after all . . . A comfort is that Robert is considered here to be looking better than he ever was known to look—and this, notwithstanding the greyness of his beard . . . which indeed, is, in my own mind, very becoming to him, the argentine touch giving a character of elevation and thought to the whole physiognomy. This greyness was suddenly developed—let me tell you how. He was in a state of bilious irritability on the morning of his arrival in Rome, from exposure to the sun or some such cause, and in a fit of suicidal impatience shaved away his whole beard . . . whiskers and all!! I *cried* when I saw him, I was so horror-struck. I might have gone into hysterics and still been reasonable—for no human being was ever so disfigured by so simple an act. Of course I said when I recovered heart and voice, that everything was at an end between him and me if he didn't let it all grow again directly, and upon the further advice of his looking-glass he yielded the point,—and the beard grew—but it grew white—which was the just punishment of the gods—our sins leave their traces.

'Well, poor darling Robert won't shock you after all—you can't choose but be satisfied with his looks. M. de Monclar swore to me that he was not changed for the intermediate years. . . .'

The family returned, however, to Siena for the summer of 1860, and from thence Mrs. Browning writes to her sister-in-law of her great anxiety concerning her sister Henrietta, Mrs. Surtees Cook,* then attacked by a fatal disease.

* The name was afterwards changed to Altham.

'. . . There is nothing or little to add to my last account of my precious Henrietta. But, dear, you think the evil less than it is—be sure that the fear is too reasonable. I am of a very hopeful temperament, and I never could go on systematically making the worst of any case. I bear up here for a few days, and then comes the expectation of a letter, which is hard. I fight with it for Robert's sake, but all the work I put myself to do does not hinder a certain effect. She is confined to her bed almost wholly and suffers acutely. . . . In fact, I am living from day to day, on the merest crumbs of hope—on the daily bread which is very bitter. Of course it has shaken me a good deal, and interfered with the advantages of the summer, but that's the least. Poor Robert's scheme for me of perfect repose has scarcely been carried out. . . .'

This anxiety was heightened during the ensuing winter in Rome, by just the circumstance from which some comfort had been expected—the second postal delivery which took place every day; for the hopes and fears which might have found a moment's forgetfulness in the longer absence of news, were, as it proved, kept at fever-heat. On one critical occasion the suspense became unbearable, because Mr. Browning, by his wife's desire, had telegraphed for news, begging for a telegraphic answer. No answer had come, and she felt convinced that the worst had happened, and that the brother to whom the message was addressed could not make up his mind to convey the fact in so abrupt a form. The telegram had been stopped by the authorities, because Mr. Odo Russell had undertaken to forward it, and his position in Rome, besides the known Liberal sympathies of Mr. and Mrs. Browning and himself, had laid it open to political suspicion.

Mrs. Surtees Cook died in the course of the winter. Mr. Browning always believed that the shock and sorrow of this event had shortened his wife's life, though it is also possible that her already lowered vitality increased the dejection into which it plunged her. Her own casual allusions to the state of her health had long marked arrested progress, if not steady decline. We are told, though this may have been a mistake, that active signs of consumption were apparent in her even before the illness of 1859, which was in a certain sense the beginning of the end. She was completely an invalid, as well as entirely a recluse, during the greater part if not the whole of this last stay in Rome.

She rallied nevertheless sufficiently to write to Miss Browning in April, in a tone fully suggestive of normal health and energy.

'. . . In my own opinion he is infinitely handsomer and more attractive than when I saw him first, sixteen years ago. . . . I believe people in general would think the same exactly. As to the modelling—well, I told you that I grudged a little the time from his own particular art. But it does not do to dishearten him about his modelling. He has given a great deal of time to anatomy with reference to the expression of form, and the clay is only the new medium which takes the place of drawing. Also, Robert is peculiar in his ways of work as a poet. I have struggled a little with him on this point, for I don't think him right; that is to say, it would not be right for me . . . But Robert waits for an inclination, works by fits and starts; he can't do otherwise he says, and his head is full of ideas which are to come out in clay or marble. I yearn for the poems, but he leaves that to me for the present. . . . You will think Robert looking very well when you see him; indeed, you may judge by the photographs meanwhile. You know, Sarianna, how I used to forbid the moustache. I insisted as long as I could, but all artists were against me, and I suppose that the bare upper lip does not harmonise with the beard. He keeps the hair now closer, and the beard is pointed. . . . As to the moony whiteness of the beard, it is beautiful, *I* think, but then I think him all beautiful, and always. . . .'

Mr. Browning's old friend, Madame du Quaire,* came to Rome in December. She had visited Florence three years before, and I am indebted to her for some details of the spiritualist controversy by which its English colony was at that time divided. She was now a widow, travelling with her brother; and Mr. Browning came whenever he could, to comfort her in her sorrow, and, as she says, discourse of nature, art, the beautiful, and all that 'conquers death'. He little knew how soon he would need the same comfort for himself. He would also declaim passages from his wife's poems; and when, on one of these occasions, Madame du Quaire had said, as so many persons now say, that she much preferred his poetry to hers, he made this characteristic answer, to be repeated in substance some years afterwards to another friend: 'You are wrong—quite wrong—she has genius; I am only a painstaking fellow. Can't you imagine a clever sort of angel who plots and plans, and tries to build up something—he wants to make you see it as he sees it—shows you one point of view, carries you off to another, hammering into your head the thing he wants you to understand; and whilst this bother is going on God Almighty turns you off a little star—that's the difference between us. The true creative power is hers, not mine.'

* Formerly Miss Blackett, and sister of the member for New Castle.

Mrs. Browning died at Casa Guidi on June 29, 1861, soon after their return to Florence. She had had a return of the bronchial affection to which she was subject; and a new doctor who was called in discovered grave mischief at the lungs, which she herself had long believed to be existent or impending. But the attack was comparatively, indeed actually, slight; and an extract from her last letter to Miss Browning, dated June 7, confirms what her family and friends have since asserted, that it was the death of Cavour which gave her the final blow.

'. . . We come home into a cloud here. I can scarcely command voice or hand to name 'Cavour'. That great soul which meditated and made Italy has gone to the diviner Country. If tears or blood could have saved him to us, he should have had mine. I feel yet as if I could scarcely comprehend the greatness of the vacancy. A hundred Garibaldis for such a man!'

Her death was signalized by the appearance—this time, I am told, unexpected—of another brilliant comet, which passed so near the earth as to come into contact with it.

Chapter 14

1861-1863

Miss Blagden—Letters from Mr. Browning to Miss Haworth and Mr. Leighton—His Feeling in regard to Funeral Ceremonies—Establishment in London—Plan of Life—Letter to Madame du Quaire—Miss Arabel Barrett—Biarritz—Letters to Miss Blagden—Conception of 'The Ring and the Book'—Biographical Indiscretion—New Edition of his Works—Mr. and Mrs. Procter.

The friend who was nearest, at all events most helpful, to Mr. Browning in this great and sudden sorrow was Miss Blagden—Isa Blagden, as she was called by all her intimates. Only a passing allusion to her could hitherto find place in this fragmentary record of the Poet's life; but the friendship which had long subsisted between her and Mrs. Browning brings her now into closer and more frequent relation to it. She was for many years a centre of English society in Florence; for her genial, hospitable nature, as well as literary tastes she wrote one or two novels, I believe not without merit, secured her the acquaintance of many interesting persons, some of whom occasionally made her house their home; and the evenings spent with her at her villa on Bellosguardo live pleasantly in the remembrance of those of our older generation who were permitted to share in them.

She carried the boy away from the house of mourning, and induced his father to spend his nights under her roof, while the last painful duties detained him in Florence. He at least gave her cause to deny, what has been so often affirmed, that great griefs are necessarily silent. She always spoke of this period as her 'apocalyptic month', so deeply poetic were the ravings which alternated with the simple human cry of the desolate heart: 'I want her, I want her!' But the ear which received these utterances has long been closed in death. The only written outbursts of Mr. Browning's frantic sorrow were addressed, I believe, to his sister, and to the friend, Madame du Quaire, whose own recent loss most naturally invoked them, and who has since thought best, so far as rested with her, to destroy the letters in which they were contained. It is enough to know by simple statement that he then suffered as he did. Life conquers Death for most of us; whether or not 'nature, art, and beauty' assist in the conquest. It was bound to conquer in Mr. Browning's case: first through his many-sided vitality; and secondly, through the special motive for living and striving which remained to him in his son. This note is struck in two letters which are given me to publish, written about three weeks after Mrs. Browning's death; and we see also that by this time his manhood was reacting against the blow, and bracing itself with such consoling remembrance as the peace and painlessness of his wife's last moments could afford to him.

Florence: July 19, '61.

Dear Leighton,—It is like your old kindness to write to me and to say what you do—I know you feel for me. I can't write about it—but there were many alleviating circumstances that you shall know one day—there seemed no pain, and what she would have felt most the knowledge of separation from us was spared her. I find these things a comfort indeed.

I shall go away from Italy for many a year—to Paris, then London for a day or two just to talk with her sister—but if I can see you it will be a great satisfaction. Don't fancy I am 'prostrated', I have enough to do for the boy and myself in carrying out her wishes. He is better than one would have thought, and behaves dearly to me. Everybody has been very kind.

Tell dear Mrs. Sartoris that I know her heart and thank her with all mine. After my day or two at London I shall go to some quiet place in France to get right again and then stay some time at Paris in order to find out leisurely what it will be best to do for Peni—but eventually I shall go to England, I suppose. I don't mean to live with anybody, even my own family, but to occupy myself thoroughly, seeing dear friends, however, like you. God bless you. Yours ever affectionately, Robert Browning.

The second is addressed to Miss Haworth.

Florence: July 20, 1861.

My dear Friend,—I well know you feel as you say, for her once and for me now. Isa Blagden, perfect in all kindness to me, will have told you something perhaps—and one day I shall see you and be able to tell you myself as much as I can. The main comfort is that she suffered very little pain, none beside that ordinarily attending the simple attacks of cold and cough she was subject to—had no presentiment of the result whatever, and was consequently spared the misery of knowing she was about to leave us; she was smilingly assuring me she was 'better', 'quite comfortable—if I would but come to bed,' to within a few minutes of the last. I think I foreboded evil at Rome, certainly from the beginning of the week's illness—but when I reasoned about it, there was no justifying fear—she said on the last evening 'it is merely the old attack, not so severe a one as that of two years ago—there is no doubt I shall soon recover,' and we talked over plans for the summer, and next year. I sent the servants away and her maid to bed—so little reason for disquietude did there seem. Through the night she slept heavily, and brokenly—that was the bad sign—but then she would sit up, take her medicine, say unrepeatable things to me and sleep again. At four o'clock there were symptoms that alarmed me, I called the maid and sent for the doctor. She smiled as I proposed to bathe her feet, 'Well, you *are* determined to make an exaggerated case of it!' Then came what my heart will keep till I see her again and longer—the most perfect expression of her love to me within my whole knowledge of her. Always smilingly, happily, and with a face like a girl's—and in a few minutes she died in my arms; her head on my cheek. These incidents so sustain me that I tell them to her beloved ones as their right: there was no lingering, nor acute pain, nor consciousness of separation, but God took her to himself as you would lift a sleeping child from a dark, uneasy bed into your arms and the light. Thank God. Annunziata thought by her earnest ways with me, happy and smiling as they were, that she must have been aware of our parting's approach—but she was quite conscious, had words at command, and yet did not even speak of Peni, who was in the next room. Her last word was when I asked 'How do you feel?' —'Beautiful.' You know I have her dearest wishes and interests to attend to *at once*—her child to care for, educate, establish properly; and my own life to fulfil as properly,—all just as she would require were she here. I shall leave Italy altogether for years—go to London for a few days' talk with Arabel—then go to my father and begin to try leisurely what will be the best for Peni—but no more 'housekeeping' for me, even with my family. I shall grow, still, I hope—but my root is taken and remains.

I know you always loved her, and me too in my degree. I shall always be grateful to those who loved her, and that, I repeat, you did.

She was, and is, lamented with extraordinary demonstrations, if one consider it. The Italians seem to have understood her by an instinct. I have received strange kindness from everybody. Pen is very well—very dear and good, anxious to comfort me as he calls it. He can't know his loss yet. After years, his will be worse than mine—he will want what he never had—that is, for the time when he could be helped by her wisdom, and genius and piety—I *have* had everything and shall not forget.

God bless you, dear friend. I believe I shall set out in a week. Isa goes with me—dear, true heart. You, too, would do what you could for us were you here and your assistance needful. A letter from you came a day or two before the end—she made me enquire about the Frescobaldi Palace for you,—Isa wrote to you in consequence. I shall be heard of at 151, rue de Grenelle St. Germain. Faithfully and affectionately yours, Robert Browning.

The first of these displays even more self-control, it might be thought less feeling, than the second; but it illustrates the reserve which, I believe, habitually characterized Mr. Browning's attitude towards men. His natural, and certainly most complete, confidants were women. At about the end of July he left Florence with his son; also accompanied by Miss Blagden, who travelled with them as far as Paris. She herself must soon have returned to Italy; since he wrote to her in September on the subject of his wife's provisional disinterment,* in a manner which shows her to have been on the spot.

* Required for the subsequent placing of the monument designed by F. Leighton.

Sept. '61.

'. . . Isa, may I ask you one favour? Will you, whenever these dreadful preliminaries, the provisional removement &c. when they are proceeded with,—will you do—all you can—suggest every regard to decency and proper feeling to the persons concerned? I have a horror of that man of the grave-yard, and needless publicity and exposure—I rely on you, dearest friend of ours, to at least lend us your influence when the time shall come—a word may be invaluable. If there is any show made, or gratification of strangers' curiosity, far better that I had left the turf untouched. These things occur through sheer thoughtlessness, carelessness, not anything worse, but the effect is irreparable. I won't think any more of it—now—at least. . . .'

The dread expressed in this letter of any offence to the delicacies of the occasion was too natural to be remarked upon here; but it connects itself with an habitual aversion for the paraphernalia of death, which was a marked peculiarity of Mr. Browning's nature. He shrank, as his wife had done, from the 'earth side' of the portentous change; but truth compels me to own that her infinite pity had little or no part in his attitude towards it. For him, a body from which the soul had passed, held nothing of the person whose earthly vesture it had been. He had no sympathy for the still human tenderness with which so many of us regard the mortal remains of those they have loved, or with the solemn or friendly interest in which that tenderness so often reflects itself in more neutral minds. He would claim all respect for the corpse, but he would turn away from it. Another aspect of this feeling shows itself in a letter to one of his brothers-in-law, Mr. George Moulton-Barrett, in reference to his wife's monument, with which Mr. Barrett had professed himself pleased. His tone is characterized by an almost religious reverence for the memory which that monument enshrines. He nevertheless writes:

'I hope to see it one day—and, although I have no kind of concern as to where the old clothes of myself shall be thrown, yet, if my fortune be such, and my survivors be not unduly troubled, I should like them to lie in the place I have retained there. It is no matter, however.'

The letter is dated October 19, 1866. He never saw Florence again.

Mr. Browning spent two months with his father and sister at St.-Enogat, near Dinard, from which place the letter to Miss Blagden was written; and then proceeded to London, where his wife's sister, Miss Arabel Barrett, was living. He had declared in his first grief that he would never keep house again, and he began his solitary life in lodgings which at his request she had engaged for him; but the discomfort of this arrangement soon wearied him of it; and before many months had passed, he had sent to Florence for his furniture, and settled himself in the house in Warwick Crescent, which possessed, besides other advantages, that of being close to Delamere Terrace, where Miss Barrett had taken up her abode.

This first period of Mr. Browning's widowed life was one of unutterable dreariness, in which the smallest and yet most unconquerable element was the prosaic ugliness of everything which surrounded him. It was fifteen years since he had spent a winter in England; he had never spent one in London. There had been nothing to break for him the transition from the stately beauty of Florence to the impressions and associations of the Harrow and Edgware Roads, and of Paddington Green. He might have escaped this neighbourhood by way of Westbourne Terrace; but his walks constantly led him in an easterly direction; and whether in an unconscious hugging of his chains, or, as was more probable, from the desire to save time, he would drag his aching heart and reluctant body through the sordidness or the squalor of this short cut, rather than seek the pleasanter thoroughfares which were open to him. Even the prettiness of Warwick Crescent was neutralized for him by the atmosphere of low or ugly life which encompassed it on almost every side. His haunting dream was one day to have done with it all; to have fulfilled his mission with his son, educated him, launched him in a suitable career, and to go back to sunshine and beauty again. He learned by degrees to regard London as a home; as the only fitting centre for the varied energies which were reviving in him; to feel pride and pleasure in its increasingly picturesque character. He even learned to appreciate the outlook from his house—that 'second from the bridge' of which so curious a presentment had entered into one of the poems of the 'Men and Women'*—in spite of the refuse of humanity which would sometimes yell at the street corner, or fling stones at his plate-glass. But all this had to come; and it is only fair to admit that twenty-nine years ago the beauties of which I have spoken were in great measure to come also. He could not then in any mood have exclaimed, as he did to a friend two or three years ago: 'Shall we not have a pretty London if things go on in this way?' They were driving on the Kensington side of Hyde Park.

* 'How it strikes a Contemporary'.

The paternal duty, which, so much against his inclination, had established Mr. Browning in England, would in every case have lain very near to his conscience and to his heart; but it especially urged itself upon them through the absence of any injunction concerning it on his wife's part. No farewell words of hers had commended their child to his father's love and care; and though he may, for the moment, have imputed this fact to unconsciousness of her approaching death, his deeper insight soon construed the silence into an expression of trust, more binding upon him than the most earnest exacted promise could have been. The growing boy's education occupied a considerable part of his time and thoughts, for he had determined not to send him to school, but, as far as possible, himself prepare him for the University. He must also, in some degree, have supervised his recreations. He had therefore, for the present, little leisure for social distractions, and probably at first very little inclination for them. His plan of life and duty, and the sense of responsibility attendant on it, had been communicated to Madame du Quaire in a letter written also from St.-Enogat.

M. Chauvin, St.-Enogat pres Dinard, Ile et Vilaine: Aug. 17, '61.

Dear Madame du Quaire,—I got your note on Sunday afternoon, but found myself unable to call on you as I had been intending to do. Next morning I left for this place near St.-Malo, but I give what they say is the proper address. I want first to beg you to forgive my withholding so long your little oval mirror—it is safe in Paris, and I am vexed at having stupidly forgotten to bring it when I tried to see you. I shall stay here till the autumn sets in, then return to Paris for a few days—the first of which will be the best, if I can see you in the course of it—afterward, I settle in London.

When I meant to pass the winter in Paris, I hoped, the first thing almost, to be near you—it now seems to me, however, that the best course for the Boy is to begin a good English education at once. I shall take quiet lodgings somewhere near Kensington Gardens, I rather think and get a Tutor. I want, if I can according to my present very imperfect knowledge to get the poor little fellow fit for the University without passing thro' a Public School. I, myself, could never have done much by either process, but he is made differently—imitates and emulates and all that. How I should be grateful if you would help me by any word that should occur to you! I may easily do wrong, begin ill, thro' too much anxiety—perhaps, however, all may be easier than seems to me just now.

I shall have a great comfort in talking to you—this writing is stiff, ineffectual work. Pen is very well, cheerful now,— has his little horse here. The place is singularly unspoiled, fresh and picturesque, and lovely to heart's content. I wish you were here!—and if you knew exactly what such a wish means, you would need no assuring in addition that I am Yours affectionately and gratefully ever Robert Browning.

The person of whom he saw most was his sister-in-law, whom he visited, I believe, every evening. Miss Barrett had been a favourite sister of Mrs. Browning's, and this constituted a sufficient title to her husband's affection. But she was also a woman to be loved for her own sake. Deeply religious and very charitable, she devoted herself to visiting the poor—a form of philanthropy which was then neither so widespread nor so fashionable as it has since become; and she founded, in 1850, the first Training School or Refuge which had ever existed for destitute little girls. It need hardly be added that Mr. and Miss Browning co-operated in the work. The little poem, 'The Twins', republished in 1855 in 'Men and Women', was first printed with Mrs. Browning's 'Plea for the Ragged Schools of London' for the benefit of this Refuge. It was in Miss Barrett's company that Mr. Browning used to attend the church of Mr. Thomas Jones, to a volume of whose 'Sermons and Addresses' he wrote a short introduction in 1884.

On February 15, 1862, he writes again to Miss Blagden.

Feb. 15, '62.

'. . . While I write, my heart is sore for a great calamity just befallen poor Rossetti, which I only heard of last night— his wife, who had been, as an invalid, in the habit of taking laudanum, swallowed an overdose—was found by the poor fellow on his return from the working-men's class in the evening, under the effects of it—help was called in, the stomach-pump used; but she died in the night, about a week ago. There has hardly been a day when I have not thought, "if I can, to-morrow, I will go and see him, and thank him for his book, and return his sister's poems." Poor, dear fellow! . . .

'. . . Have I not written a long letter, for me who hate the sight of a pen now, and see a pile of unanswered things on the table before me? —on this very table. Do you tell me in turn all about yourself. I shall be interested in the minutest thing you put down. What sort of weather is it? You cannot but be better at your new villa than in the large solitary one.

There I am again, going up the winding way to it, and seeing the herbs in red flower, and the butterflies on the top of the wall under the olive-trees! Once more, good-bye. . . .'

The hatred of writing of which he here speaks refers probably to the class of letters which he had lately been called upon to answer, and which must have been painful in proportion to the kindness by which they were inspired. But it returned to him many years later, in simple weariness of the mental and mechanical act, and with such force that he would often answer an unimportant note in person, rather than make the seemingly much smaller exertion of doing so with his pen. It was the more remarkable that, with the rarest exceptions, he replied to every letter which came to him.

The late summer of the former year had been entirely unrefreshing, in spite of his acknowledgment of the charms of St.-Enogat. There was more distraction and more soothing in the stay at Cambo and Biarritz, which was chosen for the holiday of 1862. Years afterwards, when the thought of Italy carried with it less longing and even more pain, Mr. Browning would speak of a visit to the Pyrenees, if not a residence among them, as one of the restful possibilities of his later and freer life. He wrote to Miss Blagden:

Biarritz, Maison Gastonbide: Sept. 19, '62.

'. . . I stayed a month at green pleasant little Cambo, and then came here from pure inability to go elsewhere—St.-Jean de Luz, on which I had reckoned, being still fuller of Spaniards who profit by the new railway. This place is crammed with gay people of whom I see nothing but their outsides. The sea, sands, and view of the Spanish coast and mountains, are superb and this house is on the town's outskirts. I stay till the end of the month, then go to Paris, and then get my neck back into the old collar again. Pen has managed to get more enjoyment out of his holiday than seemed at first likely—there was a nice French family at Cambo with whom he fraternised, riding with the son and escorting the daughter in her walks. His red cheeks look as they should. For me, I have got on by having a great read at Euripides—the one book I brought with me, besides attending to my own matters, my new poem that is about to be; and of which the whole is pretty well in my head,—the Roman murder story you know.

'. . . How I yearn, yearn for Italy at the close of my life! . . .'

The 'Roman murder story' was, I need hardly say, to become 'The Ring and the Book'.

It has often been told, though with curious confusion as regards the date, how Mr. Browning picked up the original parchment-bound record of the Franceschini case, on a stall of the Piazza San Lorenzo. We read in the first section of his own work that he plunged instantly into the study of this record; that he had mastered it by the end of the day; and that he then stepped out on to the terrace of his house amid the sultry blackness and silent lightnings of the June night, as the adjacent church of San Felice sent forth its chants, and voices buzzed in the street below,—and saw the tragedy as a living picture unfold itself before him. These were his last days at Casa Guidi. It was four years before he definitely began the work. The idea of converting the story into a poem cannot even have occurred to him for some little time, since he offered it for prose treatment to Miss Ogle, the author of 'A Lost Love'; and for poetic use, I am almost certain, to one of his leading contemporaries. It was this slow process of incubation which gave so much force and distinctness to his ultimate presentment of the characters; though it infused a large measure of personal imagination, and, as we shall see, of personal reminiscence, into their historical truth.

Before 'The Ring and the Book' was actually begun, 'Dramatis Personae' and 'In a Balcony' were to be completed. Their production had been delayed during Mrs. Browning's lifetime, and necessarily interrupted by her death; but we hear of the work as progressing steadily during this summer of 1862.

A painful subject of correspondence had been also for some time engaging Mr. Browning's thoughts and pen. A letter to Miss Blagden written January 19, '63, is so expressive of his continued attitude towards the questions involved that, in spite of its strong language, his family advise its publication. The name of the person referred to will alone be omitted.

'. . . Ever since I set foot in England I have been pestered with applications for leave to write the Life of my wife—I have refused—and there an end. I have last week received two communications from friends, enclosing the letters of a certain . . . of . . ., asking them for details of life and letters, for a biography he is engaged in—adding, that he "has secured the correspondence with her old friend . . ." Think of this beast working away at this, not deeming my feelings or those of her family worthy of notice—and meaning to print letters written years and years ago, on the most intimate and personal subjects to an "old friend"—which, at the poor . . . [friend's] death fell into the hands of a complete stranger, who, at once wanted to print them, but desisted through Ba's earnest expostulation enforced by my own threat to take law proceedings—as fortunately letters are copyright. I find this woman died last year, and her son writes to me this morning that . . . got them from him as autographs merely—he will try and get them back. . . , evidently a blackguard, got my letter, which gave him his deserts, on Saturday—no answer yet,—if none comes, I shall be forced to advertise in the 'Times', and obtain an injunction. But what I suffer in feeling the hands of these blackguards for I forgot to say another man has been making similar applications to friends what I undergo with their paws in my very bowels, you can guess, and God knows! No friend, of course, would ever give up the letters—if anybody ever is forced to do that which *she* would have writhed under—if it ever *were* necessary, why, *I* should be forced to do it, and, with any good to her memory and fame, my own pain in the attempt would be turned into joy—I should *do* it at whatever cost: but it is not only unnecessary but absurdly useless—and, indeed, it shall not be done if I can stop the scamp's knavery along with his breath.

'I am going to reprint the Greek Christian Poets and another essay—nothing that ought to be published shall be kept back,—and this she certainly intended to correct, augment, and re-produce—but *I* open the doubled-up paper! Warn anyone you may think needs the warning of the utter distress in which I should be placed were this scoundrel, or any other of the sort, to baffle me and bring out the letters—I can't prevent fools from uttering their folly upon her life, as they do on every other subject, but the law protects property,—as these letters are. Only last week, or so, the Bishop of Exeter stopped the publication of an announced "Life"—containing extracts from his correspondence—and so I shall do. . . .'

Mr. Browning only resented the exactions of modern biography in the same degree as most other right-minded persons; but there was, to his thinking, something specially ungenerous in dragging to light any immature or unconsidered utterance which the writer's later judgment would have disclaimed. Early work was always for him included in this category; and here it was possible to disagree with him; since the promise of genius has a legitimate interest from which no distance from its subsequent fulfilment can detract. But there could be no disagreement as to the rights and decencies involved in the present case; and, as we hear no more of the letters to Mr. . . ., we may perhaps assume that their intending publisher was acting in ignorance, but did not wish to act in defiance, of Mr. Browning's feeling in the matter.

In the course of this year, 1863, Mr. Browning brought out, through Chapman and Hall, the still well-known and well-loved three-volume edition of his works, including 'Sordello', but again excluding 'Pauline'. A selection of his poems which appeared somewhat earlier, if we may judge by the preface, dated November 1862, deserves mention as a tribute to friendship. The volume had been prepared by John Forster and Bryan Waller Procter Barry Cornwall, 'two friends,' as the preface states, 'who from the first appearance of 'Paracelsus' have regarded its writer as among the few great poets of the century.' Mr. Browning had long before signalized his feeling for Barry Cornwall by the dedication of 'Colombe's Birthday'. He discharged the present debt to Mr. Procter, if such there was, by the attentions which he rendered to his infirm old age. For many years he visited him every Sunday, in spite of a deafness ultimately so complete that it was only possible to converse with him in writing. These visits were afterwards, at her urgent request, continued to Mr. Procter's widow.

Chapter 15

1863-1869

Pornic—'James Lee's Wife'—Meeting at Mr. F. Palgrave's—Letters to Miss Blagden—His own Estimate of his Work—His Father's Illness and Death; Miss Browning—Le Croisic—Academic Honours; Letter to the Master of Balliol—Death of Miss Barrett—Audierne—Uniform Edition of his Works—His rising Fame—'Dramatis Personae'—'The Ring and the Book'; Character of Pompilia.

The most constant contributions to Mr. Browning's history are supplied during the next eight or nine years by extracts from his letters to Miss Blagden. Our next will be dated from Ste.-Marie, near Pornic, where he and his family again spent their holiday in 1864 and 1865. Some idea of the life he led there is given at the close of a letter to Frederic Leighton, August 17, 1863, in which he says:

'I live upon milk and fruit, bathe daily, do a good morning's work, read a little with Pen and somewhat more by myself, go to bed early, and get up earlyish—rather liking it all.'

This mention of a diet of milk and fruit recalls a favourite habit of Mr. Browning's: that of almost renouncing animal food whenever he went abroad. It was partly promoted by the inferior quality of foreign meat, and showed no sign of specially agreeing with him, at all events in his later years, when he habitually returned to England looking thinner and more haggard than before he left it. But the change was always congenial to his taste.

A fuller picture of these simple, peaceful, and poetic Pornic days comes to us through Miss Blagden, August 18:

'. . . This is a wild little place in Brittany, something like that village where we stayed last year. Close to the sea—a hamlet of a dozen houses, perfectly lonely—one may walk on the edge of the low rocks by the sea for miles. Our house is the Mayor's, large enough, clean and bare. If I could, I would stay just as I am for many a day. I feel out of the very earth sometimes as I sit here at the window; with the little church, a field, a few houses, and the sea. On a weekday there is nobody in the village, plenty of hay-stacks, cows and fowls; all our butter, eggs, milk, are produced in the farm-house. Such a soft sea, and such a mournful wind!

'I wrote a poem yesterday of 120 lines, and mean to keep writing whether I like it or not. . . .'

That 'window' was the 'Doorway' in 'James Lee's Wife'. The sea, the field, and the fig-tree were visible from it.

A long interval in the correspondence, at all events so far as we are concerned, carries us to the December of 1864, and then Mr. Browning wrote:

'... on the other hand, I feel such comfort and delight in doing the best I can with my own object of life, poetry—which, I think, I never could have seen the good of before, that it shows me I have taken the root I *did* take, *well*. I hope to do much more yet—and that the flower of it will be put into Her hand somehow. I really have great opportunities and advantages—on the whole, almost unprecedented ones—I think, no other disturbances and cares than those I am most grateful for being allowed to have....'

One of our very few written reminiscences of Mr. Browning's social life refers to this year, 1864, and to the evening, February 12, on which he signed his will in the presence of Mr. Francis Palgrave and Alfred Tennyson. It is inscribed in the diary of Mr. Thomas Richmond, then chaplain to St. George's Hospital; and Mr. Reginald Palgrave has kindly procured me a copy of it. A brilliant party had met at dinner at the house of Mr. F. Palgrave, York Gate, Regent's Park; Mr. Richmond, having fulfilled a prior engagement, had joined it later. 'There were, in order,' he says, 'round the dinner-table dinner being over, Gifford Palgrave, Tennyson, Dr. John Ogle, Sir Francis H. Doyle, Frank Palgrave, W. E. Gladstone, Browning, Sir John Simeon, Monsignor Patterson, Woolner, and Reginald Palgrave.'

Mr. Richmond closes his entry by saying he will never forget that evening. The names of those whom it had brought together, almost all to be sooner or later numbered among the Poet's friends, were indeed enough to stamp it as worthy of recollection. One or two characteristic utterances of Mr. Browning are, however, the only ones which it seems advisable to repeat here. The conversation having turned on the celebration of the Shakespeare ter-centenary, he said: 'Here we are called upon to acknowledge Shakespeare, we who have him in our very bones and blood, our very selves. The very recognition of Shakespeare's merits by the Committee reminds me of nothing so apt as an illustration, as the decree of the Directoire that men might acknowledge God.'

Among the subjects discussed was the advisability of making schoolboys write English verses as well as Latin and Greek. 'Woolner and Sir Francis Doyle were for this; Gladstone and Browning against it.'

Work had now found its fitting place in the Poet's life. It was no longer the overflow of an irresistible productive energy; it was the deliberate direction of that energy towards an appointed end. We hear something of his own feeling concerning this in a letter of August '65, again from Ste.-Marie, and called forth by some gossip concerning him which Miss Blagden had connected with his then growing fame.

'... I suppose that what you call "my fame within these four years" comes from a little of this gossiping and going about, and showing myself to be alive: and so indeed some folks say—but I hardly think it: for remember I was uninterruptedly almost in London from the time I published 'Paracelsus' till I ended that string of plays with 'Luria'—and I used to go out then, and see far more of merely literary people, critics &c. than I do now,—but what came of it? There were always a few people who had a certain opinion of my poems, but nobody cared to speak what he thought, or the things printed twenty-five years ago would not have waited so long for a good word; but at last a new set of men arrive who don't mind the conventionalities of ignoring one and seeing everything in another—Chapman says, "the new orders come from Oxford and Cambridge," and all my new cultivators are young men—more than that, I observe that some of my old friends don't like at all the irruption of outsiders who rescue me from their sober and private approval, and take those words out of their mouths "which they always meant to say" and never did. When there gets to be a general feeling of this kind, that there must be something in the works of an author, the reviews are obliged to notice him, such notice as it is—but what poor work, even when doing its best! I mean poor in the failure to give a general notion of the whole works; not a particular one of such and such points therein. As I begun, so I shall end,—taking my own course, pleasing myself or aiming at doing so, and thereby, I hope, pleasing God.

'As I never did otherwise, I never had any fear as to what I did going ultimately to the bad,—hence in collected editions I always reprinted everything, smallest and greatest. Do you ever see, by the way, the numbers of the selection which Moxons publish? They are exclusively poems omitted in that other selection by Forster; it seems little use sending them to you, but when they are completed, if they give me a few copies, you shall have one if you like. Just before I left London, Macmillan was anxious to print a third selection, for his Golden Treasury, which should of course be different from either—but *three* seem too absurd. There—enough of me—

'I certainly will do my utmost to make the most of my poor self before I die; for one reason, that I may help old Pen the better; I was much struck by the kind ways, and interest shown in me by the Oxford undergraduates,—those introduced to me by Jowett.—I am sure they would be the more helpful to my son. So, good luck to my great venture, the murder-poem, which I do hope will strike you and all good lovers of mine....'

We cannot wonder at the touch of bitterness with which Mr. Browning dwells on the long neglect which he had sustained; but it is at first sight difficult to reconcile this high positive estimate of the value of his poetry with the relative depreciation of his own poetic genius which constantly marks his attitude towards that of his wife. The facts are, however, quite compatible. He regarded Mrs. Browning's genius as greater, because more spontaneous, than his own: owing less to life and its opportunities; but he judged his own work as the more important, because of the larger knowledge of life which had entered into its production. He was wrong in the first terms of his comparison: for he underrated the creative, hence spontaneous element in his own nature, while claiming primarily the position of an observant thinker; and he overrated the amount of creativeness implied by the poetry of his wife. He failed to see that, given her intellectual endowments, and the lyric gift, the characteristics of her genius were due to circumstances as much as those of his own. Actual life is not the only source of poetic inspiration, though it may perhaps be the best. Mrs. Browning as a poet became what she was, not in spite of her long seclusion, but by help of it. A touching paragraph, bearing upon this subject, is dated October '65.

'. . . Another thing. I have just been making a selection of Ba's poems which is wanted—how I have done it, I can hardly say—it is one dear delight to know that the work of her goes on more effectually than ever—her books are more and more read—certainly, sold. A new edition of Aurora Leigh is completely exhausted within this year. . . .'

Of the thing next dearest to his memory, his Florentine home, he had written in the January of this year:

'. . . Yes, Florence will never be *my* Florence again. To build over or beside Poggio seems barbarous and inexcusable. The Fiesole side don't matter. Are they going to pull the old walls down, or any part of them, I want to know? Why can't they keep the old city as a nucleus and build round and round it, as many rings of houses as they please,—framing the picture as deeply as they please? Is Casa Guidi to be turned into any Public Office? I should think that its natural destination. If I am at liberty to flee away one day, it will not be to Florence, I dare say. As old Philipson said to me once of Jerusalem—"No, I don't want to go there,—I can see it in my head." . . . Well, goodbye, dearest Isa. I have been for a few minutes—nay, a good many,—so really with you in Florence that it would be no wonder if you heard my steps up the lane to your house. . . .'

Part of a letter written in the September of '65 from Ste.-Marie may be interesting as referring to the legend of Pornic included in 'Dramatis Personae'.

'. . . I suppose my "poem" which you say brings me and Pornic together in your mind, is the one about the poor girl—if so, "fancy" as I hear you say they have pulled down the church since I arrived last month—there are only the shell-like, roofless walls left, for a few weeks more; it was very old—built on a natural base of rock—small enough, to be sure—so they build a smart new one behind it, and down goes this; just as if they could not have pitched down their brick and stucco farther away, and left the old place for the fishermen—so here—the church is even more picturesque—and certain old Norman ornaments, capitals of pillars and the like, which we left erect in the doorway, are at this moment in a heap of rubbish by the road-side. The people here are good, stupid and dirty, without a touch of the sense of picturesqueness in their clodpolls. . . .'

The little record continues through 1866.

Feb. 19, '66.

'. . . I go out a great deal; but have enjoyed nothing so much as a dinner last week with Tennyson, who, with his wife and one son, is staying in town for a few weeks,—and she is just what she was and always will be—very sweet and dear: he seems to me better than ever. I met him at a large party on Saturday—also Carlyle, whom I never met at a "drum" before. . . . Pen is drawing our owl—a bird that is the light of our house, for his tameness and engaging ways. . . .'

May 19, '66.

'. . . My father has been unwell,—he is better and will go into the country the moment the east winds allow,—for in Paris,—as here,—there is a razor wrapped up in the flannel of sunshine. I hope to hear presently from my sister, and will tell you if a letter comes: he is eighty-five, almost,—you see! otherwise his wonderful constitution would keep me from inordinate apprehension. His mind is absolutely as I always remember it,—and the other day when I wanted some information about a point of mediaeval history, he wrote a regular bookful of notes and extracts thereabout. . . .'

June 20, '66.

'My dearest Isa, I was telegraphed for to Paris last week, and arrived time enough to pass twenty-four hours more with my father: he died on the 14th—quite exhausted by internal haemorrhage, which would have overcome a man of thirty. He retained all his faculties to the last—was utterly indifferent to death,—asking with surprise what it was we were affected about since he was perfectly happy?—and kept his own strange sweetness of soul to the end—nearly his last words to me, as I was fanning him, were "I am so afraid that I fatigue you, dear!" this, while his sufferings were great; for the strength of his constitution seemed impossible to be subdued. He wanted three weeks exactly to complete his eighty-fifth year. So passed away this good, unworldly, kind-hearted, religious man, whose powers natural and acquired would so easily have made him a notable man, had he known what vanity or ambition or the love of money or social influence meant. As it is, he was known by half-a-dozen friends. He was worthy of being Ba's father—out of the whole world, only he, so far as my experience goes. She loved him,—and *he* said, very recently, while gazing at her portrait, that only that picture had put into his head that there might be such a thing as the worship of the images of saints. My sister will come and live with me henceforth. You see what she loses. All her life has been spent in caring for my mother, and seventeen years after that, my father. You may be sure she does not rave and rend hair like people who have plenty to atone for in the past; but she loses very much. I returned to London last night. . . .'

During his hurried journey to Paris, Mr. Browning was mentally blessing the Emperor for having abolished the system of passports, and thus enabled him to reach his father's bedside in time. His early Italian journeys had brought him some vexatious experience of the old order of things. Once, at Venice, he had been mistaken for a well-known Liberal, Dr. Bowring, and found it almost impossible to get his passport 'vise'; and, on another occasion, it aroused suspicion by being 'too good'; though in what sense I do not quite remember.

Miss Browning did come to live with her brother, and was thenceforward his inseparable companion. Her presence with him must therefore be understood wherever I have had no special reason for mentioning it.

They tried Dinard for the remainder of the summer; but finding it unsuitable, proceeded by St.-Malo to Le Croisic, the little sea-side town of south-eastern Brittany which two of Mr. Browning's poems have since rendered famous.

The following extract has no date.

Le Croisic, Loire Inferieure.

'. . . We all found Dinard unsuitable, and after staying a few days at St. Malo resolved to try this place, and well for us, since it serves our purpose capitally. . . . We are in the most delicious and peculiar old house I ever occupied, the oldest in the town—plenty of great rooms—nearly as much space as in Villa Alberti. The little town, and surrounding country are wild and primitive, even a trifle beyond Pornic perhaps. Close by is Batz, a village where the men dress in white from head to foot, with baggy breeches, and great black flap hats;—opposite is Guerande, the old capital of Bretagne: you have read about it in Balzac's 'Beatrix',—and other interesting places are near. The sea is all round our peninsula, and on the whole I expect we shall like it very much. . . .'

Later.

'. . . We enjoyed Croisic increasingly to the last—spite of three weeks' vile weather, in striking contrast to the golden months at Pornic last year. I often went to Guerande—once Sarianna and I walked from it in two hours and something under,—nine miles:—though from our house, straight over the sands and sea, it is not half the distance. . . .'

In 1867 Mr. Browning received his first and greatest academic honours. The M.A. degree by diploma, of the University of Oxford, was conferred on him in June;* and in the month of October he was made honorary Fellow of Balliol College. Dr. Jowett allows me to publish the, as he terms it, very characteristic letter in which he acknowledged the distinction. Dr. Scott, afterwards Dean of Rochester, was then Master of Balliol.

* 'Not a lower degree than that of D.C.L., but a much higher honour, hardly given since Dr. Johnson's time except to kings and royal personages. . . .' So the Keeper of the Archives wrote to Mr. Browning at the time.

19, Warwick Crescent: Oct. 21, '67.

Dear Dr. Scott,—I am altogether unable to say how I feel as to the fact you communicate to me. I must know more intimately than you can how little worthy I am of such an honour,—you hardly can set the value of that honour, you who give, as I who take it.

Indeed, there *are* both 'duties and emoluments' attached to this position,—duties of deep and lasting gratitude, and emoluments through which I shall be wealthy my life long. I have at least loved learning and the learned, and there needed no recognition of my love on their part to warrant my professing myself, as I do, dear Dr. Scott, yours ever most faithfully, Robert Browning.

In the following year he received and declined the virtual offer of the Lord Rectorship of the University of St. Andrews, rendered vacant by the death of Mr. J. S. Mill.

He returned with his sister to Le Croisic for the summer of 1867.

In June 1868, Miss Arabel Barrett died, of a rheumatic affection of the heart. As did her sister seven years before, she passed away in Mr. Browning's arms. He wrote the event to Miss Blagden as soon as it occurred, describing also a curious circumstance attendant on it.

19th June, '68.

'. . . You know I am not superstitious—here is a note I made in a book, Tuesday, July 21, 1863. "Arabel told me yesterday that she had been much agitated by a dream which happened the night before, Sunday, July 19. She saw Her and asked 'when shall I be with you?' the reply was, 'Dearest, in five years,' whereupon Arabella woke. She knew in her dream that it was not to the living she spoke."—In five years, within a month of their completion—I had forgotten the date of the dream, and supposed it was only three years ago, and that two had still to run. Only a coincidence, but noticeable. . . .'

In August he writes again from Audierne, Finisterre Brittany.

'. . . You never heard of this place, I daresay. After staying a few days at Paris we started for Rennes,—reached Caen and halted a little—thence made for Auray, where we made excursions to Carnac, Lokmariaker, and Ste.-Anne d'Auray; all very interesting of their kind; then saw Brest, Morlaix, St.-Pol de Leon, and the sea-port Roscoff,—our intended bathing place—it was full of folk, however, and otherwise impracticable, so we had nothing for it, but to "rebrousser chemin" and get to the south-west again. At Quimper we heard for a second time that Audierne would suit us exactly, and to it we came—happily, for "suit" it certainly does. Look on the map for the most westerly point of Bretagne—and of the mainland of Europe—there is niched Audierne, a delightful quite unspoiled little fishing-town, with the open ocean in front, and beautiful woods, hills and dales, meadows and lanes behind and around,—sprinkled here and there with villages each with its fine old Church. Sarianna and I have just returned from a four hours' walk in the course of which we visited a town, Pont Croix, with a beautiful cathedral-like building amid the cluster of clean bright Breton houses,—and a little farther is another church, "Notre Dame de Comfort", with only a hovel or two round it, worth the journey from England to see; we are therefore very well off—at an inn, I should say, with singularly good, kind, and liberal people, so have no cares for the moment. May you be doing as well! The weather has been most propitious, and to-day is perfect to a wish. We bathe, but somewhat ingloriously, in a smooth creek of mill-pond quietude, there being no cabins on the bay itself, unlike the great rushing waves of Croisic—the water is much colder. . . .'

The tribute contained in this letter to the merits of le Pere Batifoulier and his wife would not, I think, be endorsed by the few other English travellers who have stayed at their inn. The writer's own genial and kindly spirit no doubt partly elicited, and still more supplied, the qualities he saw in them.

The six-volume, so long known as 'uniform' edition of Mr. Browning's works, was brought out in the autumn of this year by Messrs. Smith, Elder & Co.; practically Mr. George Murray Smith, who was to be thenceforward his exclusive publisher and increasingly valued friend. In the winter months appeared the first two volumes to be followed in the ensuing spring by the third and fourth of 'The Ring and the Book'.

With 'The Ring and the Book' Mr. Browning attained the full recognition of his genius. The 'Athenaeum' spoke of it as the 'opus magnum' of the generation; not merely beyond all parallel the supremest poetic achievement of the time, but the most precious and profound spiritual treasure that England had produced since the days of Shakespeare. His popularity was yet to come, so also the widespread reading of his hitherto neglected poems; but henceforth whatever he published was sure of ready acceptance, of just, if not always enthusiastic, appreciation. The ground had not been gained at a single leap. A passage in another letter to Miss Blagden shows that, when 'The Ring and the Book' appeared, a high place was already awaiting it outside those higher academic circles in which its author's position was secured.

'. . . I want to get done with my poem. Booksellers are making me pretty offers for it. One sent to propose, last week, to publish it at his risk, giving me *all* the profits, and pay me the whole in advance—"for the incidental advantages of my name"—the R. B. who for six months once did not sell one copy of the poems! I ask 200 Pounds for the sheets to America, and shall get it. . . .'

His presence in England had doubtless stimulated the public interest in his productions; and we may fairly credit 'Dramatis Personae' with having finally awakened his countrymen of all classes to the fact that a great creative power had arisen among them. 'The Ring and the Book' and 'Dramatis Personae' cannot indeed be dissociated in what was the culminating moment in the author's poetic life, even more than the zenith of his literary career. In their expression of all that constituted the wide range and the characteristic quality of his genius, they at once support and supplement each other. But a fact of more distinctive biographical interest connects itself exclusively with the later work.

We cannot read the emotional passages of 'The Ring and the Book' without hearing in them a voice which is not Mr. Browning's own: an echo, not of his past, but from it. The remembrance of that past must have accompanied him through every stage of the great work. Its subject had come to him in the last days of his greatest happiness. It had lived with him, though in the background of consciousness, through those of his keenest sorrow. It was his refuge in that aftertime, in which a subsiding grief often leaves a deeper sense of isolation. He knew the joy with which his wife would have witnessed the diligent performance of this his self-imposed task. The beautiful dedication contained in the first and last books was only a matter of course. But Mrs. Browning's spiritual presence on this occasion was more than a presiding memory of the heart. I am convinced that it entered largely into the conception of 'Pompilia', and, so far as this depended on it, the character of the whole work. In the outward course of her history, Mr. Browning proceeded strictly on the ground of fact. His dramatic conscience would not have allowed it otherwise. He had read the record of the case, as he has been heard to say, fully eight times over before converting it into the substance of his poem; and the form in which he finally cast it, was that which recommended itself to him as true—which, within certain limits, *was* true. The testimony of those who watched by Pompilia's death-bed is almost conclusive as to the absence of any criminal motive to her flight, or criminal circumstance connected with it. Its time proved itself to have been that of her impending, perhaps newly expected motherhood, and may have had some reference to this fact. But the real Pompilia was a simple child, who lived in bodily terror of her husband, and had made repeated efforts to escape from him. Unless my memory much deceives me, her physical condition plays no part in the historical defence of her flight. If it appeared there at all, it was as a merely practical incentive to her striving to place herself in safety. The sudden rapturous sense of maternity which, in the poetic rendering of the case, becomes her impulse to self-protection, was beyond her age and her culture; it was not suggested by the facts; and, what is more striking, it was not a natural development of Mr. Browning's imagination concerning them.

The parental instinct was among the weakest in his nature—a fact which renders the more conspicuous his devotion to his own son; it finds little or no expression in his work. The apotheosis of motherhood which he puts forth through the aged priest in 'Ivan Ivanovitch' was due to the poetic necessity of lifting a ghastly human punishment into the sphere of Divine retribution. Even in the advancing years which soften the father into the grandfather, the essential quality of early childhood was not that which appealed to him. He would admire its flower-like beauty, but not linger over it. He had no special emotion for its helplessness. When he was attracted by a child it was through the evidence of something not only distinct from, but opposed to this. 'It is the soul' I see 'in that speck of a body,' he said, not many years ago, of a tiny boy—now too big for it to be desirable that I should mention his name, but whose mother, if she reads this, will know to whom I allude—who had delighted him by an act of intelligent grace which seemed beyond his years. The ingenuously unbounded maternal pride, the almost luscious maternal sentiment, of Pompilia's dying moments can only associate themselves in our mind with Mrs. Browning's personal utterances, and some notable passages in 'Casa Guidi Windows' and 'Aurora Leigh'. Even the exalted fervour of the invocation to Caponsacchi, its blending of spiritual ecstasy with half-realized earthly emotion, has, I think, no parallel in her husband's work.

'Pompilia' bears, still, unmistakably, the stamp of her author's genius. Only he could have imagined her peculiar form of consciousness; her childlike, wondering, yet subtle, perception of the anomalies of life. He has raised the woman in her from the typical to the individual by this distinguishing touch of his supreme originality; and thus infused into her character a haunting pathos which renders it to many readers the most exquisite in the whole range of his creations. For others at the same time, it fails in the impressiveness because it lacks the reality which habitually marks them.

So much, however, is certain: Mr. Browning would never have accepted this 'murder story' as the subject of a poem, if he could not in some sense have made it poetical. It was only in an idealized Pompilia that the material for such a process could be found. We owe it, therefore, to the one departure from his usual mode of dramatic conception, that the Poet's masterpiece has been produced. I know no other instance of what can be even mistaken for reflected inspiration in the whole range of his work, the given passages in 'Pauline' excepted.

The postscript of a letter to Frederic Leighton written so far back as October 17, 1864, is interesting in its connection with the preliminary stages of this great undertaking.

'A favour, if you have time for it. Go into the church St. Lorenzo in Lucina in the Corso—and look attentively at it—so as to describe it to me on your return. The general arrangement of the building, if with a nave—pillars or not—the number of altars, and any particularity there may be—over the High Altar is a famous Crucifixion by Guido. It will be of great use to me. I don't care about the *outsid*.'

Chapter 16

1869-1873

Lord Dufferin; Helen's Tower—Scotland; Visit to Lady Ashburton—Letters to Miss Blagden—St.-Aubin; The Franco-Prussian War—'Herve Riel'—Letter to Mr. G. M. Smith—'Balaustion's Adventure'; 'Prince Hohenstiel-Schwangau'—'Fifine at the Fair'—Mistaken Theories of Mr. Browning's Work—St.-Aubin; 'Red Cotton Nightcap Country'.

From 1869 to 1871 Mr. Browning published nothing; but in April 1870 he wrote the sonnet called 'Helen's Tower', a beautiful tribute to the memory of Helen, mother of Lord Dufferin, suggested by the memorial tower which her son was erecting to her on his estate at Clandeboye. The sonnet appeared in 1883, in the 'Pall Mall Gazette', and was reprinted in 1886, in 'Sonnets of the Century', edited by Mr. Sharp; and again in the fifth part of the Browning Society's 'Papers'; but it is still I think sufficiently little known to justify its reproduction.

Who hears of Helen's Tower may dream perchance How the Greek Beauty from the Scaean Gate Gazed on old friends unanimous in hate, Death-doom'd because of her fair countenance. Hearts would leap otherwise at thy advance, Lady, to whom this Tower is consecrate! Like hers, thy face once made all eyes elate, Yet, unlike hers, was bless'd by every glance. The Tower of Hate is outworn, far and strange; A transitory shame of long ago; It dies into the sand from which it sprang; But thine, Love's rock-built Tower, shall fear no change. God's self laid stable earth's foundations so, When all the morning-stars together sang.

April 26, 1870.

Lord Dufferin is a warm admirer of Mr. Browning's genius. He also held him in strong personal regard.

In the summer of 1869 the poet, with his sister and son, changed the manner of his holiday, by joining Mr. Story and his family in a tour in Scotland, and a visit to Louisa, Lady Ashburton, at Loch Luichart Lodge; but in the August of 1870 he was again in the primitive atmosphere of a French fishing village, though one which had little to recommend it but the society of a friend; it was M. Milsand's St.-Aubin. He had written, February 24, to Miss Blagden, under the one inspiration which naturally recurred in his correspondence with her.

'... So you, too, think of Naples for an eventual resting-place! Yes, that is the proper basking-ground for "bright and aged snakes." Florence would be irritating, and, on the whole, insufferable—Yet I never hear of any one going thither but my heart is twitched. There is a good, charming, little singing German lady, Miss Regan, who told me the other day that she was just about revisiting her aunt, Madame Sabatier, whom you may know, or know of—and I felt as if I should immensely like to glide, for a long summer-day through the streets and between the old stone-walls,—unseen come and unheard go—perhaps by some miracle, I shall do so—and look up at Villa Brichieri as Arnold's Gypsy-Scholar gave one wistful look at "the line of festal light in Christ Church Hall," before he went to sleep in some forgotten grange. . . . I am so glad I can be comfortable in your comfort. I fancy exactly how you feel and see how you live: it *is* the Villa Geddes of old days, I find. I well remember the fine view from the upper room—that looking down the steep hill, by the side of which runs the road you describe—that path was always my preferred walk, for its shortness abruptness and the fine old wall to your left from the Villa which is overgrown with weeds and wild flowers—violets and ground-ivy, I remember. Oh, me! to find myself some late sunshiny Sunday afternoon, with my face turned to Florence—"ten minutes to the gate, ten minutes *home*!" I think I should fairly end it all on the spot. . . .'

He writes again from St.-Aubin, August 19, 1870:

'Dearest Isa,—Your letter came prosperously to this little wild place, where we have been, Sarianna and myself, just a week. Milsand lives in a cottage with a nice bit of garden, two steps off, and we occupy another of the most primitive kind on the sea-shore—which shore is a good sandy stretch for miles and miles on either side. I don't think we were ever quite so thoroughly washed by the sea-air from all quarters as here—the weather is fine, and we do well enough. The sadness of the war and its consequences go far to paralyse all our pleasure, however. . . .

'Well, you are at Siena—one of the places I love best to remember. You are returned—or I would ask you to tell me how the Villa Alberti wears, and if the fig-tree behind the house is green and strong yet. I have a pen-and-ink drawing of it, dated and signed the last day Ba was ever there—"my fig tree—" she used to sit under it, reading and writing. Nine years, or ten rather, since then! Poor old Landor's oak, too, and his cottage, ought not to be forgotten. Exactly opposite this house,—just over the way of the water,—shines every night the light-house of Havre—a place I know well, and love very moderately: but it always gives me a thrill as I see afar, *exactly* a particular spot which I was at along with her. At this moment, I see the white streak of the phare in the sun, from the window where I write and I *think*. . . . Milsand went to Paris last week, just before we arrived, to transport his valuables to a safer place than his house, which is near the fortifications. He is filled with as much despondency as can be—while the old dear and perfect kindness remains. I never knew or shall know his like among men. . . .'

The war did more than sadden Mr. and Miss Browning's visit to St.-Aubin; it opposed unlooked-for difficulties to their return home. They had remained, unconscious of the impending danger, till Sedan had been taken, the Emperor's downfall proclaimed, and the country suddenly placed in a state of siege. One morning M. Milsand came to them in anxious haste, and insisted on their starting that very day. An order, he said, had been issued that no native should leave the country, and it only needed some unusually thick-headed Maire for Mr. Browning to be arrested as a runaway Frenchman or a Prussian spy. The usual passenger boats from Calais and Boulogne no longer ran; but there was, he believed, a chance of their finding one at Havre. They acted on this warning, and discovered its wisdom in the various hindrances which they found on their way. Everywhere the horses had been requisitioned for the war. The boat on which they had relied to take them down the river to Caen had been stopped that very morning; and when they reached the railroad they were told that the Prussians would be at the other end before night. At last they arrived at Honfleur, where they found an English vessel which was about to convey cattle to Southampton; and in this, setting out at midnight, they made their passage to England.

Some words addressed to Miss Blagden, written I believe in 1871, once more strike a touching familiar note.

'. . . But *no*, dearest Isa. The simple truth is that *she* was the poet, and I the clever person by comparison—remember her limited experience of all kinds, and what she made of it. Remember on the other hand, how my uninterrupted health and strength and practice with the world have helped me. . . .'

'Balaustion's Adventure' and 'Prince Hohenstiel-Schwangau' were published, respectively, in August and December 1871. They had been preceded in the March of the same year by a ballad, 'Herve Riel', afterwards reprinted in the 'Pacchiarotto' volume, and which Mr. Browning now sold to the 'Cornhill Magazine' for the benefit of the French sufferers by the war.

The circumstances of this little transaction, unique in Mr. Browning's experience, are set forth in the following letter:

Feb. 4, '71.

'My dear Smith,—I want to give something to the people in Paris, and can afford so very little just now, that I am forced upon an expedient. Will you buy of me that poem which poor Simeon praised in a letter you saw, and which I like better than most things I have done of late?—Buy,—I mean,—the right of printing it in the Pall Mall and, if you please, the Cornhill also,—the copyright remaining with me. You remember you wanted to print it in the Cornhill, and I was obstinate: there is hardly any occasion on which I should be otherwise, if the printing any poem of mine in a magazine were purely for my own sake: so, any liberality you exercise will not be drawn into a precedent against you. I fancy this is a case in which one may handsomely puff one's own ware, and I venture to call my verses good for once. I send them to you directly, because expedition will render whatever I contribute more valuable: for when you make up your mind as to how liberally I shall be enabled to give, you must send me a cheque and I will send the same as the "Product of a Poem"—so that your light will shine deservedly. Now, begin proceedings by reading the poem to Mrs. Smith,—by whose judgment I will cheerfully be bound; and, with her approval, second my endeavour as best you can. Would,—for the love of France,—that this were a "Song of a Wren"—then should the guineas equal the lines; as it is, do what you safely may for the song of a Robin—Browning—who is yours very truly, into the bargain.

'P.S. The copy is so clear and careful that you might, with a good Reader, print it on Monday, nor need my help for corrections: I shall however be always at home, and ready at a moment's notice: return the copy, if you please, as I promised it to my son long ago.'

Mr. Smith gave him 100 guineas as the price of the poem.

He wrote concerning the two longer poems, first probably at the close of this year, and again in January 1872, to Miss Blagden.

'. . . By this time you have got my little book 'Hohenstiel' and seen for yourself whether I make the best or worst of the case. I think, in the main, he meant to do what I say, and, but for weakness,—grown more apparent in his last years than formerly,—would have done what I say he did not.* I thought badly of him at the beginning of his career, *et pour cause*: better afterward, on the strength of the promises he made, and gave indications of intending to redeem. I think him very weak in the last miserable year. At his worst I prefer him to Thiers' best. I am told my little thing is succeeding—sold 1,400 in the first five days, and before any notice appeared. I remember that the year I made the little rough sketch in Rome, '60, my account for the last six months with Chapman was—*nil*, not one copy disposed of! . . .

* This phrase is a little misleading.

'. . . I am glad you like what the editor of the Edinburgh calls my eulogium on the second empire,—which it is not, any more than what another wiseacre affirms it to be "a scandalous attack on the old constant friend of England"—it is just what I imagine the man might, if he pleased, say for himself.'

Mr. Browning continues:

'Spite of my ailments and bewailments I have just all but finished another poem of quite another kind, which shall amuse you in the spring, I hope! I don't go sound asleep at all events. 'Balaustion'—the second edition is in the press I think I told you. 2,500 in five months, is a good sale for the likes of me. But I met Henry Taylor of Artevelde two days ago at dinner, and he said he had never gained anything by his books, which surely is a shame—I mean, if no buyers mean no readers. . . .'

'Prince Hohenstiel-Schwangau' was written in Scotland, where Mr. Browning was the guest of Mr. Ernest Benzon: having left his sister to the care of M. and Madame Milsand at St.-Aubin. The ailment he speaks of consisted, I believe, of a severe cold. Another of the occurrences of 1871 was Mr. Browning's election as Life Governor of the London University.

A passage from a letter dated March 30, '72, bears striking testimony to the constant warmth of his affections.

'. . . The misfortune, which I did not guess when I accepted the invitation, is that I shall lose some of the last days of Milsand, who has been here for the last month: no words can express the love I have for him, you know. He is increasingly precious to me. . . . Waring came back the other day, after thirty years' absence, the same as ever,—nearly. He has been Prime Minister at New Zealand for a year and a half, but gets tired, and returns home with a poem.'*

* 'Ranolf and Amohia'.

This is my last extract from the correspondence with Miss Blagden. Her death closed it altogether within the year.

It is difficult to infer from letters, however intimate, the dominant state of the writer's mind: most of all to do so in Mr. Browning's case, from such passages of his correspondence as circumstances allow me to quote. Letters written in intimacy, and to the same friend, often express a recurrent mood, a revived set of associations, which for the moment destroys the habitual balance of feeling. The same effect is sometimes produced in personal intercourse; and the more varied the life, the more versatile the nature, the more readily in either case will a lately unused spring of emotion well up at the passing touch. We may even fancy we read into the letters of 1870 that eerie, haunting sadness of a cherished memory from which, in spite of ourselves, life is bearing us away. We may also err in so doing. But literary creation, patiently carried on through a given period, is usually a fair reflection of the general moral and mental conditions under which it has taken place; and it would be hard to imagine from Mr. Browning's work during these last ten years that any but gracious influences had been operating upon his genius, any more disturbing element than the sense of privation and loss had entered into his inner life.

Some leaven of bitterness must, nevertheless, have been working within him, or he could never have produced that piece of perplexing cynicism, 'Fifine at the Fair'—the poem referred to as in progress in a letter to Miss Blagden, and which appeared in the spring of 1872. The disturbing cause had been also of long standing; for the deeper reactive processes of Mr. Browning's nature were as slow as its more superficial response was swift; and while 'Dramatis Personae', 'The Ring and the Book', and even 'Balaustion's Adventure', represented the gradually perfected substance of his poetic imagination, 'Fifine at the Fair' was as the froth thrown up by it during the prolonged simmering which was to leave it clear. The work displays the iridescent brightness as well as the occasional impurity of this froth-like character. Beauty and ugliness are, indeed, almost inseparable in the moral impression which it leaves upon us. The author has put forth a plea for self-indulgence with a much slighter attempt at dramatic disguise than his special pleadings generally assume; and while allowing circumstances to expose the sophistry of the position, and punish its attendant act, he does not sufficiently condemn it. But, in identifying himself for the moment with the conception of a Don Juan, he has infused into it a tenderness and a poetry with which the true type had very little in common, and which retard its dramatic development. Those who knew Mr. Browning, or who thoroughly know his work, may censure, regret, fail to understand 'Fifine at the Fair'; they will never in any important sense misconstrue it.

But it has been so misconstrued by an intelligent and not unsympathetic critic; and his construction may be endorsed by other persons in the present, and still more in the future, in whom the elements of a truer judgment are wanting. It seems, therefore, best to protest at once against the misjudgment, though in so doing I am claiming for it an attention which it may not seem to deserve. I allude to Mr. Mortimer's 'Note on Browning' in the 'Scottish Art Review' for December 1889. This note contains a summary of Mr. Browning's teaching, which it resolves into the moral equivalent of the doctrine of the conservation of force. Mr. Mortimer assumes for the purpose of his comparison that the exercise of force means necessarily moving on; and according to him Mr. Browning prescribes action at any price, even that of defying the restrictions of moral law. He thus, we are told, blames the lovers in 'The Statue and the Bust' for their failure to carry out what was an immoral intention; and, in the person of his 'Don Juan', defends a husband's claim to relieve the fixity of conjugal affection by varied adventure in the world of temporary loves: the result being 'the negation of that convention under which we habitually view life, but which for some reason or other breaks down when we have to face the problems of a Goethe, a Shelley, a Byron, or a Browning.'

Mr. Mortimer's generalization does not apply to 'The Statue and the Bust', since Mr. Browning has made it perfectly clear that, in this case, the intended act is postponed without reference to its morality, and simply in consequence of a weakness of will, which would have been as paralyzing to a good purpose as it was to the bad one; but it is not without superficial sanction in 'Fifine at the Fair'; and the part which the author allowed himself to play in it did him an injustice only to be measured by the inference which it has been made to support. There could be no mistake more ludicrous, were it less regrettable, than that of classing Mr. Browning, on moral grounds, with Byron or Shelley; even in the case of Goethe the analogy breaks down. The evidence of the foregoing pages has rendered all protest superfluous. But the suggested moral resemblance to the two English poets receives a striking comment in a fact of Mr. Browning's life which falls practically into the present period of our history: his withdrawal from Shelley of the devotion of more than forty years on account of an act of heartlessness towards his first wife which he held to have been proved against him.

The sweet and the bitter lay, indeed, very close to each other at the sources of Mr. Browning's inspiration. Both proceeded, in great measure, from his spiritual allegiance to the past—that past by which it was impossible that he should linger, but which he could not yet leave behind. The present came to him with friendly greeting. He was unconsciously, perhaps inevitably, unjust to what it brought. The injustice reacted upon himself, and developed by degrees into the cynical mood of fancy which became manifest in 'Fifine at the Fair'.

It is true that, in the light of this explanation, we see an effect very unlike its cause; but the chemistry of human emotion is like that of natural life. It will often form a compound in which neither of its constituents can be recognized. This perverse poem was the last as well as the first manifestation of an ungenial mood of Mr. Browning's mind. A slight exception may be made for some passages in 'Red Cotton Nightcap Country', and for one of the poems of the 'Pacchiarotto' volume; but otherwise no sign of moral or mental disturbance betrays itself in his subsequent work. The past and the present gradually assumed for him a more just relation to each other. He learned to meet life as it offered itself to him with a more frank recognition of its good gifts, a more grateful response to them. He grew happier, hence more genial, as the years advanced.

It was not without misgiving that Mr. Browning published 'Fifine at the Fair'; but many years were to pass before he realized the kind of criticism to which it had exposed him. The belief conveyed in the letter to Miss Blagden that what proceeds from a genuine inspiration is justified by it, combined with the indifference to public opinion which had been engendered in him by its long neglect, made him slow to anticipate the results of external judgment, even where he was in some degree prepared to endorse them. For his value as a poet, it was best so.

The August of 1872 and of 1873 again found him with his sister at St.-Aubin, and the earlier visit was an important one: since it supplied him with the materials of his next work, of which Miss Annie Thackeray, there also for a few days, suggested the title. The tragic drama which forms the subject of Mr. Browning's poem had been in great part enacted in the vicinity of St.-Aubin; and the case of disputed inheritance to which it had given rise was pending at that moment in the tribunals of Caen. The prevailing impression left on Miss Thackeray's mind by this primitive district was, she declared, that of white cotton nightcaps the habitual headgear of the Normandy peasants. She engaged to write a story called 'White Cotton Nightcap Country'; and Mr. Browning's quick sense of both contrast and analogy inspired the introduction of this emblem of repose into his own picture of that peaceful, prosaic existence, and of the ghastly spiritual conflict to which it had served as background. He employed a good deal of perhaps strained ingenuity in the opening pages of the work, in making the white cap foreshadow the red, itself the symbol of liberty, and only indirectly connected with tragic events; and he would, I think, have emphasized the irony of circumstance in a manner more characteristic of himself, if he had laid his stress on the remoteness from 'the madding crowd', and repeated Miss Thackeray's title. There can, however, be no doubt that his poetic imagination, no less than his human insight, was amply vindicated by his treatment of the story.

On leaving St.-Aubin he spent a month at Fontainebleau, in a house situated on the outskirts of the forest; and here his principal indoor occupation was reading the Greek dramatists, especially Aeschylus, to whom he had returned with revived interest and curiosity. 'Red Cotton Nightcap Country' was not begun till his return to London in the later autumn. It was published in the early summer of 1873.

Chapter 17

1873-1878

London Life—Love of Music—Miss Egerton-Smith—Periodical Nervous Exhaustion—Mers; 'Aristophanes' Apology'—'Agamemnon'—'The Inn Album'—'Pacchiarotto and other Poems'—Visits to Oxford and Cambridge—Letters to Mrs. Fitz-Gerald—St. Andrews; Letter from Professor Knight—In the Savoyard Mountains—Death of Miss Egerton-Smith—'La Saisiaz'; 'The Two Poets of Croisic'—Selections from his Works.

The period on which we have now entered, covering roughly the ten or twelve years which followed the publication of 'The Ring and the Book', was the fullest in Mr. Browning's life; it was that in which the varied claims made by it on his moral, and above all his physical energies, found in him the fullest power of response. He could rise early and go to bed late—this, however, never from choice; and occupy every hour of the day with work or pleasure, in a manner which his friends recalled regretfully in later years, when of two or three engagements which ought to have divided his afternoon, a single one—perhaps only the most formally pressing—could be fulfilled. Soon after his final return to England, while he still lived in comparative seclusion, certain habits of friendly intercourse, often superficial, but always binding, had rooted themselves in his life. London society, as I have also implied, opened itself to him in ever-widening circles, or, as it would be truer to say, drew him more and more deeply into its whirl; and even before the mellowing kindness of his nature had infused warmth into the least substantial of his social relations, the imaginative curiosity of the poet—for a while the natural ambition of the man—found satisfaction in it. For a short time, indeed, he entered into the fashionable routine of country-house visiting. Besides the instances I have already given, and many others which I may have forgotten, he was heard of, during the earlier part of this decade, as the guest of Lord Carnarvon at Highclere Castle, of Lord Shrewsbury at Alton Towers, of Lord Brownlow and his mother, Lady Marian Alford, at Belton and Ashridge. Somewhat later, he stayed with Mr. and Lady Alice Gaisford at a house they temporarily occupied on the Sussex downs; with Mr. Cholmondeley at Condover, and, much more recently, at Aynhoe Park with Mr. and Mrs. Cartwright. Kind and pressing, and in themselves very tempting invitations of this nature came to him until the end of his life; but he very soon made a practice of declining them, because their acceptance could only renew for him the fatigues of the London season, while the tantalizing beauty and repose of the country lay before his eyes; but such visits, while they continued, were one of the necessary social experiences which brought their grist to his mill.

And now, in addition to the large social tribute which he received, and had to pay, he was drinking in all the enjoyment, and incurring all the fatigue which the London musical world could create for him. In Italy he had found the natural home of the other arts. The one poem, 'Old Pictures in Florence', is sufficiently eloquent of long communion with the old masters and their works; and if his history in Florence and Rome had been written in his own letters instead of those of his wife, they must have held many reminiscences of galleries and studios, and of the places in which pictures are bought and sold. But his love for music was as certainly starved as the delight in painting and sculpture was nourished; and it had now grown into a passion, from the indulgence of which he derived, as he always declared, some of the most beneficent influences of his life. It would be scarcely an exaggeration to say that he attended every important concert of the season, whether isolated or given in a course. There was no engagement possible or actual, which did not yield to the discovery of its clashing with the day and hour fixed for one of these. His frequent companion on such occasions was Miss Egerton-Smith.

Miss Smith became only known to Mr. Browning's general acquaintance through the dedicatory 'A. E. S.' of 'La Saisiaz'; but she was, at the time of her death, one of his oldest women friends. He first met her as a young woman in Florence when she was visiting there; and the love for and proficiency in music soon asserted itself as a bond of sympathy between them. They did not, however, see much of each other till he had finally left Italy, and she also had made her home in London. She there led a secluded life, although free from family ties, and enjoying a large income derived from the ownership of an important provincial paper. Mr. Browning was one of the very few persons whose society she cared to cultivate; and for many years the common musical interest took the practical, and for both of them convenient form, of their going to concerts together. After her death, in the autumn of 1877, he almost mechanically renounced all the musical entertainments to which she had so regularly accompanied him. The special motive and special facility were gone—she had been wont to call for him in her carriage; the habit was broken; there would have been first pain, and afterwards an unwelcome exertion in renewing it. Time was also beginning to sap his strength, while society, and perhaps friendship, were making increasing claims upon it. It may have been for this same reason that music after a time seemed to pass out of his life altogether. Yet its almost sudden eclipse was striking in the case of one who not only had been so deeply susceptible to its emotional influences, so conversant with its scientific construction and its multitudinous forms, but who was acknowledged as 'musical' by those who best knew the subtle and complex meaning of that often misused term.

Mr. Browning could do all that I have said during the period through which we are now following him; but he could not quite do it with impunity. Each winter brought its searching attack of cold and cough; each summer reduced him to the state of nervous prostration or physical apathy of which I have already spoken, and which at once rendered change imperative, and the exertion of seeking it almost intolerable. His health and spirits rebounded at the first draught of foreign air; the first breath from an English cliff or moor might have had the same result. But the remembrance of this fact never nerved him to the preliminary effort. The conviction renewed itself with the close of every season, that the best thing which could happen to him would be to be left quiet at home; and his disinclination to face even the idea of moving equally hampered his sister in her endeavour to make timely arrangements for their change of abode.

This special craving for rest helped to limit the area from which their summer resort could be chosen. It precluded all idea of 'pension'-life, hence of any much-frequented spot in Switzerland or Germany. It was tacitly understood that the shortening days were not to be passed in England. Italy did not yet associate itself with the possibilities of a moderately short absence; the resources of the northern French coast were becoming exhausted; and as the August of 1874 approached, the question of how and where this and the following months were to be spent was, perhaps, more than ever a perplexing one. It was now Miss Smith who became the means of its solution. She had more than once joined Mr. and Miss Browning at the seaside. She was anxious this year to do so again, and she suggested for their meeting a quiet spot called Mers, almost adjoining the fashionable Treport, but distinct from it. It was agreed that they should try it; and the experiment, which they had no reason to regret, opened also in some degree a way out of future difficulties. Mers was young, and had the defect of its quality. Only one desirable house was to be found there; and the plan of joint residence became converted into one of joint housekeeping, in which Mr. and Miss Browning at first refused to concur, but which worked so well that it was renewed in the three ensuing summers: Miss Smith retaining the initiative in the choice of place, her friends the right of veto upon it. They stayed again together in 1875 at Villers, on the coast of Normandy; in 1876 at the Isle of Arran; in 1877 at a house called La Saisiaz—Savoyard for the sun—in the Saleve district near Geneva.

The autumn months of 1874 were marked for Mr. Browning by an important piece of work: the production of 'Aristophanes' Apology'. It was far advanced when he returned to London in November, after a visit to Antwerp, where his son was studying art under M. Heyermans; and its much later appearance must have been intended to give breathing time to the readers of 'Red Cotton Nightcap Country'. Mr. Browning subsequently admitted that he sometimes, during these years, allowed active literary occupation to interfere too much with the good which his holiday might have done him; but the temptations to literary activity were this time too great to be withstood. The house occupied by him at Mers Maison Robert was the last of the straggling village, and stood on a rising cliff. In front was the open sea; beyond it a long stretch of down; everywhere comparative solitude. Here, in uninterrupted quiet, and in a room devoted to his use, Mr. Browning would work till the afternoon was advanced, and then set forth on a long walk over the cliffs, often in the face of a wind which, as he wrote of it at the time, he could lean against as if it were a wall. And during this time he was living, not only in his work, but with the man who had inspired it. The image of Aristophanes, in the half-shamed insolence, the disordered majesty, in which he is placed before the reader's mind, was present to him from the first moment in which the Defence was conceived. What was still more interesting, he could see him, hear him, think with him, speak for him, and still inevitably condemn him. No such instance of always ingenious, and sometimes earnest pleading foredoomed to complete discomfiture, occurs in Mr. Browning's works.

To Aristophanes he gave the dramatic sympathy which one lover of life can extend to another, though that other unduly extol its lower forms. To Euripides he brought the palm of the higher truth, to his work the tribute of the more pathetic human emotion. Even these for a moment ministered to the greatness of Aristophanes, in the tear shed by him to the memory of his rival, in the hour of his own triumph; and we may be quite sure that when Mr. Browning depicted that scene, and again when he translated the great tragedian's words, his own eyes were dimmed. Large tears fell from them, and emotion choked his voice, when he first read aloud the transcript of the 'Herakles' to a friend, who was often privileged to hear him.

Mr. Browning's deep feeling for the humanities of Greek literature, and his almost passionate love for the language, contrasted strongly with his refusal to regard even the first of Greek writers as models of literary style. The pretensions raised for them on this ground were inconceivable to him; and his translation of the 'Agamemnon', published 1877, was partly made, I am convinced, for the pleasure of exposing these claims, and of rebuking them. His preface to the transcript gives evidence of this. The glee with which he pointed to it when it first appeared was no less significant.

At Villers, in 1875, he only corrected the proofs of 'The Inn Album' for publication in November. When the party started for the Isle of Arran, in the autumn of 1876, the 'Pacchiarotto' volume had already appeared.

When Mr. Browning discontinued his short-lived habit of visiting away from home, he made an exception in favour of the Universities. His occasional visits to Oxford and Cambridge were maintained till the very end of his life, with increasing frequency in the former case; and the days spent at Balliol and Trinity afforded him as unmixed a pleasure as was compatible with the interruption of his daily habits, and with a system of hospitality which would detain him for many hours at table. A vivid picture of them is given in two letters, dated January 20 and March 10, 1877, and addressed to one of his constant correspondents, Mrs. Fitz-Gerald, of Shalstone Manor, Buckingham.

Dear Friend, I have your letter of yesterday, and thank you all I can for its goodness and graciousness to me unworthy . . . I returned on Thursday—the hospitality of our Master being not easy to set aside. But to begin with the beginning: the passage from London to Oxford was exceptionally prosperous—the train was full of men my friends. I was welcomed on arriving by a Fellow who installed me in my rooms,—then came the pleasant meeting with Jowett who at once took me to tea with his other guests, the Archbishop of Canterbury, Bishop of London, Dean of Westminster, the Airlies, Cardwells, male and female. Then came the banquet—I enclose you the plan having no doubt that you will recognise the name of many an acquaintance: please return it—and, the dinner done, speechifying set in vigorously. The Archbishop proposed the standing 'Floreat domus de Balliolo'—to which the Master made due and amusing answer, himself giving the health of the Primate. Lord Coleridge, in a silvery speech, drank to the University, responded to by the Vice-Chancellor. I forget who proposed the visitors—the Bishop of London, perhaps Lord Cardwell. Professor Smith gave the two Houses of Parliament,—Jowett, the Clergy, coupling with it the name of your friend Mr. Rogers—on whom he showered every kind of praise, and Mr. Rogers returned thanks very characteristically and pleasantly. Lord Lansdowne drank to the Bar Mr. Bowen, Lord Camperdown to—I really forget what: Mr. Green to Literature and Science delivering a most undeserved eulogium on myself, with a more rightly directed one on Arnold, Swinburne, and the old pride of Balliol, Clough: this was cleverly and almost touchingly answered by dear Mat Arnold. Then the Dean of Westminster gave the Fellows and Scholars—and then—twelve o'clock struck. We were, counting from the time of preliminary assemblage, six hours and a half engaged: *fully* five and a half nailed to our chairs at the table: but the whole thing was brilliant, genial, and suggestive of many and various thoughts to me—and there was a warmth, earnestness, and yet refinement about it which I never experienced in any previous public dinner. Next morning I breakfasted with Jowett and his guests, found that return would be difficult: while as the young men were to return on Friday there would be no opposition to my departure on Thursday. The morning was dismal with rain, but after luncheon there was a chance of getting a little air, and I walked for more than two hours, then heard service in New Coll.—then dinner again: my room had been prepared in the Master's house. So, on Thursday, after yet another breakfast, I left by the noon-day train, after all sorts of kindly offices from the Master. . . . No reporters were suffered to be present—the account in yesterday's Times was furnished by one or more of the guests; it is quite correct as far as it goes. There were, I find, certain little paragraphs which must have been furnished by 'guessers': Swinburne, set down as present—was absent through his Father's illness: the Cardinal also excused himself as did the Bishop of Salisbury and others. . . . Ever yours R. Browning.

The second letter, from Cambridge, was short and written in haste, at the moment of Mr. Browning's departure; but it tells the same tale of general kindness and attention. Engagements for no less than six meals had absorbed the first day of the visit. The occasion was that of Professor Joachim's investiture with his Doctor's degree; and Mr. Browning declares that this ceremony, the concert given by the great violinist, and his society, were 'each and all' worth the trouble of the journey. He himself was to receive the Cambridge degree of LL.D. in 1879, the Oxford D.C.L. in 1882. A passage in another letter addressed to the same friend, refers probably to a practical reminiscence of 'Red Cotton Nightcap Country', which enlivened the latter experience, and which Mrs. Fitz-Gerald had witnessed with disapprobation.*

* An actual red cotton nightcap had been made to flutter down on to the Poet's head.

. . . You are far too hard on the very harmless drolleries of the young men, licensed as they are moreover by immemorial usage. Indeed there used to be a regularly appointed jester, 'Filius Terrae' he was called, whose business it was to jibe and jeer at the honoured ones, by way of reminder that all human glories are merely gilded bubbles and must not be fancied metal. You saw that the Reverend Dons escaped no more than the poor Poet—or rather I should say than myself the poor Poet—for I was pleased to observe with what attention they listened to the Newdigate. . . . Ever affectionately yours, R. Browning.

In 1875 he was unanimously nominated by its Independent Club, to the office of Lord Rector of the University of Glasgow; and in 1877 he again received the offer of the Rectorship of St. Andrews, couched in very urgent and flattering terms. A letter addressed to him from this University by Dr. William Knight, Professor of Moral Philosophy there, which I have his permission to publish, bears witness to what had long been and was always to remain a prominent fact of Mr. Browning's literary career: his great influence on the minds of the rising generation of his countrymen.

The University, St. Andrews N.B.: Nov. 17, 1877.

My dear Sir,—. . . The students of this University, in which I have the honour to hold office, have nominated you as their Lord Rector; and intend unanimously, I am told, to elect you to that office on Thursday.

I believe that hitherto no Rector has been chosen by the undivided suffrage of any Scottish University. They have heard however that you are unable to accept the office: and your committee, who were deeply disappointed to learn this afternoon of the way in which you have been informed of their intentions, are, I believe, writing to you on the subject. So keen is their regret that they intend respectfully to wait upon you on Tuesday morning by deputation, and ask if you cannot waive your difficulties in deference to their enthusiasm, and allow them to proceed with your election.

Their suffrage may, I think, be regarded as one sign of how the thoughtful youth of Scotland estimate the work you have done in the world of letters.

And permit me to say that while these Rectorial elections in the other Universities have frequently turned on local questions, or been inspired by political partisanship, St. Andrews has honourably sought to choose men distinguished for literary eminence, and to make the Rectorship a tribute at once of intellectual and moral esteem.

May I add that when the 'perfervidum ingenium' of our northern race takes the form not of youthful hero-worship, but of loyal admiration and respectful homage, it is a very genuine affair. In the present instance I may say it is no mere outburst of young undisciplined enthusiasm, but an honest expression of intellectual and moral indebtedness, the genuine and distinct tribute of many minds that have been touched to some higher issues by what you have taught them. They do not presume to speak of your place in English literature. They merely tell you by this proffered honour the highest in their power to bestow, how they have felt your influence over them.

My own obligations to you, and to the author of Aurora Leigh, are such, that of them 'silence is golden'. Yours ever gratefully. William Knight.

Mr. Browning was deeply touched and gratified by these professions of esteem. He persisted nevertheless in his refusal. The Glasgow nomination had also been declined by him.

On August 17, 1877, he wrote to Mrs. Fitz-Gerald from La Saisiaz:

'How lovely is this place in its solitude and seclusion, with its trees and shrubs and flowers, and above all its live mountain stream which supplies three fountains, and two delightful baths, a marvel of delicate delight framed in with trees—I bathe there twice a day—and then what wonderful views from the chalet on every side! Geneva lying under us, with the lake and the whole plain bounded by the Jura and our own Saleve, which latter seems rather close behind our house, and yet takes a hard hour and a half to ascend—all this you can imagine since you know the environs of the town; the peace and quiet move me the most—And I fancy I shall drowse out the two months or more, doing no more of serious work than reading—and that is virtuous renunciation of the glorious view to my right here—as I sit aerially like Euripides, and see the clouds come and go and the view change in correspondence with them. It will help me to get rid of the pain which attaches itself to the recollections of Lucerne and Berne "in the old days when the Greeks suffered so much," as Homer says. But a very real and sharp pain touched me here when I heard of the death of poor Virginia March whom I knew particularly, and parted with hardly a fortnight ago, leaving her affectionate and happy as ever. The tones of her voice as on one memorable occasion she ejaculated repeatedly 'Good friend!' are fresh still. Poor Virginia! . . .'

Mr. Browning was more than quiescent during this stay in the Savoyard mountains. He was unusually depressed, and unusually disposed to regard the absence from home as a banishment; and he tried subsequently to account for this condition by the shadow which coming trouble sometimes casts before it. It was more probably due to the want of the sea air which he had enjoyed for so many years, and to that special oppressive heat of the Swiss valleys which ascends with them to almost their highest level. When he said that the Saleve seemed close behind the house, he was saying in other words that the sun beat back from, and the air was intercepted by it. We see, nevertheless, in his description of the surrounding scenery, a promise of the contemplative delight in natural beauty to be henceforth so conspicuous in his experience, and which seemed a new feature in it. He had hitherto approached every living thing with curious and sympathetic observation—this hardly requires saying of one who had animals for his first and always familiar friends. Flowers also attracted him by their perfume. But what he loved in nature was essentially its prefiguring of human existence, or its echo of it; and it never appeared, in either his works or his conversation, that he was much impressed by its inanimate forms—by even those larger phenomena of mountain and cloud-land on which the latter dwells. Such beauty as most appealed to him he had left behind with the joys and sorrows of his Italian life, and it had almost inevitably passed out of his consideration. During years of his residence in London he never thought of the country as a source of pleasurable emotions, other than those contingent on renewed health; and the places to which he resorted had often not much beyond their health-giving qualities to recommend them; his appetite for the beautiful had probably dwindled for lack of food. But when a friend once said to him: 'You have not a great love for nature, have you?' he had replied: 'Yes, I have, but I love men and women better;' and the admission, which conveyed more than it literally expressed, would have been true I believe at any, up to the present, period of his history. Even now he did not cease to love men and women best; but he found increasing enjoyment in the beauties of nature, above all as they opened upon him on the southern slopes of the Alps; and the delight of the aesthetic sense merged gradually in the satisfied craving for pure air and brilliant sunshine which marked his final struggle for physical life. A ring of enthusiasm comes into his letters from the mountains, and deepens as the years advance; doubtless enhanced by the great—perhaps too great—exhilaration which the Alpine atmosphere produced, but also in large measure independent of it. Each new place into which the summer carries him he declares more beautiful than the last. It possibly was so.

A touch of autumnal freshness had barely crept into the atmosphere of the Saleve, when a moral thunderbolt fell on the little group of persons domiciled at its base: Miss Egerton-Smith died, in what had seemed for her unusually good health, in the act of preparing for a mountain excursion with her friends—the words still almost on her lips in which she had given some directions for their comfort. Mr. Browning's impressionable nervous system was for a moment paralyzed by the shock. It revived in all the emotional and intellectual impulses which gave birth to 'La Saisiaz'.

This poem contains, besides its personal reference and association, elements of distinctive biographical interest. It is the author's first—as also last—attempt to reconstruct his hope of immortality by a rational process based entirely on the fundamental facts of his own knowledge and consciousness—God and the human soul; and while the very assumption of these facts, as basis for reasoning, places him at issue with scientific thought, there is in his way of handling them a tribute to the scientific spirit, perhaps foreshadowed in the beautiful epilogue to 'Dramatis Personae', but of which there is no trace in his earlier religious works. It is conclusive both in form and matter as to his heterodox attitude towards Christianity. He was no less, in his way, a Christian when he wrote 'La Saisiaz' than when he published 'A Death in the Desert' and 'Christmas Eve and Easter Day'; or at any period subsequent to that in which he accepted without questioning what he had learned at his mother's knee. He has repeatedly written or declared in the words of Charles Lamb:* 'If Christ entered the room I should fall on my knees;' and again, in those of Napoleon: 'I am an understander of men, and *he* was no man.' He has even added: 'If he had been, he would have been an impostor.' But the arguments, in great part negative, set forth in 'La Saisiaz' for the immortality of the soul, leave no place for the idea, however indefinite, of a Christian revelation on the subject. Christ remained for Mr. Browning a mystery and a message of Divine Love, but no messenger of Divine intention towards mankind.

* These words have more significance when taken with their context. 'If Shakespeare was to come into the room, we should all rise up to meet him; but if that Person [meaning Christ] was to come into the room, we should all fall down and try to kiss the hem of his garment.'

The dialogue between Fancy and Reason is not only an admission of uncertainty as to the future of the Soul: it is a plea for it; and as such it gathers up into its few words of direct statement, threads of reasoning which have been traceable throughout Mr. Browning's work. In this plea for uncertainty lies also a full and frank acknowledgment of the value of the earthly life; and as interpreted by his general views, that value asserts itself, not only in the means of probation which life affords, but in its existing conditions of happiness. No one, he declares, possessing the certainty of a future state would patiently and fully live out the present; and since the future can be only the ripened fruit of the present, its promise would be neutralized, as well as actual experience dwarfed, by a definite revelation. Nor, conversely, need the want of a certified future depress the present spiritual and moral life. It is in the nature of the Soul that it would suffer from the promise. The existence of God is a justification for hope. And since the certainty would be injurious to the Soul, hence destructive to itself, the doubt—in other words, the hope—becomes a sufficient approach to, a working substitute for it. It is pathetic to see how in spite of the convictions thus rooted in Mr. Browning's mind, the expressed craving for more knowledge, for more light, will now and then escape him.

Even orthodox Christianity gives no assurance of reunion to those whom death has separated. It is obvious that Mr. Browning's poetic creed could hold no conviction regarding it. He hoped for such reunion in proportion as he wished. There must have been moments in his life when the wish in its passion overleapt the bounds of hope. 'Prospice' appears to prove this. But the wide range of imagination, no less than the lack of knowledge, forbade in him any forecast of the possibilities of the life to come. He believed that if granted, it would be an advance on the present—an accession of knowledge if not an increase of happiness. He was satisfied that whatever it gave, and whatever it withheld, it would be good. In his normal condition this sufficed to him.

'La Saisiaz' appeared in the early summer of 1878, and with it 'The Two Poets of Croisic', which had been written immediately after it. The various incidents of this poem are strictly historical; they lead the way to a characteristic utterance of Mr. Browning's philosophy of life to which I shall recur later.

In 1872 Mr. Browning had published a first series of selections from his works; it was to be followed by a second in 1880. In a preface to the earlier volume, he indicates the plan which he has followed in the choice and arrangement of poems; and some such intention runs also through the second; since he declined a suggestion made to him for the introduction or placing of a special poem, on the ground of its not conforming to the end he had in view. It is difficult, in the one case as in the other, to reconstruct the imagined personality to which his preface refers; and his words on the later occasion pointed rather to that idea of a chord of feeling which is raised by the correspondence of the first and last poems of the respective groups. But either clue may be followed with interest.

Chapter 18

1878-1884

He revisits Italy; Asolo; Letters to Mrs. Fitz-Gerald—Venice—Favourite Alpine Retreats—Mrs. Arthur Bronson—Life in Venice—A Tragedy at Saint-Pierre—Mr. Cholmondeley—Mr. Browning's Patriotic Feeling; Extract from Letter to Mrs. Charles Skirrow—'Dramatic Idyls'—'Jocoseria'—'Ferishtah's Fancies'.

The catastrophe of La Saisiaz closed a comprehensive chapter in Mr. Browning's habits and experience. It impelled him finally to break with the associations of the last seventeen autumns, which he remembered more in their tedious or painful circumstances than in the unexciting pleasure and renewed physical health which he had derived from them. He was weary of the ever-recurring effort to uproot himself from his home life, only to become stationary in some more or less uninteresting northern spot. The always latent desire for Italy sprang up in him, and with it the often present thought and wish to give his sister the opportunity of seeing it.

Florence and Rome were not included in his scheme; he knew them both too well; but he hankered for Asolo and Venice. He determined, though as usual reluctantly, and not till the last moment, that they should move southwards in the August of 1878. Their route lay over the Spluegen; and having heard of a comfortable hotel near the summit of the Pass, they agreed to remain there till the heat had sufficiently abated to allow of the descent into Lombardy. The advantages of this first arrangement exceeded their expectations. It gave them solitude without the sense of loneliness. A little stream of travellers passed constantly over the mountain, and they could shake hands with acquaintances at night, and know them gone in the morning. They dined at the table d'hote, but took all other meals alone, and slept in a detached wing or 'dependance' of the hotel. Their daily walks sometimes carried them down to the Via Mala; often to the top of the ascent, where they could rest, looking down into Italy; and would even be prolonged over a period of five hours and an extent of seventeen miles. Now, as always, the mountain air stimulated Mr. Browning's physical energy; and on this occasion it also especially quickened his imaginative powers. He was preparing the first series of 'Dramatic Idylls'; and several of these, including 'Ivan Ivanovitch', were produced with such rapidity that Miss Browning refused to countenance a prolonged stay on the mountain, unless he worked at a more reasonable rate.

They did not linger on their way to Asolo and Venice, except for a night's rest on the Lake of Como and two days at Verona. In their successive journeys through Northern Italy they visited by degrees all its notable cities, and it would be easy to recall, in order and detail, most of these yearly expeditions. But the account of them would chiefly resolve itself into a list of names and dates; for Mr. Browning had seldom a new impression to receive, even from localities which he had not seen before. I know that he and his sister were deeply struck by the deserted grandeurs of Ravenna; and that it stirred in both of them a memorable sensation to wander as they did for a whole day through the pinewoods consecrated by Dante. I am nevertheless not sure that when they performed the repeated round of picture-galleries and palaces, they were not sometimes simply paying their debt to opportunity, and as much for each other's sake as for their own. Where all was Italy, there was little to gain or lose in one memorial of greatness, one object of beauty, visited or left unseen. But in Asolo, even in Venice, Mr. Browning was seeking something more: the remembrance of his own actual and poetic youth. How far he found it in the former place we may infer from a letter to Mrs. Fitz-Gerald.

Sept. 28, 1878.

And from 'Asolo', at last, dear friend! So can dreams come *false*.—S., who has been writing at the opposite side of the table, has told you about our journey and adventures, such as they were: but she cannot tell you the feelings with which I revisit this—to me—memorable place after above forty years' absence,—such things have begun and ended with me in the interval! It was *too* strange when we reached the ruined tower on the hill-top yesterday, and I said 'Let me try if the echo still exists which I discovered here,' you can produce it from only *one* particular spot on a remainder of brickwork— and thereupon it answered me plainly as ever, after all the silence: for some children from the adjoining 'podere', happening to be outside, heard my voice and its result—and began trying to perform the feat—calling 'Yes, yes'—all in vain: so, perhaps, the mighty secret will die with me! We shall probably stay here a day or two longer,—the air is so pure, the country so attractive: but we must go soon to Venice, stay our allotted time there, and then go homeward: you will of course address letters to Venice, not this place: it is a pleasure I promise myself that, on arriving I shall certainly hear you speak in a letter which I count upon finding.

The old inn here, to which I would fain have betaken myself, is gone—levelled to the ground: I remember it was much damaged by a recent earthquake, and the cracks and chasms may have threatened a downfall. This Stella d'Oro is, however, much such an unperverted 'locanda' as its predecessor—primitive indeed are the arrangements and unsophisticate the ways: but there is cleanliness, abundance of goodwill, and the sweet Italian smile at every mistake: we get on excellently.

To be sure never was such a perfect fellow-traveller, for my purposes, as S., so that I have no subject of concern—if things suit me they suit her—and vice-versa. I daresay she will have told you how we trudged together, this morning to Possagno—through a lovely country: how we saw all the wonders—and a wonder of detestability is the paint-performance of the great man!—and how, on our return, we found the little town enjoying high market day, and its privilege of roaring and screaming over a bargain. It confuses me altogether,—but at Venice I may write more comfortably. You will till then, Dear Friend, remember me ever as yours affectionately, Robert Browning.

If the tone of this does not express disappointment, it has none of the rapture which his last visit was to inspire. The charm which forty years of remembrance had cast around the little city on the hill was dispelled for, at all events, the time being. The hot weather and dust-covered landscape, with the more than primitive accommodation of which he spoke in a letter to another friend, may have contributed something to this result.

At Venice the travellers fared better in some essential respects. A London acquaintance, who passed them on their way to Italy, had recommended a cool and quiet hotel there, the Albergo dell' Universo. The house, Palazzo Brandolin-Rota, was situated on the shady side of the Grand Canal, just below the Accademia and the Suspension Bridge. The open stretches of the Giudecca lay not far behind; and a scrap of garden and a clean and open little street made pleasant the approach from back and side. It accommodated few persons in proportion to its size, and fewer still took up their abode there; for it was managed by a lady of good birth and fallen fortunes whose home and patrimony it had been; and her husband, a retired Austrian officer, and two grown-up daughters did not lighten her task. Every year the fortunes sank lower; the upper storey of the house was already falling into decay, and the fine old furniture passing into the brokers' or private buyers' hands. It still, however, afforded sufficiently comfortable, and, by reason of its very drawbacks, desirable quarters to Mr. Browning. It perhaps turned the scale in favour of his return to Venice; for the lady whose hospitality he was to enjoy there was as yet unknown to him; and nothing would have induced him to enter, with his eyes open, one of the English-haunted hotels, in which acquaintance, old and new, would daily greet him in the public rooms or jostle him in the corridors.

He and his sister remained at the Universo for a fortnight; their programme did not this year include a longer stay; but it gave them time to decide that no place could better suit them for an autumn holiday than Venice, or better lend itself to a preparatory sojourn among the Alps; and the plan of their next, and, though they did not know it, many a following summer, was thus sketched out before the homeward journey had begun.

Mr. Browning did not forget his work, even while resting from it; if indeed he did rest entirely on this occasion. He consulted a Russian lady whom he met at the hotel, on the names he was introducing in 'Ivan Ivanovitch'. It would be interesting to know what suggestions or corrections she made, and how far they adapted themselves to the rhythm already established, or compelled changes in it; but the one alternative would as little have troubled him as the other. Mrs. Browning told Mr. Prinsep that her husband could never alter the wording of a poem without rewriting it, indeed, practically converting it into another; though he more than once tried to do so at her instigation. But to the end of his life he could at any moment recast a line or passage for the sake of greater correctness, and leave all that was essential in it untouched.

Seven times more in the eleven years which remained to him, Mr. Browning spent the autumn in Venice. Once also, in 1882, he had proceeded towards it as far as Verona, when the floods which marked the autumn of that year arrested his farther course. Each time he had halted first in some more or less elevated spot, generally suggested by his French friend, Monsieur Dourlans, himself an inveterate wanderer, whose inclinations also tempted him off the beaten track. The places he most enjoyed were Saint-Pierre la Chartreuse, and Gressoney Saint-Jean, where he stayed respectively in 1881 and 1882, 1883 and 1885. Both of these had the drawbacks, and what might easily have been the dangers, of remoteness from the civilized world. But this weighed with him so little, that he remained there in each case till the weather had broken, though there was no sheltered conveyance in which he and his sister could travel down; and on the later occasions at least, circumstances might easily have combined to prevent their departure for an indefinite time. He became, indeed, so attached to Gressoney, with its beautiful outlook upon Monte Rosa, that nothing I believe would have hindered his returning, or at least contemplating a return to it, but the great fatigue to his sister of the mule ride up the mountain, by a path which made walking, wherever possible, the easier course. They did walk *down* it in the early October of 1885, and completed the hard seven hours' trudge to San Martino d'Aosta, without an atom of refreshment or a minute's rest.

One of the great attractions of Saint-Pierre was the vicinity of the Grande Chartreuse, to which Mr. Browning made frequent expeditions, staying there through the night in order to hear the midnight mass. Miss Browning also once attempted the visit, but was not allowed to enter the monastery. She slept in the adjoining convent.

The brother and sister were again at the Universo in 1879, 1880, and 1881; but the crash was rapidly approaching, and soon afterwards it came. The old Palazzo passed into other hands, and after a short period of private ownership was consigned to the purposes of an Art Gallery.

In 1880, however, they had been introduced by Mrs. Story to an American resident, Mrs. Arthur Bronson, and entered into most friendly relations with her; and when, after a year's interval, they were again contemplating an autumn in

Venice, she placed at their disposal a suite of rooms in the Palazzo Giustiniani Recanati, which formed a supplement to her own house—making the offer with a kindly urgency which forbade all thought of declining it. They inhabited these for a second time in 1885, keeping house for themselves in the simple but comfortable foreign manner they both so well enjoyed, only dining and spending the evening with their friend. But when, in 1888, they were going, as they thought, to repeat the arrangement, they found, to their surprise, a little apartment prepared for them under Mrs. Bronson's own roof. This act of hospitality involved a special kindness on her part, of which Mr. Browning only became aware at the close of a prolonged stay; and a sense of increased gratitude added itself to the affectionate regard with which his hostess had already inspired both his sister and him. So far as he is concerned, the fact need only be indicated. It is fully expressed in the preface to 'Asolando'.

During the first and fresher period of Mr. Browning's visits to Venice, he found a passing attraction in its society. It held an historical element which harmonized well with the decayed magnificence of the city, its old-world repose, and the comparatively simple modes of intercourse still prevailing there. Mrs. Bronson's 'salon' was hospitably open whenever her health allowed; but her natural refinement, and the conservatism which so strongly marks the higher class of Americans, preserved it from the heterogeneous character which Anglo-foreign sociability so often assumes. Very interesting, even important names lent their prestige to her circle; and those of Don Carlos and his family, of Prince and Princess Iturbide, of Prince and Princess Metternich, and of Princess Montenegro, were on the list of her 'habitues', and, in the case of the royal Spaniards, of her friends. It need hardly be said that the great English poet, with his fast spreading reputation and his infinite social charm, was kindly welcomed and warmly appreciated amongst them.

English and American acquaintances also congregated in Venice, or passed through it from London, Florence, and Rome. Those resident in Italy could make their visits coincide with those of Mr. Browning and his sister, or undertake the journey for the sake of seeing them; while the outward conditions of life were such as to render friendly intercourse more satisfactory, and common social civilities less irksome than they could be at home. Mr. Browning was, however, already too advanced in years, too familiar with everything which the world can give, to be long affected by the novelty of these experiences. It was inevitable that the need of rest, though often for the moment forgotten, should assert itself more and more. He gradually declined on the society of a small number of resident or semi-resident friends; and, due exception being made for the hospitalities of his temporary home, became indebted to the kindness of Sir Henry and Lady Layard, of Mr. and Mrs. Curtis of Palazzo Barbaro, and of Mr. and Mrs. Frederic Eden, for most of the social pleasure and comfort of his later residences in Venice.

Part of a letter to Mrs. Fitz-Gerald gives an insight into the character of his life there: all the stronger that it was written under a temporary depression which it partly serves to explain.

Albergo dell' Universo, Venezia, Italia: Sept. 24, '81.

'Dear Friend,—On arriving here I found your letter to my great satisfaction—and yesterday brought the 'Saturday Review'—for which, many thanks.

'We left our strange but lovely place on the 18th, reaching Chambery at evening,—stayed the next day there,—walking, among other diversions to "Les Charmettes", the famous abode of Rousseau—kept much as when he left it: I visited it with my wife perhaps twenty-five years ago, and played so much of "Rousseau's Dream" as could be effected on his antique harpsichord: this time I attempted the same feat, but only two notes or thereabouts out of the octave would answer the touch. Next morning we proceeded to Turin, and on Wednesday got here, in the middle of the last night of the Congress Carnival—rowing up the Canal to our Albergo through a dazzling blaze of lights and throng of boats,—there being, if we are told truly, 50,000 strangers in the city. Rooms had been secured for us, however: and the festivities are at an end, to my great joy,—for Venice is resuming its old quiet aspect—the only one I value at all. Our American friends wanted to take us in their gondola to see the principal illuminations *after* the "Serenade", which was not over before midnight—but I was contented with *that*—being tired and indisposed for talking, and, having seen and heard quite enough from our own balcony, went to bed: S. having betaken her to her own room long before.

'Next day we took stock of our acquaintances,—found that the Storys, on whom we had counted for company, were at Vallombrosa, though the two sons have a studio here—other friends are in sufficient number however—and last evening we began our visits by a very classical one—to the Countess Mocenigo, in her palace which Byron occupied: she is a charming widow since two years,—young, pretty and of the prettiest manners: she showed us all the rooms Byron had lived in,—and I wrote my name in her album *on* the desk himself wrote the last canto of 'Ch. Harold' and 'Beppo' upon. There was a small party: we were taken and introduced by the Layards who are kind as ever, and I met old friends—Lord Aberdare, Charles Bowen, and others. While I write comes a deliciously fresh 'bouquet' from Mrs. Bronson, an American lady,—in short we shall find a week or two amusing enough; though—where are the pinewoods, mountains and torrents, and wonderful air? Venice is under a cloud,—dull and threatening,—though we were apprehensive of heat, arriving, as we did, ten days earlier than last year. . . .'

The evening's programme was occasionally varied by a visit to one of the theatres. The plays given were chiefly in the Venetian dialect, and needed previous study for their enjoyment; but Mr. Browning assisted at one musical performance which strongly appealed to his historical and artistic sensibilities: that of the 'Barbiere' of Paisiello in the Rossini theatre and in the presence of Wagner, which took place in the autumn of 1880.

Although the manner of his sojourn in the Italian city placed all the resources of resident life at his command, Mr. Browning never abjured the active habits of the English traveller. He daily walked with his sister, as he did in the mountains, for walking's sake, as well as for the delight of what his expeditions showed him; and the facilities which they supplied for this healthful pleasurable exercise were to his mind one of the great merits of his autumn residences in Italy. He explored Venice in all directions, and learned to know its many points of beauty and interest, as those cannot who believe it is only to be seen from a gondola; and when he had visited its every corner, he fell back on a favourite stroll along the Riva to the public garden and back again; never failing to leave the house at about the same hour of the day. Later still, when a friend's gondola was always at hand, and air and sunshine were the one thing needful, he would be carried to the Lido, and take a long stretch on its farther shore.

The letter to Mrs. Fitz-Gerald, from which I have already quoted, concludes with the account of a tragic occurrence which took place at Saint-Pierre just before his departure, and in which Mr. Browning's intuitions had played a striking part.

'And what do you think befell us in this abode of peace and innocence? Our journey was delayed for three hours in consequence of the one mule of the village being requisitioned by the 'Juge d'Instruction' from Grenoble, come to enquire into a murder committed two days before. My sister and I used once a day to walk for a couple of hours up a mountain-road of the most lovely description, and stop at the summit whence we looked down upon the minute hamlet of St.-Pierre d'Entremont,—even more secluded than our own: then we got back to our own aforesaid. And in this Paradisial place, they found, yesterday week, a murdered man—frightfully mutilated—who had been caught apparently in the act of stealing potatoes in a field: such a crime had never occurred in the memory of the oldest of our folk. Who was the murderer is the mystery—whether the field's owner—in his irritation at discovering the robber,—or one of a band of similar 'charbonniers' for they suppose the man to be a Piedmontese of that occupation remains to be proved: they began by imprisoning the owner, who denies his guilt energetically. Now the odd thing is, that, either the day of, or after the murder,—as I and S. were looking at the utter solitude, I had the fancy "What should I do if I suddenly came upon a dead body in this field? Go and proclaim it—and subject myself to all the vexations inflicted by the French way of procedure which begins by assuming that you may be the criminal—or neglect an obvious duty, and return silently." I, of course, saw that the former was the only proper course, whatever the annoyance involved. And, all the while, there was just about to be the very same incident for the trouble of somebody.'

Here the account breaks off; but writing again from the same place, August 16, 1882, he takes up the suspended narrative with this question:

'Did I tell you of what happened to me on the last day of my stay here last year?' And after repeating the main facts continues as follows:

'This morning, in the course of my walk, I entered into conversation with two persons of whom I made enquiry myself. They said the accused man, a simple person, had been locked up in a high chamber,—protesting his innocence strongly,—and troubled in his mind by the affair altogether and the turn it was taking, had profited by the gendarme's negligence, and thrown himself out of the window—and so died, continuing to the last to protest as before. My presentiment of what such a person might have to undergo was justified you see—though I should not in any case have taken *that* way of getting out of the difficulty. The man added, "it was not he who committed the murder, but the companions of the man, an Italian charcoal-burner, who owed him a grudge, killed him, and dragged him to the field—filling his sack with potatoes as if stolen, to give a likelihood that the field's owner had caught him stealing and killed him,—so M. Perrier the greffier told me." Enough of this grim story.

. . . . .

'My sister was anxious to know exactly where the body was found: "Vouz savez la croix au sommet de la colline? A cette distance de cela!" That is precisely where I was standing when the thought came over me.'

A passage in a subsequent letter of September 3 clearly refers to some comment of Mrs. Fitz-Gerald's on the peculiar nature of this presentiment:

'No—I attribute no sort of supernaturalism to my fancy about the thing that was really about to take place. By a law of the association of ideas—*contraries* come into the mind as often as *similarities*—and the peace and solitude readily called up the notion of what would most jar with them. I have often thought of the trouble that might have befallen me if poor Miss Smith's death had happened the night before, when we were on the mountain alone together—or next morning when we were on the proposed excursion—only *then* we should have had companions.'

The letter then passes to other subjects.

'This is the fifth magnificent day—like magnificence, unfit for turning to much account—for we cannot walk till sunset. I had two hours' walk, or nearly, before breakfast, however: It is the loveliest country I ever had experience of, and we shall prolong our stay perhaps—apart from the concern for poor Cholmondeley and his friends, I should be glad to apprehend no long journey—besides the annoyance of having to pass Florence and Rome unvisited, for S.'s sake, I mean: even Naples would have been with its wonderful environs a tantalizing impracticability.

'Your "Academy" came and was welcomed. The newspaper is like an electric eel, as one touches it and expects a shock. I am very anxious about the Archbishop who has always been strangely kind to me.'

He and his sister had accepted an invitation to spend the month of October with Mr. Cholmondeley at his villa in Ischia; but the party assembled there was broken up by the death of one of Mr. Cholmondeley's guests, a young lady who had imprudently attempted the ascent of a dangerous mountain without a guide, and who lost her life in the experiment.

A short extract from a letter to Mrs. Charles Skirrow will show that even in this complete seclusion Mr. Browning's patriotism did not go to sleep. There had been already sufficient evidence that his friendship did not; but it was not in the nature of his mental activities that they should be largely absorbed by politics, though he followed the course of his country's history as a necessary part of his own life. It needed a crisis like that of our Egyptian campaign, or the subsequent Irish struggle, to arouse him to a full emotional participation in current events. How deeply he could be thus aroused remained yet to be seen.

'If the George Smiths are still with you, give them my love, and tell them we shall expect to see them at Venice,—which was not so likely to be the case when we were bound for Ischia. As for Lady Wolseley—one dares not pretend to vie with her in anxiety just now; but my own pulses beat pretty strongly when I open the day's newspaper—which, by some new arrangement, reaches us, oftener than not, on the day after publication. Where is your Bertie? I had an impassioned letter, a fortnight ago, from a nephew of mine, who is in the second division [battalion?] of the Black Watch; he was ordered to Edinburgh, and the regiment not dispatched, after all,—it having just returned from India; the poor fellow wrote in his despair "to know if I could do anything!" He may be wanted yet: though nothing seems wanted in Egypt, so capital appears to be the management.'

In 1879 Mr. Browning published the first series of his 'Dramatic Idyls'; and their appearance sent a thrill of surprised admiration through the public mind. In 'La Saisiaz' and the accompanying poems he had accomplished what was virtually a life's work. For he was approaching the appointed limit of man's existence; and the poetic, which had been nourished in him by the natural life—which had once outstripped its developments, but on the whole remained subject to them—had therefore, also, passed through the successive phases of individual growth. He had been inspired as dramatic poet by the one avowed conviction that little else is worth study but the history of a soul; and outward act or circumstance had only entered into his creations as condition or incident of the given psychological state. His dramatic imagination had first, however unconsciously, sought its materials in himself; then gradually been projected into the world of men and women, which his widening knowledge laid open to him; it is scarcely necessary to say that its power was only fully revealed when it left the remote regions of poetical and metaphysical self-consciousness, to invoke the not less mysterious and far more searching utterance of the general human heart. It was a matter of course that in this expression of his dramatic genius, the intellectual and emotional should exhibit the varying relations which are developed by the natural life: that feeling should begin by doing the work of thought, as in 'Saul', and thought end by doing the work of feeling, as in 'Fifine at the Fair'; and that the two should alternate or combine in proportioned intensity in such works of an intermediate period as 'Cleon', 'A Death in the Desert', the 'Epistle of Karshish', and 'James Lee's Wife'; the sophistical ingenuities of 'Bishop Blougram', and 'Sludge'; and the sad, appealing tenderness of 'Andrea del Sarto' and 'The Worst of It'.

It was also almost inevitable that so vigorous a genius should sometimes falsify calculations based on the normal life. The long-continued force and freshness of Mr. Browning's general faculties was in itself a protest against them. We saw without surprise that during the decade which produced 'Prince Hohenstiel-Schwangau', 'Fifine at the Fair', and 'Red Cotton Nightcap Country', he could give us 'The Inn Album', with its expression of the higher sexual love unsurpassed, rarely equalled, in the whole range of his work: or those two unique creations of airy fancy and passionate symbolic romance, 'Saint Martin's Summer', and 'Numpholeptos'. It was no ground for astonishment that the creative power in him should even ignore the usual period of decline, and defy, so far as is humanly possible, its natural laws of modification. But in the 'Dramatic Idyls' he did more than proceed with unflagging powers on a long-trodden, distinctive course; he took a new departure.

Mr. Browning did not forsake the drama of motive when he imagined and worked out his new group of poems; he presented it in a no less subtle and complex form. But he gave it the added force of picturesque realization; and this by means of incidents both powerful in themselves, and especially suited for its development. It was only in proportion to this higher suggestiveness that a startling situation ever seemed to him fit subject for poetry. Where its interest and excitement exhausted themselves in the external facts, it became, he thought, the property of the chronicler, but supplied no material for the poet; and he often declined matter which had been offered him for dramatic treatment because it belonged to the more sensational category.

It is part of the vital quality of the 'Dramatic Idyls' that, in them, the act and the motive are not yet finally identified with each other. We see the act still palpitating with the motive; the motive dimly striving to recognize or disclaim itself in the act. It is in this that the psychological poet stands more than ever strongly revealed. Such at least is the case in 'Martin

Relph', and the idealized Russian legend, 'Ivan Ivanovitch'. The grotesque tragedy of 'Ned Bratts' has also its marked psychological aspects, but they are of a simpler and broader kind.

The new inspiration slowly subsided through the second series of 'Idyls', 1880, and 'Jocoseria', 1883. In 'Ferishtah's Fancies', 1884, Mr. Browning returned to his original manner, though carrying into it something of the renewed vigour which had marked the intervening change. The lyrics which alternate with its parables include some of the most tender, most impassioned, and most musical of his love-poems.

The moral and religious opinions conveyed in this later volume may be accepted without reserve as Mr. Browning's own, if we subtract from them the exaggerations of the figurative and dramatic form. It is indeed easy to recognize in them the under currents of his whole real and imaginative life. They have also on one or two points an intrinsic value which will justify a later allusion.

Chapter 19

1881-1887

The Browning Society; Mr. Furnivall; Miss E. H. Hickey—His Attitude towards the Society; Letter to Mrs. Fitz-Gerald—Mr. Thaxter, Mrs. Celia Thaxter—Letter to Miss Hickey; 'Strafford'—Shakspere and Wordsworth Societies—Letters to Professor Knight—Appreciation in Italy; Professor Nencioni—The Goldoni Sonnet—Mr. Barrett Browning; Palazzo Manzoni—Letters to Mrs. Charles Skirrow—Mrs. Bloomfield Moore—Llangollen; Sir Theodore and Lady Martin—Loss of old Friends—Foreign Correspondent of the Royal Academy—'Parleyings with certain People of Importance in their Day'.

This Indian summer of Mr. Browning's genius coincided with the highest manifestation of public interest, which he, or with one exception, any living writer, had probably yet received: the establishment of a Society bearing his name, and devoted to the study of his poetry. The idea arose almost simultaneously in the mind of Dr., then Mr. Furnivall, and of Miss E. H. Hickey. One day, in the July of 1881, as they were on their way to Warwick Crescent to pay an appointed visit there, Miss Hickey strongly expressed her opinion of the power and breadth of Mr. Browning's work; and concluded by saying that much as she loved Shakespeare, she found in certain aspects of Browning what even Shakespeare could not give her. Mr. Furnivall replied to this by asking what she would say to helping him to found a Browning Society; and it then appeared that Miss Hickey had recently written to him a letter, suggesting that he should found one; but that it had miscarried, or, as she was disposed to think, not been posted. Being thus, at all events, agreed as to the fitness of the undertaking, they immediately spoke of it to Mr. Browning, who at first treated the project as a joke; but did not oppose it when once he understood it to be serious. His only proviso was that he should remain neutral in respect to its fulfilment. He refused even to give Mr. Furnivall the name or address of any friends, whose interest in himself or his work might render their co-operation probable.

This passive assent sufficed. A printed prospectus was now issued. About two hundred members were soon secured. A committee was elected, of which Mr. J. T. Nettleship, already well known as a Browning student, was one of the most conspicuous members; and by the end of October a small Society had come into existence, which held its inaugural meeting in the Botanic Theatre of University College. Mr. Furnivall, its principal founder, and responsible organizer, was Chairman of the Committee, and Miss E. H. Hickey, the co-founder, was Honorary Secretary. When, two or three years afterwards, illness compelled her to resign this position, it was assumed by Mr. J. Dykes Campbell.

Although nothing could be more unpretending than the action of this Browning Society, or in the main more genuine than its motive, it did not begin life without encountering ridicule and mistrust. The formation of a Ruskin Society in the previous year had already established a precedent for allowing a still living worker to enjoy the fruits of his work, or, as some one termed it, for making a man a classic during his lifetime. But this fact was not yet generally known; and meanwhile a curious contradiction developed itself in the public mind. The outer world of Mr. Browning's acquaintance continued to condemn the too great honour which was being done to him; from those of the inner circle he constantly received condolences on being made the subject of proceedings which, according to them, he must somehow regard as an offence.

This was the last view of the case which he was prepared to take. At the beginning, as at the end, he felt honoured by the intentions of the Society. He probably, it is true, had occasional misgivings as to its future. He could not be sure that its action would always be judicious, still less that it would be always successful. He was prepared for its being laughed at, and for himself being included in the laughter. He consented to its establishment for what seemed to him the one unanswerable reason, that he had, even on the ground of taste, no just cause for forbidding it. No line, he considered, could be drawn between the kind of publicity which every writer seeks, which, for good or evil, he had already obtained, and that which the Browning Society was conferring on him. His works would still, as before, be read, analyzed, and discussed 'viva voce' and in print. That these proceedings would now take place in other localities than drawing-rooms or clubs, through other organs than newspapers or magazines, by other and larger groups of persons than those usually gathered round a dinner-or a tea-table, involved no real change in the situation. In any case, he had made himself public property; and those who thus organized their study of him were exercising an individual right. If his own rights had been assailed he would have guarded them also; but the circumstances of the case precluded such a contingency. And he had his reward. How he felt towards the Society at the close of its first session is better indicated in the following letter to Mrs. Fitz-Gerald than in the note to Mr. Yates which Mr. Sharp has published, and which was written with more reserve and, I believe, at a rather earlier date. Even the shade of condescension which lingers about his words will have been effaced by subsequent experience; and many letters written to Dr. Furnivall must, since then, have attested his grateful and affectionate appreciation of kindness intended and service done to him.

. . . They always treat me gently in 'Punch'—why don't you do the same by the Browning Society? I see you emphasize Miss Hickey's acknowledgement of defects in time and want of rehearsal: but I look for no great perfection in a number of kindly disposed strangers to me personally, who try to interest people in my poems by singing and reading them. They give their time for nothing, offer their little entertainment for nothing, and certainly get next to nothing in the way of thanks—unless from myself who feel grateful to the faces I shall never see, the voices I shall never hear. The kindest notices I have had, or at all events those that have given me most pleasure, have been educed by this Society—A. Sidgwick's paper, that of Professor Corson, Miss Lewis' article in this month's 'Macmillan'—and I feel grateful for it all, for my part,—and none the less for a little amusement at the wonder of some of my friends that I do not jump up and denounce the practices which must annoy me so much. Oh! my 'gentle Shakespeare', how well you felt and said—'never anything can be amiss when simpleness and duty tender it.' So, dear Lady, here is my duty and simplicity tendering itself to you, with all affection besides, and I being ever yours, R. Browning.

That general disposition of the London world which left the ranks of the little Society to be three-fourths recruited among persons, many living at a distance, whom the poet did not know, became also in its way a satisfaction. It was with him a matter of course, though never of indifference, that his closer friends of both sexes were among its members; it was one of real gratification that they included from the beginning such men as Dean Boyle of Salisbury, the Rev. Llewellyn Davies, George Meredith, and James Cotter Morison—that they enjoyed the sympathy and co-operation of such a one as Archdeacon Farrar. But he had an ingenuous pride in reading the large remainder of the Society's lists of names, and pointing out the fact that there was not one among them which he had ever heard. It was equivalent to saying, 'All these people care for me as a poet. No social interest, no personal prepossession, has attracted them to my work.' And when the unknown name was not only appended to a list; when it formed the signature of a paper—excellent or indifferent as might be—but in either case bearing witness to a careful and unobtrusive study of his poems, by so much was the gratification increased. He seldom weighed the intrinsic merit of such productions; he did not read them critically. No man was ever more adverse to the seeming ungraciousness of analyzing the quality of a gift. In real life indeed this power of gratitude sometimes defeated its own end, by neutralizing his insight into the motive or effort involved in different acts of kindness, and placing them all successively on the same plane.

In the present case, however, an ungraduated acceptance of the labour bestowed on him was part of the neutral attitude which it was his constant endeavour to maintain. He always refrained from noticing any erroneous statement concerning himself or his works which might appear in the Papers of the Society: since, as he alleged, if he once began to correct, he would appear to endorse whatever he left uncorrected, and thus make himself responsible, not only for any interpretation that might be placed on his poems, but, what was far more serious, for every eulogium that was bestowed upon them. He could not stand aloof as entirely as he or even his friends desired, since it was usual with some members of the Society to seek from him elucidations of obscure passages which, without these, it was declared, would be a stumbling-block to future readers. But he disliked being even to this extent drawn into its operation; and his help was, I believe, less and less frequently invoked. Nothing could be more false than the rumour which once arose that he superintended those performances of his plays which took place under the direction of the Society. Once only, and by the urgent desire of some of the actors, did he witness a last rehearsal of one of them.

It was also a matter of course that men and women brought together by a pre-existing interest in Mr. Browning's work should often ignore its authorized explanations, and should read and discuss it in the light of personal impressions more congenial to their own mind; and the various and circumstantial views sometimes elicited by a given poem did not serve to render it more intelligible. But the merit of true poetry lies so largely in its suggestiveness, that even mistaken impressions of it have their positive value and also their relative truth; and the intellectual friction which was thus created, not only in the parent society, but in its offshoots in England and America, was not their least important result.

These Societies conferred, it need hardly be said, no less real benefits on the public at large. They extended the sale of Mr. Browning's works, and with it their distinct influence for intellectual and moral good. They not only created in many minds an interest in these works, but aroused the interest where it was latent, and gave it expression where it had hitherto found no voice. One fault, alone, could be charged against them; and this lay partly in the nature of all friendly concerted action: they stirred a spirit of enthusiasm in which it was not easy, under conditions equally genuine, to distinguish the individual element from that which was due to contagion; while the presence among us of the still living poet often infused into that enthusiasm a vaguely emotional element, which otherwise detracted from its intellectual worth. But in so far as this was a drawback to the intended action of the Societies, it was one only in the most negative sense; nor can we doubt, that, to a certain extent, Mr. Browning's best influence was promoted by it. The hysterical sensibilities which, for some years past, he had unconsciously but not unfrequently aroused in the minds of women, and even of men, were a morbid development of that influence, which its open and systematic extension tended rather to diminish than to increase.

It is also a matter of history that Robert Browning had many deep and constant admirers in England, and still more in America,* long before this organized interest had developed itself. Letters received from often remote parts of the United States had been for many years a detail of his daily experience; and even when they consisted of the request for an autograph, an application to print selections from his works, or a mere expression of schoolboy pertness or schoolgirl sentimentality, they bore witness to his wide reputation in that country, and the high esteem in which he was held there.** The names of Levi and Celia Thaxter of Boston had long, I believe, been conspicuous in the higher ranks of his disciples, though they first occur in his correspondence at about this date. I trust I may take for granted Mrs. Thaxter's permission to publish a letter from her.

* The cheapening of his works in America, induced by the absence of international copyright, accounts of course in some degree for their wider diffusion, and hence earlier appreciation there. ** One of the most curious proofs of this was the Californian Railway time-table edition of his poems.

Newtonville, Massachusetts: March 14, 1880.

My dear Mr. Browning:

Your note reached me this morning, but it belonged to my husband, for it was he who wrote to you; so I gave it to him, glad to put into his hands so precious a piece of manuscript, for he has for you and all your work an enthusiastic appreciation such as is seldom found on this planet: it is not possible that the admiration of one mortal for another can exceed his feeling for you. You might have written for him,

I've a friend over the sea, ... It all grew out of the books I write, &c.

You should see his fine wrath and scorn for the idiocy that doesn't at once comprehend you!

He knows every word you have ever written; long ago 'Sordello' was an open book to him from title-page to closing line, and *all* you have printed since has been as eagerly and studiously devoured. He reads you aloud and his reading is a fine art to crowds of astonished people, he swears by you, he thinks no one save Shakspere has a right to be mentioned in the same century with you. You are the great enthusiasm of his life.

Pardon me, you are smiling, I dare say. You hear any amount of such things, doubtless. But a genuine living appreciation is always worth having in this old world, it is like a strong fresh breeze from off the brine, that puts a sense of life and power into a man. You cannot be the worse for it. Yours very sincerely, Celia Thaxter.

When Mr. Thaxter died, in February 1885, his son wrote to Mr. Browning to beg of him a few lines to be inscribed on his father's tombstone. The little poem by which the request was answered has not yet, I believe, been published.

'Written to be inscribed on the gravestone of Levi Thaxter.'

Thou, whom these eyes saw never,—say friends true Who say my soul, helped onward by my song, Though all unwittingly, has helped thee too? I gave but of the little that I knew: How were the gift requited, while along Life's path I pace, could'st thou make weakness strong, Help me with knowledge—for Life's old, Death's new! R. B. April 19, '85.

A publication which connected itself with the labours of the Society, without being directly inspired by it, was the annotated 'Strafford' prepared by Miss Hickey for the use of students. It may be agreeable to those who use the little work to know the estimate in which Mr. Browning held it. He wrote as follows:

19, Warwick Crescent, W.: February 15, 1884.

Dear Miss Hickey,—I have returned the Proofs by post,—nothing can be better than your notes—and with a real wish to be of use, I read them carefully that I might detect never so tiny a fault,—but I found none—unless to show you how minutely I searched, it should be one that by 'thriving in your contempt,' I meant simply 'while you despise them, and for all that, they thrive and are powerful to do you harm.' The idiom you prefer—quite an authorized one—comes to much the same thing after all.

You must know how much I grieve at your illness—temporary as I will trust it to be—I feel all your goodness to me—or whatever in my books may be taken for me—well, I wish you knew how thoroughly I feel it—and how truly I am and shall ever be Yours affectionately, Robert Browning.

From the time of the foundation of the New Shakspere Society, Mr. Browning was its president. In 1880 he became a member of the Wordsworth Society. Two interesting letters to Professor Knight, dated respectively 1880 and 1887, connect themselves with the working of the latter; and, in spite of their distance in time, may therefore be given together. The poem which formed the subject of the first was 'The Daisy';* the selection referred to in the second was that made in

1888 by Professor Knight for the Wordsworth Society, with the co-operation of Mr. Browning and other eminent literary men.

* That beginning 'In youth from rock to rock, I went.'

19, Warwick Crescent, W.: July 9, '80.

My dear Sir,—You pay me a compliment in caring for my opinion—but, such as it is, a very decided one it must be. On every account, your method of giving the original text, and subjoining in a note the variations, each with its proper date, is incontestably preferable to any other. It would be so, if the variations were even improvements—there would be pleasure as well as profit in seeing what was good grow visibly better. But—to confine ourselves to the single 'proof' you have sent me—in every case the change is sadly for the worse: I am quite troubled by such spoilings of passage after passage as I should have chuckled at had I chanced upon them in some copy pencil-marked with corrections by Jeffrey or Gifford: indeed, they are nearly as wretched as the touchings-up of the 'Siege of Corinth' by the latter. If ever diabolic agency was caught at tricks with 'apostolic' achievement see page 9—and 'apostolic', with no 'profanity' at all, I esteem these poems to be—surely you may bid it 'aroint' 'about and all about' these desecrated stanzas—each of which, however, thanks to your piety, we may hail, I trust, with a hearty

Thy long-lost praise thou shalt regain Nor be less dear to future men Than in old time!

Believe me, my dear Sir, Yours very sincerely, Robert Browning.

19, Warwick Crescent, W.: March 23, '87.

Dear Professor Knight,—I have seemed to neglect your commission shamefully enough: but I confess to a sort of repugnance to classifying the poems as even good and less good: because in my heart I fear I should do it almost chronologically—so immeasureably superior seem to me the 'first sprightly runnings'. Your selection would appear to be excellent; and the partial admittance of the later work prevents one from observing the too definitely distinguishing black line between supremely good and—well, what is fairly tolerable—from Wordsworth, always understand! I have marked a few of the early poems, not included in your list—I could do no other when my conscience tells me that I never can be tired of loving them: while, with the best will in the world, I could never do more than try hard to like them.*

* By 'them' Mr. Browning clearly means the later poems, and probably has omitted a few words which would have shown this.

You see, I go wholly upon my individual likings and distastes: that other considerations should have their weight with other people is natural and inevitable. Ever truly yours, Robert Browning.

Many thanks for the volume just received—that with the correspondence. I hope that you restore the swan simile so ruthlessly cut away from 'Dion'.

In 1884 he was again invited, and again declined, to stand for the Lord Rectorship of the University of St. Andrews. In the same year he received the LL.D. degree of the University of Edinburgh; and in the following was made Honorary President of the Associated Societies of that city.* During the few days spent there on the occasion of his investiture, he was the guest of Professor Masson, whose solicitous kindness to him is still warmly remembered in the family.

* This Association was instituted in 1833, and is a union of literary and debating societies. It is at present composed of five: the Dialectic, Scots Law, Diagnostic, Philosophical, and Philomathic.

The interest in Mr. Browning as a poet is beginning to spread in Germany. There is room for wonder that it should not have done so before, though the affinities of his genius are rather with the older than with the more modern German mind. It is much more remarkable that, many years ago, his work had already a sympathetic exponent in Italy. Signor Nencioni, Professor of Literature in Florence, had made his acquaintance at Siena, and was possibly first attracted to him through his wife, although I never heard that it was so. He was soon, however, fascinated by Mr. Browning's poetry, and made it an object of serious study; he largely quoted from, and wrote on it, in the Roman paper 'Fanfulla della Domenica', in 1881 and 1882; and published last winter what is, I am told, an excellent article on the same subject, in the 'Nuova Antologia'. Two years ago he travelled from Rome to Venice accompanied by Signor Placci, for the purpose of seeing him. He is fond of reciting passages from the works, and has even made attempts at translation: though he understands them too well not to pronounce them, what they are for every Latin language, untranslatable.

In 1883 Mr. Browning added another link to the 'golden' chain of verse which united England and Italy. A statue of Goldoni was about to be erected in Venice. The ceremonies of the occasion were to include the appearance of a volume—or album—of appropriate poems; and Cavaliere Molmenti, its intending editor, a leading member of the 'Erection Committee', begged Mr. Browning to contribute to it. It was also desired that he should be present at the unveiling.* He was unable to grant this request, but consented to write a poem. This sonnet to Goldoni also deserves to be more widely known, both for itself and for the manner of its production. Mr. Browning had forgotten, or not understood, how soon the promise concerning it must be fulfilled, and it was actually scribbled off while a messenger, sent by Signor Molmenti, waited for it.

* It was, I think, during this visit to Venice that he assisted at a no less interesting ceremony: the unveiling of a commemorative tablet to Baldassaro Galuppi, in his native island of Burano.

Goldoni,—good, gay, sunniest of souls,—Glassing half Venice in that verse of thine,—What though it just reflect the shade and shine Of common life, nor render, as it rolls Grandeur and gloom? Sufficient for thy shoals Was Carnival: Parini's depths enshrine Secrets unsuited to that opaline Surface of things which laughs along thy scrolls. There throng the people: how they come and go Lisp the soft language, flaunt the bright garb,—see,—On Piazza, Calle, under Portico And over Bridge! Dear king of Comedy, Be honoured! Thou that didst love Venice so, Venice, and we who love her, all love thee!

Venice, Nov. 27, 1883.

A complete bibliography would take account of three other sonnets, 'The Founder of the Feast', 1884, 'The Names', 1884, and 'Why I am a Liberal', 1886, to which I shall have occasion to refer; but we decline insensibly from these on to the less important or more fugitive productions which such lists also include, and on which it is unnecessary or undesirable that any stress should be laid.

In 1885 he was joined in Venice by his son. It was 'Penini's' first return to the country of his birth, his first experience of the city which he had only visited in his nurse's arms; and his delight in it was so great that the plan shaped itself in his father's mind of buying a house there, which should serve as 'pied-a-terre' for the family, but more especially as a home for him. Neither the health nor the energies of the younger Mr. Browning had ever withstood the influence of the London climate; a foreign element was undoubtedly present in his otherwise thoroughly English constitution. Everything now pointed to his settling in Italy, and pursuing his artist life there, only interrupting it by occasional visits to London and Paris. His father entered into negotiations for the Palazzo Manzoni, next door to the former Hotel de l'Univers; and the purchase was completed, so far as he was concerned, before he returned to England. The fact is related, and his own position towards it described in a letter to Mrs. Charles Skirrow, written from Venice.

Palazzo Giustiniani Recanati, S. Moise: Nov. 15, '85.

My two dear friends will have supposed, with plenty of reason, that I never got the kind letter some weeks ago. When it came, I was in the middle of an affair, conducted by letters of quite another kind, with people abroad: and as I fancied that every next day might bring me news very interesting to me and likely to be worth telling to the dear friends, I waited and waited—and only two days since did the matter come to a satisfactory conclusion—so, as the Irish song has it, 'Open your eyes and die with surprise' when I inform you that I have purchased the Manzoni Palace here, on the Canal Grande, of its owner, Marchese Montecucculi, an Austrian and an absentee—hence the delay of communication. I did this purely for Pen—who became at once simply infatuated with the city which won my whole heart long before he was born or thought of. I secure him a perfect domicile, every facility for his painting and sculpture, and a property fairly worth, even here and now, double what I gave for it—such is the virtue in these parts of ready money! I myself shall stick to London—which has been so eminently good and gracious to me—so long as God permits; only, when the inevitable outrage of Time gets the better of my body—I shall not believe in his reaching my soul and proper self—there will be a capital retreat provided: and meantime I shall be able to 'take mine ease in mine own inn' whenever so minded. There, my dear friends! I trust now to be able to leave very shortly; the main business cannot be formally concluded before two months at least—through the absence of the Marchese,—who left at once to return to his duties as commander of an Austrian ship; but the necessary engagement to sell and buy at a specified price is made in due legal form, and the papers will be sent to me in London for signature. I hope to get away the week after next at latest,—spite of the weather in England which to-day's letters report as 'atrocious',—and ours, though variable, is in the main very tolerable and sometimes perfect; for all that, I yearn to be at home in poor Warwick Crescent, which must do its best to make me forget my new abode. I forget you don't know Venice. Well then, the Palazzo Manzoni is situate on the Grand Canal, and is described by Ruskin,—to give no other authority,—as 'a perfect and very rich example of Byzantine Renaissance: its warm yellow marbles are magnificent.' And again—'an exquisite example of Byzantine Renaissance as applied to domestic architecture.' So testify the 'Stones of Venice'. But we will talk about the place, over a photograph, when I am happy enough to be with you again.

Of Venetian gossip there is next to none. We had an admirable Venetian Company,—using the dialect,—at the Goldoni Theatre. The acting of Zago, in his various parts, and Zenon-Palladini, in her especial character of a Venetian piece of volubility and impulsiveness in the shape of a servant, were admirable indeed. The manager, Gallina, is a playwright of much reputation, and gave us some dozen of his own pieces, mostly good and clever. S. is very well,—much improved in health: we walk sufficiently in this city where walking is accounted impossible by those who never attempt it. Have I tired your good temper? No! you ever wished me well, and I love you both with my whole heart. S.'s love goes with mine—who am ever yours Robert Browning.

He never, however, owned the Manzoni Palace. The Austrian gentlemen* whose property it was, put forward, at the last moment, unexpected and to his mind unreasonable claims; and he was preparing to contest the position, when a timely warning induced him to withdraw from it altogether. The warning proceeded from his son, who had remained on the spot, and was now informed on competent authority that the foundations of the house were insecure.

* Two or three brothers.

In the early summer of 1884, and again in 1886, Miss Browning had a serious illness; and though she recovered, in each case completely, and in the first rapidly, it was considered desirable that she should not travel so far as usual from home. She and her brother therefore accepted for the August and September of 1884 the urgent invitation of an American friend, Mrs. Bloomfield Moore, to stay with her at a villa which she rented for some seasons at St. Moritz. Mr. Browning was delighted with the Engadine, where the circumstances of his abode, and the thoughtful kindness of his hostess, allowed him to enjoy the benefits of comparative civilization together with almost perfect repose. The weather that year was brilliant until the end of September, if not beyond it; and his letters tell the old pleasant story of long daily walks and a general sense of invigoration. One of these, written to Mr. and Mrs. Skirrow, also contains some pungent remarks on contemporary events, with an affectionate allusion to one of the chief actors in them.

'Anyhow, I have the sincerest hope that Wolseley may get done as soon, and kill as few people, as possible,—keeping himself safe and sound—brave dear fellow—for the benefit of us all.'

He also speaks with great sympathy of the death of Mr. Charles Sartoris, which had just taken place at St.-Moritz.

In 1886, Miss Browning was not allowed to leave England; and she and Mr. Browning established themselves for the autumn at the Hand Hotel at Llangollen, where their old friends, Sir Theodore and Lady Martin, would be within easy reach. Mr. Browning missed the exhilarating effects of the Alpine air; but he enjoyed the peaceful beauty of the Welsh valley, and the quiet and comfort of the old-fashioned English inn. A new source of interest also presented itself to him in some aspects of the life of the English country gentleman. He was struck by the improvements effected by its actual owner* on a neighbouring estate, and by the provisions contained in them for the comfort of both the men and the animals under his care; and he afterwards made, in reference to them, what was for a professing Liberal, a very striking remark: 'Talk of abolishing that class of men! They are the salt of the earth!' Every Sunday afternoon he and his sister drank tea—weather permitting—on the lawn with their friends at Brintysilio; and he alludes gracefully to these meetings in a letter written in the early summer of 1888, when Lady Martin had urged him to return to Wales.

* I believe a Captain Best.

The poet left another and more pathetic remembrance of himself in the neighbourhood of Llangollen: his weekly presence at the afternoon Sunday service in the parish church of Llantysilio. Churchgoing was, as I have said, no part of his regular life. It was no part of his life in London. But I do not think he ever failed in it at the Universities or in the country. The assembling for prayer meant for him something deeper in both the religious and the human sense, where ancient learning and piety breathed through the consecrated edifice, or where only the figurative 'two or three' were 'gathered together' within it. A memorial tablet now marks the spot at which on this occasion the sweet grave face and the venerable head were so often seen. It has been placed by the direction of Lady Martin on the adjoining wall.

It was in the September of this year that Mr. Browning heard of the death of M. Joseph Milsand. This name represented for him one of the few close friendships which were to remain until the end, unclouded in fact and in remembrance; and although some weight may be given to those circumstances of their lives which precluded all possibility of friction and risk of disenchantment, I believe their rooted sympathy, and Mr. Browning's unfailing powers of appreciation would, in all possible cases, have maintained the bond intact. The event was at the last sudden, but happily not quite unexpected.

Many other friends had passed by this time out of the poet's life—those of a younger, as well as his own and an older generation. Miss Haworth died in 1883. Charles Dickens, with whom he had remained on the most cordial terms, had walked between him and his son at Thackeray's funeral, to receive from him, only seven years later, the same pious office. Lady Augusta Stanley, the daughter of his old friend, Lady Elgin, was dead, and her husband, the Dean of Westminster. So also were 'Barry Cornwall' and John Forster, Alfred Domett, and Thomas Carlyle, Mr. Cholmondeley and Lord Houghton; others still, both men and women, whose love for him might entitle them to a place in his Biography, but whom I could at most only mention by name.

For none of these can his feeling have been more constant or more disinterested than that which bound him to Carlyle. He visited him at Chelsea in the last weary days of his long life, as often as their distance from each other and his own engagements allowed. Even the man's posthumous self-disclosures scarcely availed to destroy the affectionate reverence which he had always felt for him. He never ceased to defend him against the charge of unkindness to his wife, or to believe that in the matter of their domestic unhappiness she was the more responsible of the two.* Yet Carlyle had never rendered him that service, easy as it appears, which one man of letters most justly values from another: that of proclaiming the admiration which he privately expresses for his works. The fact was incomprehensible to Mr. Browning—it was so foreign to his own nature; and he commented on it with a touch, though merely a touch, of bitterness, when repeating to a friend some almost extravagant eulogium which in earlier days he had received from him tete-a-tete. 'If only,' he said, 'those words had been ever repeated in public, what good they might have done me!'

* He always thought her a hard and unlovable woman, and I believe little liking was lost between them. He told a comical story of how he had once, unintentionally but rather stupidly, annoyed her. She had asked him, as he was standing by her tea-table, to put the kettle back on the fire. He took it out of her hands, but, preoccupied by the conversation he was

carrying on, deposited it on the hearthrug. It was some time before he could be made to see that this was wrong; and he believed Mrs. Carlyle never ceased to think that he had a mischievous motive for doing it.

In the spring of 1886, he accepted the post of Foreign Correspondent to the Royal Academy, rendered vacant by the death of Lord Houghton. He had long been on very friendly terms with the leading Academicians, and a constant guest at the Banquet; and his fitness for the office admitted of no doubt. But his nomination by the President, and the manner in which it was ratified by the Council and general body, gave him sincere pleasure.

Early in 1887, the 'Parleyings' appeared. Their author is still the same Robert Browning, though here and there visibly touched by the hand of time. Passages of sweet or majestic music, or of exquisite fancy, alternate with its long stretches of argumentative thought; and the light of imagination still plays, however fitfully, over statements of opinion to which constant repetition has given a suggestion of commonplace. But the revision of the work caused him unusual trouble. The subjects he had chosen strained his powers of exposition; and I think he often tried to remedy by mere verbal correction, what was a defect in the logical arrangement of his ideas. They would slide into each other where a visible dividing line was required. The last stage of his life was now at hand; and the vivid return of fancy to his boyhood's literary loves was in pathetic, perhaps not quite accidental, coincidence with the fact. It will be well to pause at this beginning of his decline, and recall so far as possible the image of the man who lived, and worked, and loved, and was loved among us, during that brief old age, and the lengthened period of level strength which had preceded it. The record already given of his life and work supplies the outline of the picture; but a few more personal details are required for its completion.

Chapter 20

Constancy to Habit—Optimism—Belief in Providence—Political Opinions—His Friendships—Reverence for Genius—Attitude towards his Public—Attitude towards his Work—Habits of Work—His Reading—Conversational Powers—Impulsiveness and Reserve—Nervous Peculiarities—His Benevolence—His Attitude towards Women.

When Mr. Browning wrote to Miss Haworth, in the July of 1861, he had said: 'I shall still grow, I hope; but my root is taken, and remains.' He was then alluding to a special offshoot of feeling and association, on the permanence of which it is not now necessary to dwell; but it is certain that he continued growing up to a late age, and that the development was only limited by those general roots, those fixed conditions of his being, which had predetermined its form. This progressive intellectual vitality is amply represented in his works; it also reveals itself in his letters in so far as I have been allowed to publish them. I only refer to it to give emphasis to a contrasted or corresponding characteristic: his aversion to every thought of change. I have spoken of his constancy to all degrees of friendship and love. What he loved once he loved always, from the dearest man or woman to whom his allegiance had been given, to the humblest piece of furniture which had served him. It was equally true that what he had done once he was wont, for that very reason, to continue doing. The devotion to habits of feeling extended to habits of life; and although the lower constancy generally served the purposes of the higher, it also sometimes clashed with them. It conspired with his ready kindness of heart to make him subject to circumstances which at first appealed to him through that kindness, but lay really beyond its scope. This statement, it is true, can only fully apply to the latter part of his life. His powers of reaction must originally have been stronger, as well as freer from the paralysis of conflicting motive and interest. The marked shrinking from effort in any untried direction, which was often another name for his stability, could scarcely have coexisted with the fresher and more curious interest in men and things; we know indeed from recorded facts that it was a feeling of later growth; and it visibly increased with the periodical nervous exhaustion of his advancing years. I am convinced, nevertheless, that, when the restiveness of boyhood had passed away, Mr. Browning's strength was always more passive than active; that he habitually made the best of external conditions rather than tried to change them. He was a 'fighter' only by the brain. And on this point, though on this only, his work is misleading.

The acquiescent tendency arose in some degree from two equally prominent characteristics of Mr. Browning's nature: his optimism, and his belief in direct Providence; and these again represented a condition of mind which was in certain respects a quality, but must in others be recognized as a defect. It disposed him too much to make a virtue of happiness. It tended also to the ignoring or denying of many incidental possibilities, and many standing problems of human suffering. The first part of this assertion is illustrated by 'The Two Poets of Croisic', in which Mr. Browning declares that, other conditions being equal, the greater poet will have been he who led the happier life, who most completely—and we must take this in the human as well as religious sense—triumphed over suffering. The second has its proof in the contempt for poetic melancholy which flashes from the supposed utterance of Shakespeare in 'At the Mermaid'; its negative justification in the whole range of his work.

Such facts may be hard to reconcile with others already known of Mr. Browning's nature, or already stated concerning it; but it is in the depths of that nature that the solution of this, as of more than one other anomaly, must be sought. It is true that remembered pain dwelt longer with him than remembered pleasure. It is true that the last great sorrow of his life was long felt and cherished by him as a religion, and that it entered as such into the courage with which he first confronted it. It is no less true that he directly and increasingly cultivated happiness; and that because of certain sufferings which had been connected with them, he would often have refused to live his happiest days again.

It seems still harder to associate defective human sympathy with his kind heart and large dramatic imagination, though that very imagination was an important factor in the case. It forbade the collective and mathematical estimate of human suffering, which is so much in favour with modern philanthropy, and so untrue a measure for the individual life; and he indirectly condemns it in 'Ferishtah's Fancies' in the parable of 'Bean Stripes'. But his dominant individuality also barred the recognition of any judgment or impression, any thought or feeling, which did not justify itself from his own point of view. The barrier would melt under the influence of a sympathetic mood, as it would stiffen in the atmosphere of disagreement. It would yield, as did in his case so many other things, to continued indirect pressure, whether from his love of justice, the strength of his attachments, or his power of imaginative absorption. But he was bound by the conditions of an essentially creative nature. The subjectiveness, if I may for once use that hackneyed word, had passed out of his work only to root itself more strongly in his life. He was self-centred, as the creative nature must inevitably be. He appeared, for this reason, more widely sympathetic in his works than in his life, though even in the former certain grounds of vicarious feeling remained untouched. The sympathy there displayed was creative and obeyed its own law. That which was demanded from him by reality was responsive, and implied submission to the law of other minds.

Such intellectual egotism is unconnected with moral selfishness, though it often unconsciously does its work. Were it otherwise, I should have passed over in silence this aspect, comprehensive though it is, of Mr. Browning's character. He was capable of the largest self-sacrifice and of the smallest self-denial; and would exercise either whenever love or duty clearly pointed the way. He would, he believed, cheerfully have done so at the command, however arbitrary, of a Higher Power; he often spoke of the absence of such injunction, whether to endurance or action, as the great theoretical difficulty of life for those who, like himself, rejected or questioned the dogmatic teachings of Christianity. This does not mean that he ignored the traditional moralities which have so largely taken their place. They coincided in great measure with his own instincts; and few occasions could have arisen in which they would not be to him a sufficient guide. I may add, though this is a digression, that he never admitted the right of genius to defy them; when such a right had once been claimed for it in his presence, he rejoined quickly, 'That is an error! *noblesse oblige*.' But he had difficulty in acknowledging any abstract law which did not derive from a Higher Power; and this fact may have been at once cause and consequence of the special conditions of his own mind. All human or conventional obligation appeals finally to the individual judgment; and in his case this could easily be obscured by the always militant imagination, in regard to any subject in which his feelings were even indirectly concerned. No one saw more justly than he, when the object of vision was general or remote. Whatever entered his personal atmosphere encountered a refracting medium in which objects were decomposed, and a succession of details, each held as it were close to the eye, blocked out the larger view.

We have seen, on the other hand, that he accepted imperfect knowledge as part of the discipline of experience. It detracted in no sense from his conviction of direct relations with the Creator. This was indeed the central fact of his theology, as the absolute individual existence had been the central fact of his metaphysics; and when he described the fatal leap in 'Red Cotton Nightcap Country' as a frantic appeal to the Higher Powers for the 'sign' which the man's religion did not afford, and his nature could not supply, a special dramatic sympathy was at work within him. The third part of the epilogue to 'Dramatis Personae' represented his own creed; though this was often accentuated in the sense of a more personal privilege, and a perhaps less poetic mystery, than the poem conveys. The Evangelical Christian and the subjective idealist philosopher were curiously blended in his composition.

The transition seems violent from this old-world religion to any system of politics applicable to the present day. They were, nevertheless, closely allied in Mr. Browning's mind. His politics were, so far as they went, the practical aspect of his religion. Their cardinal doctrine was the liberty of individual growth; removal of every barrier of prejudice or convention by which it might still be checked. He had been a Radical in youth, and probably in early manhood; he remained, in the truest sense of the word, a Liberal; and his position as such was defined in the sonnet prefixed in 1886 to Mr. Andrew Reid's essay, 'Why I am a Liberal', and bearing the same name. Its profession of faith did not, however, necessarily bind him to any political party. It separated him from all the newest developments of so-called Liberalism. He respected the rights of property. He was a true patriot, hating to see his country plunged into aggressive wars, but tenacious of her position among the empires of the world. He was also a passionate Unionist; although the question of our political relations with Ireland weighed less with him, as it has done with so many others, than those considerations of law and order, of honesty and humanity, which have been trampled under foot in the name of Home Rule. It grieved and surprised him to find himself on this subject at issue with so many valued friends; and no pain of Lost Leadership was ever more angry or more intense, than that which came to him through the defection of a great statesman whom he had honoured and loved, from what he believed to be the right cause.

The character of Mr. Browning's friendships reveals itself in great measure in even a simple outline of his life. His first friends of his own sex were almost exclusively men of letters, by taste if not by profession; the circumstances of his entrance into society made this a matter of course. In later years he associated on cordial terms with men of very various interests and professions; and only writers of conspicuous merit, whether in prose or poetry, attracted him as such. No intercourse was more congenial to him than that of the higher class of English clergymen. He sympathized in their beliefs even when he did not share them. Above all he loved their culture; and the love of culture in general, of its old classic forms in particular, was as strong in him as if it had been formed by all the natural and conventional associations of a university career. He had hearty friends and appreciators among the dignitaries of the Church—successive Archbishops and Bishops, Deans of Westminster and St. Paul's. They all knew the value of the great freelance who fought like the gods of old with the regular army. No name, however, has been mentioned in the poet's family more frequently or with more affection than that of the Rev. J. D. W. Williams, Vicar of Bottisham in Cambridgeshire. The mutual acquaintance, which was made through Mr. Browning's brother-in-law, Mr. George Moulton-Barrett, was prepared by Mr. Williams' great love for his poems, of which he translated many into Latin and Greek; but I am convinced that Mr. Browning's delight in his friend's classical attainments was quite as great as his gratification in the tribute he himself derived from them.

His love of genius was a worship: and in this we must include his whole life. Nor was it, as this feeling so often is, exclusively exercised upon the past. I do not suppose his more eminent contemporaries ever quite knew how generous his enthusiasm for them had been, how free from any under-current of envy, or impulse to avoidable criticism. He could not endure even just censure of one whom he believed, or had believed to be great. I have seen him wince under it, though no third person was present, and heard him answer, 'Don't! don't!' as if physical pain were being inflicted on him. In the early days he would make his friend, M. de Monclar, draw for him from memory the likenesses of famous writers whom he had known in Paris; the sketches thus made of George Sand and Victor Hugo are still in the poet's family. A still more striking and very touching incident refers to one of the winters, probably the second, which he spent in Paris. He was one day walking with little Pen, when Beranger came in sight, and he bade the child 'run up to' or 'run past that gentleman, and put his hand for a moment upon him.' This was a great man, he afterwards explained, and he wished his son to be able by-and-by to say that if he had not known, he had at all events touched him. Scientific genius ranked with him only second to the poetical.

Mr. Browning's delicate professional sympathies justified some sensitiveness on his own account; but he was, I am convinced, as free from this quality as a man with a poet-nature could possibly be. It may seem hazardous to conjecture how serious criticism would have affected him. Few men so much 'reviewed' have experienced so little. He was by turns derided or ignored, enthusiastically praised, zealously analyzed and interpreted: but the independent judgment which could embrace at once the quality of his mind and its defects, is almost absent—has been so at all events during later years—from the volumes which have been written about him. I am convinced, nevertheless, that he would have accepted serious, even adverse criticism, if it had borne the impress of unbiassed thought and genuine sincerity. It could not be otherwise with one in whom the power of reverence was so strongly marked.

He asked but one thing of his reviewers, as he asked but one thing of his larger public. The first demand is indicated in a letter to Mrs. Frank Hill, of January 31, 1884.

Dear Mrs. Hill,—Could you befriend me? The 'Century' prints a little insignificance of mine—an impromptu sonnet—but prints it *correctly*. The 'Pall Mall' pleases to extract it—and produces what I enclose: one line left out, and a note of admiration ! turned into an I, and a superfluous 'the' stuck in—all these blunders with the correctly printed text before it! So does the charge of unintelligibility attach itself to your poor friend—who can kick nobody. Robert Browning.

The carelessness often shown in the most friendly quotation could hardly be absent from that which was intended to support a hostile view; and the only injustice of which he ever complained, was what he spoke of as falsely condemning him out of his own mouth. He used to say: 'If a critic declares that any poem of mine is unintelligible, the reader may go to it and judge for himself; but, if it is made to appear unintelligible by a passage extracted from it and distorted by misprints, I have no redress.' He also failed to realize those conditions of thought, and still more of expression, which made him often on first reading difficult to understand; and as the younger generation of his admirers often deny those difficulties where they exist, as emphatically as their grandfathers proclaimed them where they did not, public opinion gave him little help in the matter.

The second unspoken request was in some sense an antithesis to the first. Mr. Browning desired to be read accurately but not literally. He deprecated the constant habit of reading him into his work; whether in search of the personal meaning of a given passage or poem, or in the light of a foregone conclusion as to what that meaning must be. The latter process was that generally preferred, because the individual mind naturally seeks its own reflection in the poet's work, as it does in the facts of nature. It was stimulated by the investigations of the Browning Societies, and by the partial familiarity with his actual life which constantly supplied tempting, if untrustworthy clues. It grew out of the strong personal as well as literary interest which he inspired. But the tendency to listen in his work for a single recurrent note always struck him as analogous to the inspection of a picture gallery with eyes blind to every colour but one; and the act of sympathy often involved in this mode of judgment was neutralized for him by the limitation of his genius which it presupposed. His general objection to being identified with his works is set forth in 'At the Mermaid', and other poems of the same volume, in which it takes the form of a rather captious protest against inferring from the poet any habit or quality of the man; and where also, under the impulse of the dramatic mood, he enforces the lesson by saying more than he can possibly mean. His readers might object that his human personality was so often plainly revealed in his poetic utterance whether or not that of Shakespeare was, and so often also avowed by it, that the line which divided them became impossible to draw. But he again would have rejoined that the Poet could never express himself with any large freedom, unless a fiction of impersonality were granted to him. He might also have alleged, he often did allege, that in his case the fiction would hold a great deal of truth; since, except in the rarest cases, the very fact of poetic, above all of dramatic reproduction, detracts from the reality of the thought or feeling reproduced. It introduces the alloy of fancy without which the fixed outlines of even living experience cannot be welded into poetic form. He claimed, in short, that in judging of his work, one should allow for the action in it of the constructive imagination, in the exercise of which all deeper poetry consists. The form of literalism, which showed itself in seeking historical authority for every character or incident which he employed by way of illustration, was especially irritating to him.

I may as indeed I must concede this much, without impugning either the pleasure or the gratitude with which he recognized the increasing interest in his poems, and, if sometimes exhibited in a mistaken form, the growing appreciation of them.

There was another and more striking peculiarity in Mr. Browning's attitude towards his works: his constant conviction that the latest must be the best, because the outcome of the fullest mental experience, and of the longest practice in his art. He was keenly alive to the necessary failings of youthful literary production; he also practically denied to it that quality which so often places it at an advantage over that, not indeed of more mature manhood, but at all events of advancing age. There was much in his own experience to blind him to the natural effects of time; it had been a prolonged triumph over them. But the delusion, in so far as it was one, lay deeper than the testimony of such experience, and would I think have survived it. It was the essence of his belief that the mind is superior to physical change; that it may be helped or hindered by its temporary alliance with the body, but will none the less outstrip it in their joint course; and as intellect was for him the life of poetry, so was the power of poetry independent of bodily progress and bodily decline. This conviction pervaded his life. He learned, though happily very late, to feel age an impediment; he never accepted it as a disqualification.

He finished his work very carefully. He had the better right to resent any garbling of it, that this habitually took place through his punctuation, which was always made with the fullest sense of its significance to any but the baldest style, and of its special importance to his own. I have heard him say: 'People accuse me of not taking pains! I take nothing *but* pains!' And there was indeed a curious contrast between the irresponsible, often strangely unquestioned, impulse to which the substance of each poem was due, and the conscientious labour which he always devoted to its form. The laborious habit must have grown upon him; it was natural that it should do so as thought gained the ascendency over emotion in what he had to say. Mrs. Browning told Mr. Val Prinsep that her husband 'worked at a great rate;' and this fact probably connected itself with the difficulty he then found in altering the form or wording of any particular phrase; he wrote most frequently under that lyrical inspiration in which the idea and the form are least separable from each other. We know, however, that in the later editions of his old work he always corrected where he could; and if we notice the changed lines in 'Paracelsus' or 'Sordello', as they appear in the edition of 1863, or the slighter alterations indicated for the last reprint of his works, we are struck by the care evinced in them for greater smoothness of expression, as well as for greater accuracy and force.

He produced less rapidly in later life, though he could throw off impromptu verses, whether serious or comical, with the utmost ease. His work was then of a kind which required more deliberation; and other claims had multiplied upon his time and thoughts. He was glad to have accomplished twenty or thirty lines in a morning. After lunch-time, for many years, he avoided, when possible, even answering a note. But he always counted a day lost on which he had not written something; and in those last years on which we have yet to enter, he complained bitterly of the quantity of ephemeral correspondence which kept him back from his proper work. He once wrote, on the occasion of a short illness which confined him to the house, 'All my power of imagination seems gone. I might as well be in bed!' He repeatedly determined to write a poem every day, and once succeeded for a fortnight in doing so. He was then in Paris, preparing 'Men and Women'. 'Childe Roland' and 'Women and Roses' were among those produced on this plan; the latter having been suggested by some flowers sent to his wife. The lyrics in 'Ferishtah's Fancies' were written, I believe, on consecutive days; and the intention renewed itself with his last work, though it cannot have been maintained.

He was not as great a reader in later as in earlier years; he had neither time nor available strength to be so if he had wished; and he absorbed almost unconsciously every item which added itself to the sum of general knowledge. Books had indeed served for him their most important purpose when they had satisfied the first curiosities of his genius, and enabled it to establish its independence. His mind was made up on the chief subjects of contemporary thought, and what was novel or controversial in its proceeding had no attraction for him. He would read anything, short of an English novel, to a friend whose eyes required this assistance; but such pleasure as he derived from the act was more often sympathetic than spontaneous, even when he had not, as he often had, selected for it a book which he already knew. In the course of his last decade he devoted himself for a short time to the study of Spanish and Hebrew. The Spanish dramatists yielded him a fund of new enjoyment; and he delighted in his power of reading Hebrew in its most difficult printed forms. He also tried, but with less result, to improve his knowledge of German. His eyesight defied all obstacles of bad paper and ancient type, and there was anxiety as well as pleasure to those about him in his unfailing confidence in its powers. He never wore spectacles, nor had the least consciousness of requiring them. He would read an old closely printed volume by the waning light of a winter afternoon, positively refusing to use a lamp. Indeed his preference of the faintest natural light to the best that could be artificially produced was perhaps the one suggestion of coming change. He used for all purposes a single eye; for the two did not combine in their action, the right serving exclusively for near, the left for distant objects. This was why in walking he often closed the right eye; while it was indispensable to his comfort in reading, not only that the light should come from the right side, but that the left should be shielded from any luminous object, like the fire, which even at the distance of half the length of a room would strike on his field of vision and confuse the near sight.

His literary interest became increasingly centred on records of the lives of men and women; especially of such men and women as he had known; he was generally curious to see the newly published biographies, though often disappointed by them. He would also read, even for his amusement, good works of French or Italian fiction. His allegiance to Balzac remained unshaken, though he was conscious of lengthiness when he read him aloud. This author's deep and hence often poetic realism was, I believe, bound up with his own earliest aspirations towards dramatic art. His manner of reading aloud a story which he already knew was the counterpart of his own method of construction. He would claim his listener's attention for any apparently unimportant fact which had a part to play in it: he would say: 'Listen to this description: it will be important. Observe this character: you will see a great deal more of him or her.' We know that in his own work nothing was thrown away; no note was struck which did not add its vibration to the general utterance of the poem; and his habitual generosity towards a fellow-worker prompted him to seek and recognize the same quality, even in productions where it was less conspicuous than in his own. The patient reading which he required for himself was justified by that which he always demanded for others; and he claimed it less in his own case for his possible intricacies of thought or style, than for that compactness of living structure in which every detail or group of details was essential to the whole, and in a certain sense contained it. He read few things with so much pleasure as an occasional chapter in the Old Testament.

Mr. Browning was a brilliant talker; he was admittedly more a talker than a conversationalist. But this quality had nothing in common with self-assertion or love of display. He had too much respect for the acquirements of other men to wish to impose silence on those who were competent to speak; and he had great pleasure in listening to a discussion on any subject in which he was interested, and on which he was not specially informed. He never willingly monopolized the conversation; but when called upon to take a prominent part in it, either with one person or with several, the flow of remembered knowledge and revived mental experience, combined with the ingenuous eagerness to vindicate some point in dispute would often carry him away; while his hearers, nearly as often, allowed him to proceed from absence of any desire to interrupt him. This great mental fertility had been prepared by the wide reading and thorough assimilation of his early days; and it was only at a later, and in certain respects less vigorous period, that its full bearing could be seen. His memory for passing occurrences, even such as had impressed him, became very weak; it was so before he had grown really old; and he would urge this fact in deprecation of any want of kindness or sympathy, which a given act of forgetfulness might seem to involve. He had probably always, in matters touching his own life, the memory of feelings more than that of facts. I think this has been described as a peculiarity of the poet-nature; and though this memory is probably the more tenacious of the two, it is no safe guide to the recovery of facts, still less to that of their order and significance. Yet up to the last weeks, even the last conscious days of his life, his remembrance of historical incident, his aptness of literary illustration, never failed him. His dinner-table anecdotes supplied, of course, no measure for this spontaneous reproductive power; yet some weight must be given to the number of years during which he could abound in such stories, and attest their constant appropriateness by not repeating them.

This brilliant mental quality had its drawback, on which I have already touched in a rather different connection: the obstacle which it created to even serious and private conversation on any subject on which he was not neutral. Feeling, imagination, and the vividness of personal points of view, constantly thwarted the attempt at a dispassionate exchange of ideas. But the balance often righted itself when the excitement of the discussion was at an end; and it would even become apparent that expressions or arguments which he had passed over unheeded, or as it seemed unheard, had stored themselves in his mind and borne fruit there.

I think it is Mr. Sharp who has remarked that Mr. Browning combined impulsiveness of manner with much real reserve. He was habitually reticent where his deeper feelings were concerned; and the impulsiveness and the reticence were both equally rooted in his poetic and human temperament. The one meant the vital force of his emotions, the other their sensibility. In a smaller or more prosaic nature they must have modified each other. But the partial secretiveness had also occasionally its conscious motives, some unselfish, and some self-regarding; and from this point of view it stood in marked apparent antagonism to the more expansive quality. He never, however, intentionally withheld from others such things as it concerned them to know. His intellectual and religious convictions were open to all who seriously sought them; and if, even on such points, he did not appear communicative, it was because he took more interest in any subject of conversation which did not directly centre in himself.

Setting aside the delicacies which tend to self-concealment, and for which he had been always more or less conspicuous; excepting also the pride which would co-operate with them, all his inclinations were in the direction of truth; there was no quality which he so much loved and admired. He thought aloud wherever he could trust himself to do so. Impulse predominated in all the active manifestations of his nature. The fiery child and the impatient boy had left their traces in the man; and with them the peculiar childlike quality which the man of genius never outgrows, and which, in its mingled waywardness and sweetness, was present in Robert Browning till almost his dying day. There was also a recurrent touch of hardness, distinct from the comparatively ungenial mood of his earlier years of widowhood; and this, like his reserve, seemed to conflict with his general character, but in reality harmonized with it. It meant, not that feeling was suspended in him, but that it was compressed. It was his natural response to any opposition which his reasonings could not shake nor his will overcome, and which, rightly or not, conveyed to him the sense of being misunderstood. It reacted in pain for others, but it lay with an aching weight on his own heart, and was thrown off in an upheaval of the pent-up kindliness and affection, the moment their true springs were touched. The hardening power in his composition, though fugitive and comparatively seldom displayed, was in fact proportioned to his tenderness; and no one who had not seen him in the revulsion from a hard mood, or the regret for it, knew what that tenderness could be.

Underlying all the peculiarities of his nature, its strength and its weakness, its exuberance and its reserves, was the nervous excitability of which I have spoken in an earlier chapter. I have heard him say: 'I am nervous to such a degree that I might fancy I could not enter a drawing-room, if I did not know from long experience that I can do it.' He did not desire to conceal this fact, nor need others conceal it for him; since it was only calculated to disarm criticism and to strengthen sympathy. The special vital power which he derived from this organization need not be reaffirmed. It carried also its inevitable disablements. Its resources were not always under his own control; and he frequently complained of the lack of presence of mind which would seize him on any conventional emergency not included in the daily social routine. In a real one he was never at fault. He never failed in a sympathetic response or a playful retort; he was always provided with the exact counter requisite in a game of words. In this respect indeed he had all the powers of the conversationalist; and the perfect ease and grace and geniality of his manner on such occasions, arose probably far more from his innate human and social qualities than from even his familiar intercourse with the world. But he could not extemporize a speech. He could not on the spur of the moment string together the more or less set phrases which an after-dinner oration demands. All his friends knew this, and spared him the necessity of refusing. He had once a headache all day, because at a dinner, the night before, a false report had reached him that he was going to be asked to speak. This alone would have sufficed to prevent him from accepting any public post. He confesses the disability in a pretty note to Professor Knight, written in reference to a recent meeting of the Wordsworth Society.

19, Warwick Crescent, W.: May 9, '84.

My dear Professor Knight,—I seem ungracious and ungrateful, but am neither; though, now that your festival is over, I wish I could have overcome my scruples and apprehensions. It is hard to say—when kind people press one to 'just speak for a minute'—that the business, so easy to almost anybody, is too bewildering for oneself. Ever truly yours, Robert Browning.

A Rectorial Address need probably not have been extemporized, but it would also have been irksome to him to prepare. He was not accustomed to uttering himself in prose except within the limits, and under the incitements, of private correspondence. The ceremonial publicity attaching to all official proceedings would also have inevitably been a trial to him. He did at one of the Wordsworth Society meetings speak a sentence from the chair, in the absence of the appointed chairman, who had not yet arrived; and when he had received his degree from the University of Edinburgh he was persuaded to say a few words to the assembled students, in which I believe he thanked them for their warm welcome; but such exceptions only proved the rule.

We cannot doubt that the excited stream of talk which sometimes flowed from him was, in the given conditions of mind and imagination, due to a nervous impulse which he could not always restrain; and that the effusiveness of manner with which he greeted alike old friends and new, arose also from a momentary want of self-possession. We may admit this the more readily that in both cases it was allied to real kindness of intention, above all in the latter, where the fear of seeming cold towards even a friend's friend, strove increasingly with the defective memory for names and faces which were not quite familiar to him. He was also profoundly averse to the idea of posing as a man of superior gifts; having indeed, in regard to social intercourse, as little of the fastidiousness of genius as of its bohemianism. He, therefore, made it a rule, from the moment he took his place as a celebrity in the London world, to exert himself for the amusement of his fellow-guests at a dinner-table, whether their own mental resources were great or small; and this gave rise to a frequent effort at conversation, which converted itself into a habit, and ended by carrying him away. This at least was his own conviction in the matter. The loud voice, which so many persons must have learned to think habitual with him, bore also traces of this half-unconscious nervous stimulation.* It was natural to him in anger or excitement, but did not express his gentler or more equable states of feeling; and when he read to others on a subject which moved him, his utterance often subsided into a tremulous softness which left it scarcely audible.

* Miss Browning reminds me that loud speaking had become natural to him through the deafness of several of his intimate friends: Landor, Kirkup, Barry Cornwall, and previously his uncle Reuben, whose hearing had been impaired in early life by a blow from a cricket ball. This fact necessarily modifies my impression of the case, but does not quite destroy it.

The mental conditions under which his powers of sympathy were exercised imposed no limits on his spontaneous human kindness. This characteristic benevolence, or power of love, is not fully represented in Mr. Browning's works; it is certainly not prominent in those of the later period, during which it found the widest scope in his life; but he has in some sense given its measure in what was intended as an illustration of the opposite quality. He tells us, in 'Fifine at the Fair', that while the best strength of women is to be found in their love, the best product of a man is only yielded to hate. It is the 'indignant wine' which has been wrung from the grape plant by its external mutilation. He could depict it dramatically in more malignant forms of emotion; but he could only think of it personally as the reaction of a nobler feeling which has been gratuitously outraged or repressed.

He more directly, and still more truly, described himself when he said at about the same time, 'I have never at any period of my life been deaf to an appeal made to me in the name of love.' He was referring to an experience of many years before, in which he had even yielded his better judgment to such an appeal; and it was love in the larger sense for which the concession had been claimed.

It was impossible that so genuine a poet, and so real a man, should be otherwise than sensitive to the varied forms of feminine attraction. He avowedly preferred the society of women to that of men; they were, as I have already said, his habitual confidants, and, evidently, his most frequent correspondents; and though he could have dispensed with woman friends as he dispensed with many other things—though he most often won them without knowing it—his frank interest in their sex, and the often caressing kindness of manner in which it was revealed, might justly be interpreted by individual women into a conscious appeal to their sympathy. It was therefore doubly remarkable that on the ground of benevolence, he scarcely discriminated between the claim on him of a woman, and that of a man; and his attitude towards women was in this respect so distinctive as to merit some words of notice. It was large, generous, and unconventional; but, for that very reason, it was not, in the received sense of the word, chivalrous. Chivalry proceeds on the assumption that women not only cannot, but should not, take care of themselves in any active struggle with life; Mr. Browning had no theoretical objection to a woman's taking care of herself. He saw no reason why, if she was hit, she should not hit back again, or even why, if she hit, she should not receive an answering blow. He responded swiftly to every feminine appeal to his kindness or his protection, whether arising from physical weakness or any other obvious cause of helplessness or suffering; but the appeal in such cases lay first to his humanity, and only in second order to his consideration of sex. He would have had a man flogged who beat his wife; he would have had one flogged who ill-used a child—or an animal: he was notedly opposed to any sweeping principle or practice of vivisection. But he never quite understood that the strongest women are weak, or at all events vulnerable, in the very fact of their sex, through the minor traditions and conventions with which society justly, indeed necessarily, surrounds them. Still less did he understand those real, if impalpable, differences between men and women which correspond to the difference of position. He admitted the broad distinctions which have become proverbial, and are therefore only a rough measure of the truth. He could say on occasion: 'You ought to *be* better; you are a woman; I ought to *know* better; I am a man.' But he had had too large an experience of human nature to attach permanent weight to such generalizations; and they found certainly no expression in his works. Scarcely an instance of a conventional, or so-called man's woman, occurs in their whole range. Excepting perhaps the speaker in 'A Woman's Last Word', 'Pompilia' and 'Mildred' are the nearest approach to it; and in both of these we find qualities of imagination or thought which place them outside the conventional type. He instinctively judged women, both morally and intellectually, by the same standards as men; and when confronted by some divergence of thought or feeling, which meant, in the woman's case, neither quality nor defect in any strict sense of the word, but simply a nature trained to different points of view, an element of perplexity entered into his probable opposition. When the difference presented itself in a neutral aspect, it affected him like the casual peculiarities of a family or a group, or a casual disagreement between things of the same kind. He would say to a woman friend: 'You women are so different from men!' in the tone in which he might have said, 'You Irish, or you Scotch, are so different from Englishmen;' or again, 'It is impossible for a man to judge how a woman would act in such or such a case; you are so different;' the case being sometimes one in which it would be inconceivable to a normal woman, and therefore to the generality of men, that she should act in any but one way.

The vague sense of mystery with which the poet's mind usually invests a being of the opposite sex, had thus often in him its counterpart in a puzzled dramatic curiosity which constituted an equal ground of interest.

This virtual admission of equality between the sexes, combined with his Liberal principles to dispose him favourably towards the movement for Female Emancipation. He approved of everything that had been done for the higher instruction of women, and would, not very long ago, have supported their admission to the Franchise. But he was so much displeased by the more recent action of some of the lady advocates of Women's Rights, that, during the last year of his life, after various modifications of opinion, he frankly pledged himself to the opposite view. He had even visions of writing a tragedy or drama in support of it. The plot was roughly sketched, and some dialogue composed, though I believe no trace of this remains.

It is almost implied by all I have said, that he possessed in every mood the charm of perfect simplicity of manner. On this point he resembled his father. His tastes lay also in the direction of great simplicity of life, though circumstances did not allow of his indulging them to the same extent. It may interest those who never saw him to know that he always dressed as well as the occasion required, and always with great indifference to the subject. In Florence he wore loose clothes which were adapted to the climate; in London his coats were cut by a good tailor in whatever was the prevailing fashion; the change was simply with him an incident of the situation. He had also a look of dainty cleanliness which was heightened by the smooth healthy texture of the skin, and in later life by the silvery whiteness of his hair.

His best photographic likenesses were those taken by Mr. Fradelle in 1881, Mr. Cameron and Mr. William Grove in 1888 and 1889.

Chapter 21

1887-1889

Marriage of Mr. Barrett Browning—Removal to De Vere Gardens—Symptoms of failing Strength—New Poems; New Edition of his Works—Letters to Mr. George Bainton, Mr. Smith, and Lady Martin—Primiero and Venice—Letters to Miss Keep—The last Year in London—Asolo—Letters to Mrs. Fitz-Gerald, Mrs. Skirrow, and Mr. G. M. Smith.

The last years of Mr. Browning's life were introduced by two auspicious events, in themselves of very unequal importance, but each in its own way significant for his happiness and his health. One was his son's marriage on October 4, 1887, to Miss Fannie Coddington, of New York, a lady towards whom Mr. Barrett Browning had been strongly attracted when he was a very young man and she little more than a child; the other, his own removal from Warwick Crescent to De Vere Gardens, which took place in the previous June. The change of residence had long been with him only a question of opportunity. He was once even in treaty for a piece of ground at Kensington, and intended building a house. That in which he had lived for so many years had faults of construction and situation which the lapse of time rendered only more conspicuous; the Regent's Canal Bill had also doomed it to demolition; and when an opening presented itself for securing one in all essentials more suitable, he was glad to seize it, though at the eleventh hour. He had mentally fixed on the new locality in those earlier days in which he still thought his son might eventually settle in London; and it possessed at the same time many advantages for himself. It was warmer and more sheltered than any which he could have found on the north side of the Park; and, in that close vicinity to Kensington Gardens, walking might be contemplated as a pleasure, instead of mere compulsory motion from place to place. It was only too soon apparent that the time had passed when he could reap much benefit from the event; but he became aware from the first moment of his installation in the new home that the conditions of physical life had become more favourable for him. He found an almost pathetic pleasure in completing the internal arrangements of the well-built, commodious house. It seems, on looking back, as if the veil had dropped before his eyes which sometimes shrouds the keenest vision in face of an impending change; and he had imagined, in spite of casual utterances which disclaimed the hope, that a new lease of life was being given to him. He had for several years been preparing for the more roomy dwelling which he would probably some day inhabit; and handsome pieces of old furniture had been stowed away in the house in Warwick Crescent, pending the occasion for their use. He loved antiquities of this kind, in a manner which sometimes recalled his father's affection for old books; and most of these had been bought in Venice, where frequent visits to the noted curiosity-shops had been his one bond of habit with his tourist countrymen in that city. They matched the carved oak and massive gildings and valuable tapestries which had carried something of Casa Guidi into his first London home. Brass lamps that had once hung inside chapels in some Catholic church, had long occupied the place of the habitual gaselier; and to these was added in the following year one of silver, also brought from Venice—the Jewish 'Sabbath lamp'. Another acquisition, made only a few months, if indeed so long, before he left London for the last time, was that of a set of casts representing the Seasons, which were to stand at intervals on brackets in a certain unsightly space on his drawing-room wall; and he had said of these, which I think his son was procuring for him: 'Only my four little heads, and then I shall not buy another thing for the house'—in a tone of childlike satisfaction at his completed work.

This summer he merely went to St. Moritz, where he and his sister were, for the greater part of their stay, again guests of Mrs. Bloomfield Moore. He was determined to give the London winter a fuller trial in the more promising circumstances of his new life, and there was much to be done in De Vere Gardens after his return. His father's six thousand books, together with those he had himself accumulated, were for the first time to be spread out in their proper array, instead of crowding together in rows, behind and behind each other. The new bookcases, which could stand in the large new study, were waiting to receive them. He did not know until he tried to fulfil it how greatly the task would tax his strength. The library was, I believe, never completely arranged.

During this winter of 1887-8 his friends first perceived that a change had come over him. They did not realize that his life was drawing to a close; it was difficult to do so when so much of the former elasticity remained; when he still proclaimed himself 'quite well' so long as he was not definitely suffering. But he was often suffering; one terrible cold followed another. There was general evidence that he had at last grown old. He, however, made no distinct change in his mode of life. Old habits, suspended by his longer imprisonments to the house, were resumed as soon as he was set free. He still dined out; still attended the private view of every, or almost every art exhibition. He kept up his unceasing correspondence—in one or two cases voluntarily added to it; though he would complain day after day that his fingers ached from the number of hours through which he had held his pen. One of the interesting letters of this period was written to Mr. George Bainton, of Coventry, to be used, as that gentleman tells me, in the preparation of a lecture on the 'Art of Effective Written Composition'. It confirms the statement I have had occasion to make, that no extraneous influence ever permanently impressed itself on Mr. Browning's style.

29, De Vere Gardens: Oct. 6, '87.

Dear Sir,—I was absent from London when your kind letter reached this house, to which I removed some time ago—hence the delay in acknowledging your kindness and replying, in some degree, to your request. All I can say, however, is this much—and very little—that, by the indulgence of my father and mother, I was allowed to live my own life and choose my own course in it; which, having been the same from the beginning to the end, necessitated a permission to read nearly all sorts of books, in a well-stocked and very miscellaneous library. I had no other direction than my parents' taste for whatever was highest and best in literature; but I found out for myself many forgotten fields which proved the richest of pastures: and, so far as a preference of a particular 'style' is concerned, I believe mine was just the same at first as at last. I cannot name any one author who exclusively influenced me in that respect,—as to the fittest expression of thought—but thought itself had many impulsions from very various sources, a matter not to your present purpose. I repeat, this is very little to say, but all in my power—and it is heartily at your service—if not as of any value, at least as a proof that I gratefully feel your kindness, and am, dear Sir Yours very truly, Robert Browning.

In December 1887 he wrote 'Rosny', the first poem in 'Asolando', and that which perhaps most displays his old subtle dramatic power; it was followed by 'Beatrice Signorini' and 'Flute-Music'. Of the 'Bad Dreams' two or three were also written in London, I think, during that winter. The 'Ponte dell' Angelo' was imagined during the next autumn in Venice. 'White Witchcraft' had been suggested in the same summer by a letter from a friend in the Channel Islands which spoke of the number of toads to be seen there. In the spring of 1888 he began revising his works for the last, and now entirely uniform edition, which was issued in monthly volumes, and completed by the July of 1889. Important verbal corrections were made in 'The Inn Album', though not, I think, in many of the later poems; but that in which he found most room for improvement was, very naturally, 'Pauline'; and he wrote concerning it to Mr. Smith the following interesting letter.

29, De Vere Gardens, W.: Feb. 27, '88.

My dear Smith,—When I received the Proofs of the 1st. vol. on Friday evening, I made sure of returning them next day—so accurately are they printed. But on looking at that unlucky 'Pauline', which I have not touched for half a century, a sudden impulse came over me to take the opportunity of just correcting the most obvious faults of expression, versification and construction,—letting the *thoughts*—such as they are—remain exactly as at first: I have only treated the imperfect expression of these just as I have now and then done for an amateur friend, if he asked me and I liked him enough to do so. Not a line is displaced, none added, none taken away. I have just sent it to the printer's with an explanatory word: and told him that he will have less trouble with all the rest of the volumes put together than with this little portion. I expect to return all the rest to-morrow or next day.

As for the sketch—the portrait—it admits of no very superior treatment: but, as it is the only one which makes me out youngish,—I should like to know if an artist could not strengthen the thing by a pencil touch or two in a few minutes—improve the eyes, eyebrows, and mouth somewhat. The head too wants improvement: were Pen here he could manage it all in a moment. Ever truly yours, Robert Browning.

Any attempt at modifying the expressed thoughts of his twenty-first year would have been, as he probably felt, a futile tampering with the work of another man; his literary conscience would have forbidden this, if it had been otherwise possible. But he here proves by his own words what I have already asserted, that the power of detail correction either was, or had become by experience, very strong in him.

The history of this summer of 1888 is partly given in a letter to Lady Martin.

29, De Vere Gardens, W.: Aug. 12, '88.

Dear Lady Martin,—The date of your kind letter,—June 18,—would affect me indeed, but for the good conscience I retain despite of appearances. So uncertain have I been as to the course we should take,—my sister and myself—when the time came for leaving town, that it seemed as if 'next week' might be the eventful week when all doubts would disappear—perhaps the strange cold weather and interminable rain made it hard to venture from under one's roof even in fancy of being better lodged elsewhere. This very day week it was the old story—cold—then followed the suffocating eight or nine tropical days which forbade any more delay, and we leave to-morrow for a place called Primiero, near Feltre—where my son and his wife assure us we may be comfortably—and coolly—housed, until we can accompany them to Venice, which we may stay at for a short time. You remember our troubles at Llangollen about the purchase of a Venetian house . . . ? My son, however, nothing daunted, and acting under abler counsels than I was fortunate enough to obtain,* has obtained a still more desirable acquisition, in the shape of the well-known Rezzonico Palace that of Pope Clement 13th—and, I believe, is to be congratulated on his bargain. I cannot profess the same interest in this as in the earlier object of his ambition, but am quite satisfied by the evident satisfaction of the 'young people'. So,—by the old law of compensation,—while we may expect pleasant days abroad—our chance is gone of once again enjoying your company in your own lovely Vale of Llangollen;—had we not been pulled otherwise by the inducements we could not resist,—another term of delightful weeks—each tipped with a sweet starry Sunday at the little church leading to the House Beautiful where we took our rest of an evening spent always memorably—this might have been our fortunate lot once again! As it is, perhaps we need more energetic treatment than we should get with you —for both of us are more oppressed than ever by the exigencies of the lengthy season, and require still more bracing air than the gently lulling temperature of Wales. May it be doing you, and dear Sir Theodore, all the good you deserve—throwing in the share due to us, who must forego it! With all love from us both, ever affectionately yours Robert Browning.

* Those of Mr. Alexander Malcolm.

He did start for Italy on the following day, but had become so ill, that he was on the point of postponing his departure. He suffered throughout the journey as he had never suffered on any journey before; and during his first few days at Primiero, could only lead the life of an invalid. He rallied, however, as usual, under the potent effects of quiet, fresh air, and sunshine; and fully recovered his normal state before proceeding to Venice, where the continued sense of physical health combined with many extraneous circumstances to convert his proposed short stay into a long one. A letter from the mountains, addressed to a lady who had never been abroad, and to whom he sometimes wrote with more descriptive detail than to other friends, gives a touching glimpse of his fresh delight in the beauties of nature, and his tender constant sympathy with the animal creation.

Primiero: Sept. 7, '88.

. . . . .

'The weather continues exquisitely temperate, yet sunny, ever since the clearing thunderstorm of which I must have told you in my last. It is, I am more and more confirmed in believing, the most beautiful place I was ever resident in: far more so than Gressoney or even St.-Pierre de Chartreuse. You would indeed delight in seeing the magnificence of the mountains,—the range on either side, which morning and evening, in turn, transmute literally to gold,—I mean what I say. Their utterly bare ridges of peaks and crags of all shape, quite naked of verdure, glow like yellow ore; and, at times, there is a silver change, as the sun prevails or not.

'The valley is one green luxuriance on all sides; Indian corn, with beans, gourds, and even cabbages, filling up the interstices; and the flowers, though not presenting any novelty to my uninstructed eyes, yet surely more large and purely developed than I remember to have seen elsewhere. For instance, the tiger-lilies in the garden here must be above ten feet high, every bloom faultless, and, what strikes me as peculiar, every leaf on the stalk from bottom to top as perfect as if no insect existed to spoil them by a notch or speck. . . .

'. . . Did I tell you we had a little captive fox,—the most engaging of little vixens? To my great joy she has broken her chain and escaped, never to be recaptured, I trust. The original wild and untameable nature was to be plainly discerned even in this early stage of the whelp's life: she dug herself, with such baby feet, a huge hole, the use of which was evident, when, one day, she pounced thence on a stray turkey—allured within reach by the fragments of fox's breakfast,—the intruder escaping with the loss of his tail. The creature came back one night to explore the old place of captivity,—ate some food and retired. For myself,—I continue absolutely well: I do not walk much, but for more than amends, am in the open air all day long.'

No less striking is a short extract from a letter written in Venice to the same friend, Miss Keep.

Ca' Alvise: Oct. 16, '88.

'Every morning at six, I see the sun rise; far more wonderfully, to my mind, than his famous setting, which everybody glorifies. My bedroom window commands a perfect view: the still, grey lagune, the few seagulls flying, the islet of S. Giorgio in deep shadow, and the clouds in a long purple rack, behind which a sort of spirit of rose burns up till presently all the rims are on fire with gold, and last of all the orb sends before it a long column of its own essence apparently: so my day begins.'

We feel, as we read these late, and even later words, that the lyric imagination was renewing itself in the incipient dissolution of other powers. It is the Browning of 'Pippa Passes' who speaks in them.

He suffered less on the whole during the winter of 1888-9. It was already advanced when he returned to England; and the attacks of cold and asthma were either shorter or less frequent. He still maintained throughout the season his old social routine, not omitting his yearly visit, on the anniversary of Waterloo, to Lord Albemarle, its last surviving veteran. He went for some days to Oxford during the commemoration week, and had for the first, as also last time, the pleasure of Dr. Jowett's almost exclusive society at his beloved Balliol College. He proceeded with his new volume of poems. A short letter written to Professor Knight, June 16, and of which the occasion speaks for itself, fitly closes the labours of his life; for it states his view of the position and function of poetry, in one brief phrase, which might form the text to an exhaustive treatise upon them.

29, De Vere Gardens, W.: June 16, 1889.

My dear Professor Knight,—I am delighted to hear that there is a likelihood of your establishing yourself in Glasgow, and illustrating Literature as happily as you have expounded Philosophy at St. Andrews. It is certainly the right order of things: Philosophy first, and Poetry, which is its highest outcome, afterward—and much harm has been done by reversing the natural process. How capable you are of doing justice to the highest philosophy embodied in poetry, your various studies of Wordsworth prove abundantly; and for the sake of both Literature and Philosophy I wish you success with all my heart.

Believe me, dear Professor Knight, yours very truly, Robert Browning.

But he experienced, when the time came, more than his habitual disinclination for leaving home. A distinct shrinking from the fatigue of going to Italy now added itself to it; for he had suffered when travelling back in the previous winter, almost as much as on the outward journey, though he attributed the distress to a different cause: his nerves were, he thought, shaken by the wearing discomforts incidental on a broken tooth. He was for the first time painfully sensitive to the vibration of the train. He had told his friends, both in Venice and London, that so far as he was able to determine, he would never return to Italy. But it was necessary he should go somewhere, and he had no alternative plan. For a short time in this last summer he entertained the idea of a visit to Scotland; it had indeed definitely shaped itself in his mind; but an incident, trivial in itself, though he did not think it so, destroyed the first scheme, and it was then practically too late to form another. During the second week in August the weather broke. There could no longer be any question of the northward journey without even a fixed end in view. His son and daughter had taken possession of their new home, the Palazzo Rezzonico, and were anxious to see him and Miss Browning there; their wishes naturally had weight. The casting vote in favour of Venice was given by a letter from Mrs. Bronson, proposing Asolo as the intermediate stage. She had fitted up for herself a little summer retreat there, and promised that her friends should, if they joined her, be also comfortably installed. The journey was this time propitious. It was performed without imprudent haste, and Mr. Browning reached Asolo unfatigued and to all appearance well.

He saw this, his first love among Italian cities, at a season of the year more favourable to its beauty than even that of his first visit; yet he must himself have been surprised by the new rapture of admiration which it created in him, and which seemed to grow with his lengthened stay. This state of mind was the more striking, that new symptoms of his physical decline were now becoming apparent, and were in themselves of a depressing kind. He wrote to a friend in England, that the atmosphere of Asolo, far from being oppressive, produced in him all the effects of mountain air, and he was conscious of difficulty of breathing whenever he walked up hill. He also suffered, as the season advanced, great inconvenience from cold. The rooms occupied by himself and his sister were both unprovided with fireplaces; and though the daily dinner with Mrs. Bronson obviated the discomfort of the evenings, there remained still too many hours of the autumnal day in which the impossibility of heating their own little apartment must have made itself unpleasantly felt. The latter drawback would have been averted by the fulfilment of Mr. Browning's first plan, to be in Venice by the beginning of October, and return to the comforts of his own home before the winter had quite set in; but one slight motive for delay succeeded another, till at last a more serious project introduced sufficient ground of detention. He seemed possessed by a strange buoyancy—an almost feverish joy in life, which blunted all sensations of physical distress, or helped him to misinterpret them. When warned against the imprudence of remaining where he knew he suffered from cold, and believed, rightly or wrongly, that his asthmatic tendencies were increased, he would reply that he was growing acclimatized—that he was quite well. And, in a fitful or superficial sense, he must have been so.

His letters of that period are one continuous picture, glowing with his impressions of the things which they describe. The same words will repeat themselves as the same subject presents itself to his pen; but the impulse to iteration scarcely ever affects us as mechanical. It seems always a fresh response to some new stimulus to thought or feeling, which he has received. These reach him from every side. It is not only the Asolo of this peaceful later time which has opened before him, but the Asolo of 'Pippa Passes' and 'Sordello'; that which first stamped itself on his imagination in the echoes of the Court life of Queen Catharine,* and of the barbaric wars of the Eccelini. Some of his letters dwell especially on these early historical associations: on the strange sense of reopening the ancient chronicle which he had so deeply studied fifty years before. The very phraseology of the old Italian text, which I am certain he had never glanced at from that distant time, is audible in an account of the massacre of San Zenone, the scene of which he has been visiting. To the same correspondent he says that his two hours' drive to Asolo 'seemed to be a dream;' and again, after describing, or, as he thinks, only trying to describe some beautiful feature of the place, 'but it is indescribable!'

* Catharine Cornaro, the dethroned queen of Cyprus.

A letter addressed to Mrs. FitzGerald, October 8, 1889, is in part a fitting sequel to that which he had written to her from the same spot, eleven years before.

'. . . Fortunately there is little changed here: my old Albergo,—ruinous with earthquake—is down and done with— but few novelties are observable—except the regrettable one that the silk industry has been transported elsewhere—to Cornuda and other places nearer the main railway. No more Pippas—at least of the silk-winding sort!

'But the pretty type is far from extinct.

'Autumn is beginning to paint the foliage, but thin it as well; and the sea of fertility all round our height, which a month ago showed pomegranates and figs and chestnuts,—walnuts and apples all rioting together in full glory,—all this is daily disappearing. I say nothing of the olive and the vine. I find the Turret rather the worse for careful weeding—the hawks which used to build there have been "shot for food"—and the echo is sadly curtailed of its replies; still, things are the same in the main. Shall I ever see them again, when—as I suppose—we leave for Venice in a fortnight? . . .'

In the midst of this imaginative delight he carried into his walks the old keen habits of observation. He would peer into the hedges for what living things were to be found there. He would whistle softly to the lizards basking on the low walls which border the roads, to try his old power of attracting them.

On the 15th of October he wrote to Mrs. Skirrow, after some preliminary description:

Then—such a view over the whole Lombard plain; not a site in view, or *approximate* view at least, without its story. Autumn is now painting all the abundance of verdure,—figs, pomegranates, chestnuts, and vines, and I don't know what else,—all in a wonderful confusion,—and now glowing with all the colours of the rainbow. Some weeks back, the little town was glorified by the visit of a decent theatrical troop who played in a theatre *in*side the old palace of Queen Catharine Cornaro—utilized also as a prison in which I am informed are at present full five if not six malefactors guilty of stealing grapes, and the like enormities. Well, the troop played for a fortnight together exceedingly well—high tragedy and low comedy—and the stage-box which I occupied cost 16 francs. The theatre had been out of use for six years, for we are out of the way and only a baiting-place for a company pushing on to Venice. In fine, we shall stay here probably for a week or more,—and then proceed to Pen, at the Rezzonico; a month there, and then homewards! . . .

I delight in finding that the beloved Husband and precious friend manages to do without the old yoke about his neck, and enjoys himself as never anybody had a better right to do. I continue to congratulate him on his emancipation and ourselves on a more frequent enjoyment of his company in consequence.* Give him my true love; take mine, dearest friend,—and my sister's love to you both goes with it. Ever affectionately yours Robert Browning.

* Mr. Skirrow had just resigned his post of Master in Chancery.

The cry of 'homewards!' now frequently recurs in his letters. We find it in one written a week later to Mr. G. M. Smith, otherwise very expressive of his latest condition of mind and feeling.

Asolo, Veneto, Italia: Oct. 22, '89.

My dear Smith,—I was indeed delighted to get your letter two days ago— for there *are* such accidents as the loss of a parcel, even when it has been despatched from so important a place as this city—for a regular city it is, you must know, with all the rights of one,—older far than Rome, being founded by the Euganeans who gave their name to the adjoining hills. 'Fortified' is was once, assuredly, and the walls still surround it most picturesquely though mainly in utter ruin, and you even overrate the population, which does not now much exceed 900 souls—in the city Proper, that is—for the territory below and around contains some 10,000. But we are at the very top of things, garlanded about, as it were, with a narrow line of houses,—some palatial, such as you would be glad to see in London,—and above all towers the old dwelling of Queen Cornaro, who was forced to exchange her Kingdom of Cyprus for this pretty but petty dominion where she kept state in a mimic Court, with Bembo, afterwards Cardinal, for her secretary—who has commemorated the fact in his 'Asolani' or dialogues inspired by the place: and I do assure you that, after some experience of beautiful sights in Italy and elsewhere I know nothing comparable to the view from the Queen's tower and palace, still perfect in every respect. Whenever you pay Pen and his wife the visit you are pledged to, * it will go hard but you spend five hours in a journey to Asolo. The one thing I am disappointed in is to find that the silk-cultivation with all the pretty girls who were engaged in it are transported to Cornuda and other places,—nearer the railway, I suppose: and to this may be attributed the decrease in the number of inhabitants. The weather when I wrote last *was* 'blue and blazing—at noon-day—' but we share in the general plague of rain,—had a famous storm yesterday: while to-day is blue and sunny as ever. Lastly, for your admonition: we *have* a perfect telegraphic communication; and at the passage above, where I put a * I was interrupted by the arrival of a telegram: thank you all the same for your desire to relieve my anxiety. And now, to our immediate business— which is only to keep thanking you for your constant goodness, present and future: do with the book just as you will. I fancy it is bigger in bulk than usual. As for the 'proofs'—I go at the end of the month to Venice, whither you will please to send whatever is necessary. . . . I shall do well to say as little as possible of my good wishes for you and your family, for it comes to much the same thing as wishing myself prosperity: no matter, my sister's kindest regards shall excuse mine, and I will only add that I am, as ever, Affectionately yours Robert Browning.

A general quickening of affectionate impulse seemed part of this last leap in the socket of the dying flame.

Chapter 22

1889

Proposed Purchase of Land at Asolo—Venice—Letter to Mr. G. Moulton-Barrett—Lines in the 'Athenaeum'—Letter to Miss Keep—Illness—Death— Funeral Ceremonial at Venice—Publication of 'Asolando'—Interment in Poets' Corner.

He had said in writing to Mrs. FitzGerald, 'Shall I ever see them' the things he is describing 'again?' If not then, soon afterwards, he conceived a plan which was to insure his doing so. On a piece of ground belonging to the old castle, stood the shell of a house. The two constituted one property which the Municipality of Asolo had hitherto refused to sell. It had been a dream of Mr. Browning's life to possess a dwelling, however small, in some beautiful spot, which should place him beyond the necessity of constantly seeking a new summer resort, and above the alternative of living at an inn, or accepting—as he sometimes feared, abusing—the hospitality of his friends. He was suddenly fascinated by the idea of buying this piece of ground; and, with the efficient help which his son could render during his absence, completing the house, which should be christened 'Pippa's Tower'. It was evident, he said in one of his letters, that for his few remaining years his summer wanderings must always end in Venice. What could he do better than secure for himself this resting-place by the way?

His offer of purchase was made through Mrs. Bronson, to Count Loredano and other important members of the municipality, and their personal assent to it secured. But the town council was on the eve of re-election; no important business could be transacted by it till after this event; and Mr. Browning awaited its decision till the end of October at Asolo, and again throughout November in Venice, without fully understanding the delay. The vote proved favourable; but the night on which it was taken was that of his death.

The consent thus given would have been only a first step towards the accomplishment of his wish. It was necessary that it should be ratified by the Prefecture of Treviso, in the district of which Asolo lies; and Mr. Barrett Browning, who had determined to carry on the negotiations, met with subsequent opposition in the higher council. This has now, however, been happily overcome.

A comprehensive interest attaches to one more letter of the Asolo time. It was addressed to Mr. Browning's brother-in-law, Mr. George Moulton-Barrett.

Asolo, Veneto: Oct. 22, '89.

My dear George,—It was a great pleasure to get your kind letter; though after some delay. We were not in the Tyrol this year, but have been for six weeks or more in this little place which strikes me,—as it did fifty years ago, which is something to say, considering that, properly speaking, it was the first spot of Italian soil I ever set foot upon— having proceeded to Venice by sea—and thence here. It is an ancient city, older than Rome, and the scene of Queen Catharine Cornaro's exile, where she held a mock court, with all its attendants, on a miniature scale; Bembo, afterwards Cardinal, being her secretary. Her palace is still above us all, the old fortifications surround the hill-top, and certain of the houses are stately—though the population is not above 1,000 souls: the province contains many more of course. But the immense charm of the surrounding country is indescribable—I have never seen its like—the Alps on one side, the Asolan mountains all round,—and opposite, the vast Lombard plain,—with indications of Venice, Padua, and the other cities, visible to a good eye on a clear day; while everywhere are sites of battles and sieges of bygone days, described in full by the historians of the Middle Ages.

We have a valued friend here, Mrs. Bronson, who for years has been our hostess at Venice, and now is in possession of a house here built into the old city wall—she was induced to choose it through what I have said about the beauties of the place: and through her care and kindness we are comfortably lodged close by. We think of leaving in a week or so for Venice—guests of Pen and his wife; and after a short stay with them we shall return to London. Pen came to see us for a couple of days: I was hardly prepared for his surprise and admiration which quite equalled my own and that of my sister. All is happily well with them—their palazzo excites the wonder of everybody, so great is Pen's cleverness, and extemporised architectural knowledge, as apparent in all he has done there; why, *why* will you not go and see him there? He and his wife are very hospitable and receive many visitors. Have I told you that there was a desecrated chapel which he has restored in honour of his mother— putting up there the inscription by Tommaseo now above Casa Guidi?

Fannie is all you say,—and most dear and precious to us all. . . . Pen's medal to which you refer, is awarded to him in spite of his written renunciation of any sort of wish to contend for a prize. He will now resume painting and sculpture— having been necessarily occupied with the superintendence of his workmen—a matter capitally managed, I am told. For the rest, both Sarianna and myself are very well; I have just sent off my new volume of verses for publication. The complete edition of the works of E. B. B. begins in a few days.

The second part of this letter is very forcibly written, and, in a certain sense, more important than the first; but I suppress it by the desire of Mr. Browning's sister and son, and in complete concurrence with their judgment in the matter. It was a systematic defence of the anger aroused in him by a lately published reference to his wife's death; and though its reasonings were unanswerable as applied to the causes of his emotion, they did not touch the manner in which it had been displayed. The incident was one which deserved only to be forgotten; and if an injudicious act had not preserved its memory, no word of mine should recall it. Since, however, it has been thought fit to include the 'Lines to Edward Fitzgerald' in a widely circulated Bibliography of Mr. Browning's Works,* I owe it to him to say—what I believe is only known to his sister and myself—that there was a moment in which he regretted those lines, and would willingly have withdrawn them. This was the period, unfortunately short, which intervened between his sending them to the 'Athenaeum', and their appearance there. When once public opinion had expressed itself upon them in its too extreme forms of sympathy and condemnation, the pugnacity of his mind found support in both, and regret was silenced if not destroyed. In so far as his published words remained open to censure, I may also, without indelicacy, urge one more plea in his behalf. That which to the merely sympathetic observer appeared a subject for disapprobation, perhaps disgust, had affected him with the directness of a sharp physical blow. He spoke of it, and for hours, even days, was known to feel it, as such. The events of that distant past, which he had lived down, though never forgotten, had flashed upon him from the words which so unexpectedly met his eye, in a vividness of remembrance which was reality. 'I felt as if she had died yesterday,' he said some days later to a friend, in half deprecation, half denial, of the too great fierceness of his reaction. He only recovered his balance in striking the counter-blow. That he could be thus affected at an age usually destructive of the more violent emotions, is part of the mystery of those closing days which had already overtaken him.

* That contained in Mr. Sharp's 'Life'. A still more recent publication gives the lines in full.

By the first of November he was in Venice with his son and daughter; and during the three following weeks was apparently well, though a physician whom he met at a dinner party, and to whom he had half jokingly given his pulse to feel, had learned from it that his days were numbered. He wrote to Miss Keep on the 9th of the month:

'. . . Mrs. Bronson has bought a house at Asolo, and beautified it indeed,—niched as it is in an old tower of the fortifications still partly surrounding the city for a city it is, and eighteen towers, more or less ruinous, are still discoverable there: it is indeed a delightful place. Meantime, to go on,—we came here, and had a pleasant welcome from our hosts— who are truly magnificently lodged in this vast palazzo which my son has really shown himself fit to possess, so surprising are his restorations and improvements: the whole is all but complete, decorated,—that is, renewed admirably in all respects.

'What strikes me as most noteworthy is the cheerfulness and comfort of the huge rooms.

'The building is warmed throughout by a furnace and pipes.

'Yesterday, on the Lido, the heat was hardly endurable: bright sunshine, blue sky,—snow-tipped Alps in the distance. No place, I think, ever suited my needs, bodily and intellectual, so well.

'The first are satisfied—I am *quite* well, every breathing inconvenience gone: and as for the latter, I got through whatever had given me trouble in London. . . .'

But it was winter, even in Venice, and one day began with an actual fog. He insisted, notwithstanding, on taking his usual walk on the Lido. He caught a bronchial cold of which the symptoms were aggravated not only by the asthmatic tendency, but by what proved to be exhaustion of the heart; and believing as usual that his liver alone was at fault, he took little food, and refused wine altogether.*

* He always declined food when he was unwell; and maintained that in this respect the instinct of animals was far more just than the idea often prevailing among human beings that a failing appetite should be assisted or coerced.

He did not yield to the sense of illness; he did not keep his bed. Some feverish energy must have supported him through this avoidance of every measure which might have afforded even temporary strength or relief. On Friday, the 29th, he wrote to a friend in London that he had waited thus long for the final answer from Asolo, but would wait no longer. He would start for England, if possible, on the Wednesday or Thursday of the following week. It was true 'he had caught a cold; he felt sadly asthmatic, scarcely fit to travel; but he hoped for the best, and would write again soon.' He wrote again the following day, declaring himself better. He had been punished, he said, for long-standing neglect of his 'provoking liver'; but a simple medicine, which he had often taken before, had this time also relieved the oppression of his chest; his friend was not to be uneasy about him; 'it was in his nature to get into scrapes of this kind, but he always managed, somehow or other, to extricate himself from them.' He concluded with fresh details of his hopes and plans.

In the ensuing night the bronchial distress increased; and in the morning he consented to see his son's physician, Dr. Cini, whose investigation of the case at once revealed to him its seriousness. The patient had been removed two days before, from the second storey of the house, which the family then inhabited, to an entresol apartment just above the ground-floor, from which he could pass into the dining-room without fatigue. Its lower ceilings gave him erroneously an impression of greater warmth, and he had imagined himself benefited by the change. A freer circulation of air was now considered imperative, and he was carried to Mrs. Browning's spacious bedroom, where an open fireplace supplied both warmth and ventilation, and large windows admitted all the sunshine of the Grand Canal. Everything was done for him which professional skill and loving care could do. Mrs. Browning, assisted by her husband, and by a young lady who was then her guest,* filled the place of the trained nurses until these could arrive; for a few days the impending calamity seemed even to have been averted. The bronchial attack was overcome. Mr. Browning had once walked from the bed to the sofa; his sister, whose anxiety had perhaps been spared the full knowledge of his state, could send comforting reports to his friends at home. But the enfeebled heart had made its last effort. Attacks of faintness set in. Special signs of physical strength maintained themselves until within a few hours of the end. On Wednesday, December 11, a consultation took place between Dr. Cini, Dr. da Vigna, and Dr. Minich; and the opinion was then expressed for the first time that recovery, though still possible, was not within the bounds of probability. Weakness, however, rapidly gained upon him towards the close of the following day. Two hours before midnight of this Thursday, December 12, he breathed his last.

* Miss Evelyn Barclay, now Mrs. Douglas Giles.

He had been a good patient. He took food and medicine whenever they were offered to him. Doctors and nurses became alike warmly interested in him. His favourite among the latter was, I think, the Venetian, a widow, Margherita Fiori, a simple kindly creature who had known much sorrow. To her he said, about five hours before the end, 'I feel much worse. I know now that I must die.' He had shown at intervals a perception, even conviction, of his danger; but the excitement of the brain, caused by exhaustion on the one hand and the necessary stimulants on the other, must have precluded all systematic consciousness of approaching death. He repeatedly assured his family that he was not suffering.

A painful and urgent question now presented itself for solution: Where should his body find its last rest? He had said to his sister in the foregoing summer, that he wished to be buried wherever he might die: if in England, with his mother; if in France, with his father; if in Italy, with his wife. Circumstances all pointed to his removal to Florence; but a recent decree had prohibited further interment in the English Cemetery there, and the town had no power to rescind it. When this was known in Venice, that city begged for itself the privilege of retaining the illustrious guest, and rendering him the last honours. For the moment the idea even recommended itself to Mr. Browning's son. But he felt bound to make a last effort in the direction of the burial at Florence; and was about to despatch a telegram, in which he invoked the mediation of Lord Dufferin, when all difficulties were laid at rest by a message from the Dean of Westminster, conveying his assent to an interment in the Abbey.* He had already telegraphed for information concerning the date of the funeral, with a view to the memorial service, which he intended to hold on the same day. Nor would the further honour have remained for even twenty-four hours ungranted, because unasked, but for the belief prevailing among Mr. Browning's friends that there was no room for its acceptance.

* The assent thus conveyed had assumed the form of an offer, and was characterized as such by the Dean himself.

It was still necessary to provide for the more immediate removal of the body. Local custom forbade its retention after the lapse of two days and nights; and only in view of the special circumstances of the case could a short respite be granted to the family. Arrangements were therefore at once made for a private service, to be conducted by the British Chaplain in one of the great halls of the Rezzonico Palace; and by two o'clock of the following day, Sunday, a large number of visitors and residents had assembled there. The subsequent passage to the mortuary island of San Michele had been organized by the city, and was to display so much of the character of a public pageant as the hurried preparation allowed. The chief municipal officers attended the service. When this had been performed, the coffin was carried by eight firemen pompieri, arrayed in their distinctive uniform, to the massive, highly decorated municipal barge Barca delle Pompe funebri which waited to receive it. It was guarded during the transit by four 'uscieri' in 'gala' dress, two sergeants of the Municipal Guard, and two of the firemen bearing torches: the remainder of these following in a smaller boat. The barge was towed by a steam launch of the Royal Italian Marine. The chief officers of the city, the family and friends in their separate gondolas, completed the procession. On arriving at San Michele, the firemen again received their burden, and bore it to the chapel in which its place had been reserved.

When 'Pauline' first appeared, the Author had received, he never learned from whom, a sprig of laurel enclosed with this quotation from the poem,

Trust in signs and omens.

Very beautiful garlands were now piled about his bier, offerings of friendship and affection. Conspicuous among these was the ceremonial structure of metallic foliage and porcelain flowers, inscribed 'Venezia a Roberto Browning', which represented the Municipality of Venice. On the coffin lay one comprehensive symbol of the fulfilled prophecy: a wreath of laurel-leaves which his son had placed there.

A final honour was decreed to the great English Poet by the city in which he had died; the affixing of a memorial tablet to the outer wall of the Rezzonico Palace. Since these pages were first written, the tablet has been placed. It bears the following inscription:
A ROBERTO BROWNING MORTO IN QUESTO PALAZZO IL 12 DICEMBRE 1889 VENEZIA POSE
Below this, in the right-hand corner appear two lines selected from his works:
Open my heart and you will see Graved inside of it, 'Italy'.
Nor were these the only expressions of Italian respect and sympathy. The municipality of Florence sent its message of condolence. Asolo, poor in all but memories, itself bore the expenses of a mural tablet for the house which Mr. Browning had occupied. It is now known that Signor Crispi would have appealed to Parliament to rescind the exclusion from the Florentine cemetery, if the motive for doing so had been less promptly removed.

Mr. Browning's own country had indeed opened a way for the reunion of the husband and wife. The idea had rapidly shaped itself in the public mind that, since they might not rest side by side in Italy, they should be placed together among the great of their own land; and it was understood that the Dean would sanction Mrs. Browning's interment in the Abbey, if a formal application to this end were made to him. But Mr. Barrett Browning could not reconcile himself to the thought of disturbing his mother's grave, so long consecrated to Florence by her warm love and by its grateful remembrance; and at the desire of both surviving members of the family the suggestion was set aside.

Two days after his temporary funeral, privately and at night, all that remained of Robert Browning was conveyed to the railway station; and thence, by a trusted servant, to England. The family followed within twenty-four hours, having made the necessary preparations for a long absence from Venice; and, travelling with the utmost speed, arrived in London on the same day. The house in De Vere Gardens received its master once more.

'Asolando' was published on the day of Mr. Browning's death. The report of his illness had quickened public interest in the forthcoming work, and his son had the satisfaction of telling him of its already realized success, while he could still receive a warm, if momentary, pleasure from the intelligence. The circumstances of its appearance place it beyond ordinary criticism; they place it beyond even an impartial analysis of its contents. It includes one or two poems to which we would gladly assign a much earlier date; I have been told on good authority that we may do this in regard to one of them. It is difficult to refer the 'Epilogue' to a coherent mood of any period of its author's life. It is certain, however, that by far the greater part of the little volume was written in 1888-89, and I believe all that is most serious in it was the product of the later year. It possesses for many readers the inspiration of farewell words; for all of us it has their pathos.

He was buried in Westminster Abbey, in Poets' Corner, on the 31st of December, 1889. In this tardy act of national recognition England claimed her own. A densely packed, reverent and sympathetic crowd of his countrymen and countrywomen assisted at the consignment of the dead poet to his historic resting place. Three verses of Mrs. Browning's poem, 'The Sleep', set to music by Dr. Bridge, were sung for the first time on this occasion.

Conclusion

A few words must still be said upon that purport and tendency of Robert Browning's work, which has been defined by a few persons, and felt by very many as his 'message'.

The definition has been disputed on the ground of Art. We are told by Mr. Sharp, though in somewhat different words, that the poet, qua poet, cannot deliver a 'message' such as directly addresses itself to the intellectual or moral sense; since his special appeal to us lies not through the substance, but through the form, or presentment, of what he has had to say; since, therefore by implication, in claiming for it an intellectual—as distinct from an aesthetic—character, we ignore its function as poetry.

It is difficult to argue justly, where the question at issue turns practically on the meaning of a word. Mr. Sharp would, I think, be the first to admit this; and it appears to me that, in the present case, he so formulates his theory as to satisfy his artistic conscience, and yet leave room for the recognition of that intellectual quality so peculiar to Mr. Browning's verse. But what one member of the aesthetic school may express with a certain reserve is proclaimed unreservedly by many more; and Mr. Sharp must forgive me, if for the moment I regard him as one of these; and if I oppose his arguments in the words of another poet and critic of poetry, whose claim to the double title is I believe undisputed—Mr. Roden Noel. I quote from an unpublished fragment of a published article on Mr. Sharp's 'Life of Browning'.

'Browning's message is an integral part of himself as writer; whether as poet, since we agree that he is a poet, were surely a too curious and vain discussion; but some of his finest things assuredly are the outcome of certain very definite personal convictions. "The question," Mr. Sharp says, "is not one of weighty message, but of artistic presentation." There seems to be no true contrast here. "The primary concern of the artist must be with his vehicle of expression"—no—not the primary concern. Since the critic adds—for a poet "this vehicle is language emotioned to the white heat of rhythmic music by impassioned thought or sensation." Exactly—"thought" it may be. Now part of this same "thought" in Browning is the message. And therefore it is part of his "primary concern". "It is with presentment," says Mr. Sharp, "that the artist has fundamentally to concern himself." Granted: but it must surely be presentment of *something*. . . . I do not understand how to separate the substance from the form in true poetry. . . . If the message be not well delivered, it does not constitute literature. But if it be well delivered, the primary concern of the poet lay with the message after all!'

More cogent objection has been taken to the character of the 'message' as judged from a philosophic point of view. It is the expression or exposition of a vivid a priori religious faith confirmed by positive experience; and it reflects as such a double order of thought, in which totally opposite mental activities are often forced into co-operation with each other. Mr. Sharp says, this time quoting from Mr. Mortimer 'Scottish Art Review', December 1889:

'His position in regard to the thought of the age is paradoxical, if not inconsistent. He is in advance of it in every respect but one, the most important of all, the matter of fundamental principles; in these he is behind it. His processes of thought are often scientific in their precision of analysis; the sudden conclusion which he imposes upon them is transcendental and inept.'

This statement is relatively true. Mr. Browning's positive reasonings often do end with transcendental conclusions. They also start from transcendental premises. However closely his mind might follow the visible order of experience, he never lost what was for him the consciousness of a Supreme Eternal Will as having existed before it; he never lost the vision of an intelligent First Cause, as underlying all minor systems of causation. But such weaknesses as were involved in his logical position are inherent to all the higher forms of natural theology when once it has been erected into a dogma. As maintained by Mr. Browning, this belief held a saving clause, which removed it from all dogmatic, hence all admissible grounds of controversy: the more definite or concrete conceptions of which it consists possessed no finality for even his own mind; they represented for him an absolute truth in contingent relations to it. No one felt more strongly than he the contradictions involved in any conceivable system of Divine creation and government. No one knew better that every act and motive which we attribute to a Supreme Being is a virtual negation of His existence. He believed nevertheless that such a Being exists; and he accepted His reflection in the mirror of the human consciousness, as a necessarily false image, but one which bears witness to the truth.

His works rarely indicate this condition of feeling; it was not often apparent in his conversation. The faith which he had contingently accepted became absolute for him from all practical points of view; it became subject to all the conditions of his humanity. On the ground of abstract logic he was always ready to disavow it; the transcendental imagination and the acknowledged limits of human reason claimed the last word in its behalf. This philosophy of religion is distinctly suggested in the fifth parable of 'Ferishtah's Fancies'.

But even in defending what remains, from the most widely accepted point of view, the validity of Mr. Browning's 'message', we concede the fact that it is most powerful when conveyed in its least explicit form; for then alone does it bear, with the full weight of his poetic utterance, on the minds to which it is addressed. His challenge to Faith and Hope imposes itself far less through any intellectual plea which he can advance in its support, than through the unconscious testimony of all creative genius to the marvel of conscious life; through the passionate affirmation of his poetic and human nature, not only of the goodness and the beauty of that life, but of its reality and its persistence.

We are told by Mr. Sharp that a new star appeared in Orion on the night on which Robert Browning died. The alleged fact is disproved by the statement of the Astronomer Royal, to whom it has been submitted; but it would have been a beautiful symbol of translation, such as affectionate fancy might gladly cherish if it were true. It is indeed true that on that twelfth of December, a vivid centre of light and warmth was extinguished upon our earth. The clouded brightness of many lives bears witness to the poet spirit which has departed, the glowing human presence which has passed away. We mourn the poet whom we have lost far less than we regret the man: for he had done his appointed work; and that work remains to us. But the two beings were in truth inseparable. The man is always present in the poet; the poet was dominant in the man. This fact can never be absent from our loving remembrance of him. No just estimate of his life and character will fail to give it weight.

Made in the USA
Middletown, DE
30 May 2019